Dolls & Toys

from **A** to **Z**

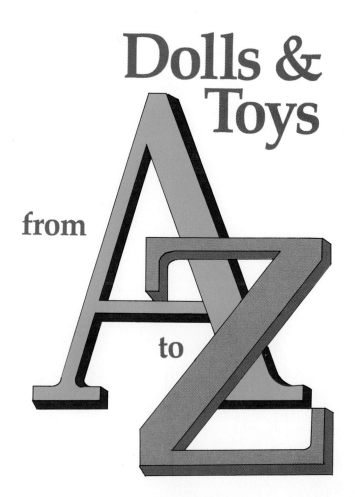

from McCall's

Needlework & Crafts

Dolls & Toys

from **A** to **Z**

from McCall's
Needlework & Crafts

Sedgewood® Press   NEW YORK

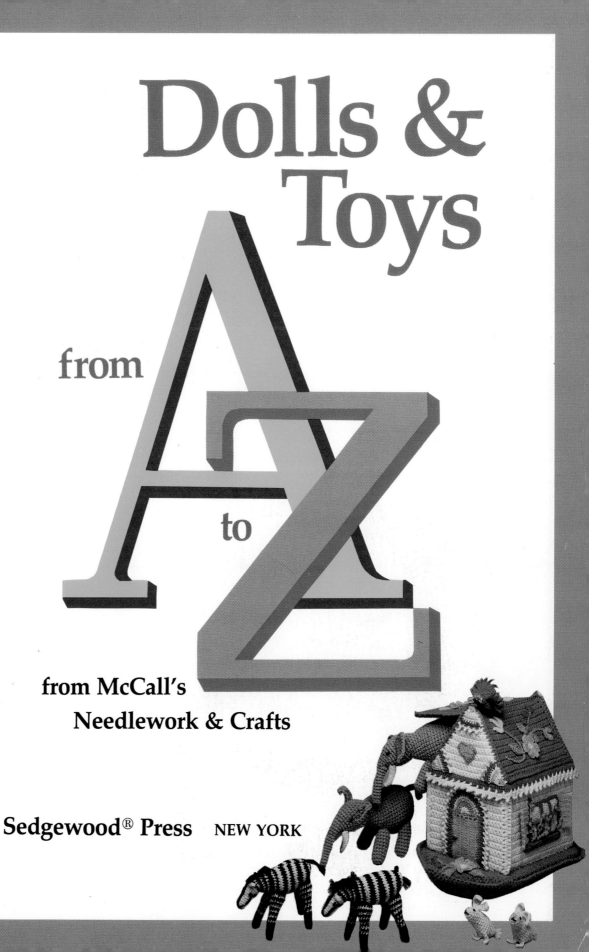

For Sedgewood® Press

Editorial Director: *Elizabeth P. Rice*

Project Editor: *Willa Speiser*

Associate Editor: *Leslie Gilbert*

Designer: *Bentwood Studio/Jos. Trautwein*

Production Manager: *Bill Rose*

Distributed by Macmillan Publishing Company, a division of Macmillan, Inc.
ISBN 0-02-496750-5
Library of Congress Catalog Card Number: 85-50564
Manufactured in the United States of America

Contents

Introduction

A doll can be a very special companion for a child—someone to care for, play with, and pretend with during the day; someone to hold close and cuddle when it's time to go to sleep. For some of us, that childhood fascination with dolls lives on whenever we hold a soft and cuddly baby doll. We remember fondly our first doll, handmade by a loved one especially for us.

DOLLS & TOYS FROM A TO Z *is a collection of projects that will delight doll fanciers of all ages. You'll find patterns for big beautiful dolls like Katie, and detailed instructions for ethnic and novelty dolls like Etthen-Oolah and Jacques, as well as a menagerie of X-traordinary Animals.*

Children will love the Noah's Ark and Old MacDonald's Farm crocheted play sets, filled with lots of easy-to-make animals. The Under the Big Top Puppets with their own circus-tent carrying case will keep little ones occupied for hours.

Some of the projects are easy to make, using scrap-basket materials you have on hand. Other dolls require more work, but your pride and pleasure in the finished doll will make the project well worth the effort. You will be able to utilize many different needlework techniques: sewing, embroidery, needlepoint, knitting, crochet, and more. The How-To's, pages 179-190, will provide instructions for all the techniques used in the book; the step-by-step diagrams will make it easy for you to learn new crafts or to refresh your memory about old favorites.

As you read through the book, you'll find an exciting variety of dolls, each with its own personality. Perhaps there's even a doll named for a special someone you know. With DOLLS & TOYS FROM A TO Z you can create a wonderful, one-of-a-kind doll that will be cherished for years to come.

ngelica *This little angel has crocheted hair, halo, wings, and robe . . . and a heavenly smile.*

SIZE
About 20″ high.

EQUIPMENT
Pencil. Ruler. Tracing paper. Tape measure. Light and dark-colored dressmaker's tracing (carbon) paper. Dry ballpoint pen. Small embroidery hoop. Embroidery and regular scissors. Embroidery and sewing needles. Crochet hook size G (4¼ mm). Sharp-pointed yarn needle. Knitting needle. Straight pins. Sewing machine. Iron. Compass.

MATERIALS
Closely woven cotton fabric such as muslin or kettle cloth 44″ wide, ½ yard off-white. Off-white sewing thread. Six-strand cotton embroidery floss: black, white, brown, red. Pink crayon. Knitting worsted: 8 ozs. white, 6 ozs. gold. Two white ⅝″ buttons. Polyester fiberfill for stuffing.

GENERAL DIRECTIONS
Enlarge patterns by copying on paper ruled in 1″ squares. Complete half-patterns indicated by long dash lines. Use dressmaker's carbon and dry ballpoint pen to transfer patterns to wrong side of fabrics, unless otherwise directed, placing them ½″ from fabric edges and ½″ apart; reverse asymmetrical patterns for each second and fourth piece. Cut out pieces ¼″ beyond marked lines for seam allowance, unless otherwise directed. When cutting additional pieces without patterns, do not add seam allowance. To assemble doll and clothes, pin pieces together with right sides facing and raw edges even. Stitch on marked lines, making ¼″ seams, unless otherwise directed. When assembling clothes, press seams open after stitching, unless otherwise directed. Clip into seam allowance at curves and corners; turn piece to right side and poke out corners with knitting needle.

DIRECTIONS FOR DOLL
From off-white fabric, cut two heads (front and back), one head center, two bodies, two arms, four legs, and two soles. Referring to photograph for placement, transfer eyes and mouth to right side of head front.

Head: Insert face area of head front in hoop. Work embroidery as follows (*see Embroidery Stitch Details, page 185*): Using two strands of black floss in needle, work lashes with straight stitch and outline eyes with outline stitch; using brown floss, fill in eyes with satin stitch. Using white, stitch small crosses for "highlights" in pupils (*see pattern*). Use two strands of red floss to work backstitch for mouth. Use crayon to lightly "rouge" cheeks with pink. Using compass, make pattern for 1¼″-diameter circle; use to cut circle from off-white fabric for nose. Using sewing needle and thread, baste ⅛″ in from edge of circle all around. On wrong side, place small piece of fiberfill in center of circle; pull basting thread and gather edges around fiberfill to form nose. Stitch nose to face at dot (*see pattern*).

Body: Fold arm in half lengthwise, right side in. Stitch raw arm and hand edges, leaving top straight edges open. Turn; stuff firmly.

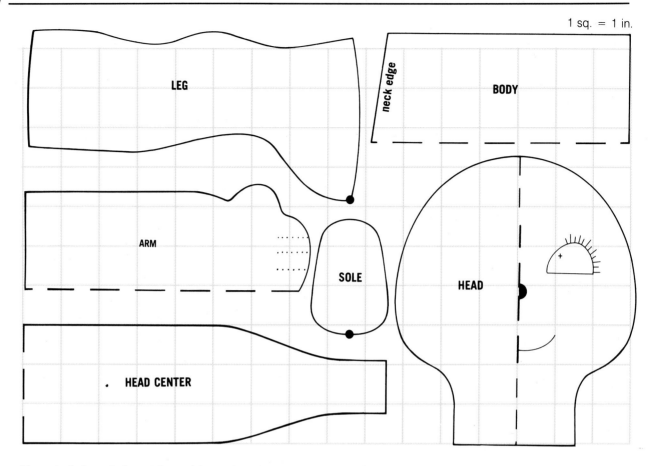

1 sq. = 1 in.

Topstitch hand along dotted lines (*see pattern*), forming fingers. Baste each arm closed ⅛" in from raw edges, enclosing stuffing. Stitch legs together in pairs at front and back, leaving top and bottom edges open. Stitch soles to bottom openings, matching dots; turn and stuff. Baste each leg top as for arm, but with seams centered. On right side of one body (front), pin arms ½" down from shoulders, so that arms cross, thumbs point down, and side edges are even; stitch. Pin and stitch legs to body bottom in similar manner, so that toes point toward shoulders. Place body front on work surface with limbs on top, now extending outward. Fold left arm across body so that hand extends above right shoulder and seam allowance faces out. Pin left side of body back, wrong side up, to body front; stitch left side. Pin and stitch right side of body in same manner (body will look like a tube, with hands extending above and legs below). Push legs up through tube, so that

only seam allowance extends at bottom; pin and stitch body bottom. Turn and stuff body. Turn raw edges ¼" to inside; slipstitch opening closed. Using matching thread, slipstitch head, centered, over shoulders.

Hair: Using gold yarn and crochet hook, work as follows: Beg at crown of head, ch 14. Sc in 2nd ch from hook and in 11 ch, 3 sc in last ch; working along opposite side of ch, sc in each ch, 3 sc in last ch. Working in back loop of each sc, sc around, increasing as necessary until piece fits head. End off. For curls, join gold in front loop of first st on top of piece. Working in front loop of each st, * ch 6, sl st in next st, repeat from * around entire piece. End off. With matching yarn, sew hair to head around edge of hair.

CROCHETED CLOTHES
Gauge: 7 sts = 2".

Dress: *Front bodice* Beg at top, with white, ch 24.

Row 1 (right side): Hdc in 2nd ch from hook and in each ch across—23 hdc. Ch 2, turn.

Row 2: Sk first st (ch 2 counts as first dc); holding back on hook last loop of each dc, 3 dc in next st, yo and through 4 loops on hook (3-dc cluster made), * dc in each of next 3 sts, cluster in next st, repeat from * across, dc in last st. Ch 1, turn.

Row 3: Hdc in each st across—23 hdc. Ch 2, turn.

Row 4: Sk first st, dc in next 2 sts, * cluster in next st, dc in each of next 3 sts, repeat from * across.

Row 5: Repeat row 3.

Row 6: Repeat row 2.

Row 7: Repeat row 3.

Row 8: Repeat row 4.

Row 9: Repeat row 3. End off.

Back bodice (make 2 pieces): Beg at top, with white, ch 13.

Row 1: Hdc in 2nd ch from hook and in each ch—12 hdc. Ch 2; turn.

Row 2: Sk first st, dc in each st across. Ch 1, turn.

Row 3: Hdc in each st across. Ch 2, turn.

Rows 4-9: Repeat rows 2 and 3. End off. Sew front and backs tog, 4 sts at top for each shoulder, 3 rows at bottom for sides.

Sleeves Join white to bottom of armhole, work 22 sc around armhole. Sl st in first sc.

Rnd 2: Ch 3, dc in joining st; working in back loops only, * sk 1 st, 2 dc in next st, repeat from * around, sl st in top of ch 3.

Rnds 3-8: Repeat rnd 2.

Rnd 9: Ch 4, tr in same st, sk 1 dc, (2 tr in next dc, sk 1 dc) twice, (2 dc in next dc, sk 1 dc) 6 times, (2 tr in next dc, sk 1 dc) twice. Sl st in top of ch 4.

Rnd 10: Ch 1, sk 1 st, (2 dc, ch 2, 2 dc all in next st, sk next st, sl st in next st, sk next st) 5 times, 2 dc, ch 2, 2 dc in ch 1 at beg of rnd, sl st in first dc. End off.

Skirt Join white to first st on waist edge of right back, ch 3, dc in same st; working in back loops, * sk 1 st, 2 dc in next st, repeat from * across to last st on left back. Ch 3, turn.

Row 2: Dc in same st as ch 3; working in back loops, * sk 1 st, 2 dc in next st, repeat from * across, inc 4 dc evenly spaced across by working 1 dc in 4 sts instead of skipping the sts. Sl st in top of ch 3 to join skirt at center back. Turn.

Rnd 1 (right side): Sl st in next st, ch 3, dc in same st; working in back loops (throughout skirt), * sk 1 st, 2 dc in next st, repeat from * around, inc 4 dc evenly around. Join each rnd.

Rnds 2-4: Ch 3, dc in same st, * sk 1 st, 2 dc in next st, repeat from * around.

Rnd 5: Ch 3, dc in same st, * sk 1 st, 2 dc in next st, repeat from * around, inc 4 dc evenly around.

Rnds 6 and 7: Repeat rnd 2.

Rnd 8: Repeat rnd 5.

Rnds 9 and 10: Repeat rnd 2.

Rnd 11: Ch 3, dc in same st, * sk 1 st, 2 dc in next st, repeat from * around, inc 8 dc evenly spaced around.

Rnds 12 and 13: Repeat rnd 2.

Rnds 14-16: Repeat rnds 11-13.

Rnd 17: Ch 3, dc in same st, * 2 dc in next st, 3 dc in next st, repeat from * around. Join; end off.

Collar With white, dc in each st around neck. Ch 3, turn.

Row 2: Dc in each st across. End off.

Waist ruffle **Row 1:** Join white at top of skirt in front loop of first st on right back bodice. Working in front loop of each st around waist, ch 3 for first dc, * 2 dc in next st, 3 dc in next st, repeat from * around. Ch 3, turn.

Row 2: Dc in each dc across, ch 3, turn.

Row 3: Dc in each dc across. End off.

Edging Work this edging around collar, sleeve ends, ruffle, and bottom of skirt. With gold, working in back loops, sl st in first st, * ch 1, sl st in next st, repeat from * around. Sew two buttons to back opening. Use spaces between dc's as buttonholes.

Panties: With white, ch 44; join with sl st in first ch to form ring.

Rnd 1: Ch 3, dc in each ch around. Join.

Rnds 2-6: Ch 3, dc in each dc around. Join. At end of rnd 6, ch 1, sc in same st, sc in next st, ch 1, turn. Sc in 2 sc. End off. Sew to 2 sts on opposite edge to form crotch.

Shoes: With gold, ch 8.

Rnd 1: Sc in 2nd ch from hook and in next 5 ch, 3 sc in last ch. Working along opposite side of ch, sc in 5 ch, 2 sc in last ch.

Rnd 2: (Sc in 7 sc, 3 sc in next sc) twice.

Rnd 3: Sc in 8 sc, 3 sc in next sc, sc in 11 sc.

Rnd 4: Sc in 9 sc, 3 sc in next sc, sc in 12 sc.

Rnd 5: Sc in 9 sc, 2 sc in each of next 3 sc, sc in 12 sc.

Rnds 6-9: Sc in each sc around—27 sc.

Rnd 10: Sc in 12 sc, (sc 2 tog) twice, sc in 11 sc.

Rnd 11: Sc in each sc around—25 sc.

Rnd 12: Sc in 11 sc, (sc 2 tog) twice, sc in 10 sc. End off.

Rnd 13: With white, sc in back loop of each sc around.

Rnd 14: Ch 3, sc in next sc, repeat from * around. End off.

Ankle strap With gold, ch 50. Attach ends to center front of shoe. Tie in bow at back of leg.

Wing (make 2): With white, ch 12.

Row 1: Sc in 2nd ch from hook and in next 9 ch, 3 sc in last ch. Working along opposite side of ch, sc in 10 sc. Ch 1, turn.

Rows 2 and 3: Sc in each sc to center sc, 3 sc in center sc, sc in each remaining sc. Ch 1, turn—27 sc.

Row 4: Sc in 5 sc, hdc in next 5 sc, sc in 2 sc, 2 sc in each of next 3 sc, sc in 2 sc, hdc in 5 sc, sc in last 5 sc. Ch 1, turn.

Row 5: Sc in 5 sc, hdc in 5 hdc, sc in 3 sc, 2 sc in each of next 4 sc, sc in 3 sc, hdc in 5 hdc, sc in last 5 sc. Ch 1, turn.

Row 6: Sc in 5 sc, hdc in next 10 sts, 2 hdc in each of next 4 sts, hdc in next 10 sts, sc in last 5 sc. Ch 1, turn.

Row 7: Sc in 3 sc, hdc in next 3 sts, dc in next 12 sts, 2 dc in each of next 2 sts, dc in next 12 sts, hdc in next 3 sts, sc in last 3 sc. Ch 1, turn.

Row 8: Sc in 3 sc, hdc in 3 hdc, dc in 12 dc, 2 dc in each of 4 dc, dc in 12 dc, hdc in 3 hdc, sc in 3 sc. Ch 1, turn.

Row 9: Sl st in first st, * sk 1 st, (2 dc, ch 2, 2 dc) in next st, sk 1 st, sl st in next st, repeat from * around, then sl st in every other row across ends of rows to gather bottom of wing. End off.

With gold, sc down center wing along original ch. With gold, sc around wing between rows 7 and 8. Edge wing same as dress.

Joining piece With white, ch 16.

Row 1: Sc in 2nd ch from hook and in each ch across. Ch 1, turn each row.

Row 2: Dec 1 sc, sc across to last 2 sc, dec 1 sc—13 sc.

Row 3: Sc in each sc across.

Rows 4-12: Repeat rows 2 and 3—3 sc. End off. Sew wings to sides of joining piece. With gold, ch 90. Sl st in each ch across. Make another ch the same. Weave a ch through bottom of each wing where wing is sewn to joining piece. Tie wings on doll with bows in front.

Halo: With gold, make a ch to fit around head. Dc in 4th ch from hook and in each ch across. Sew ends tog. With white, work dress edging on each side of halo.

Bethany & Bo-Peep

Bethany wears a rainbow of ribbons in her cornrowed hair. Bo-Peep has crocheted curls and a dainty smocked dress.

Bethany

SIZE
About 20″ high.

EQUIPMENT
Pencil. Ruler. Tracing paper. Scissors. Tape measure. Dressmaker's tracing (carbon) paper. Dry ball-point pen. Straight pins. Sewing needle. Knitting needle. Sewing machine with zigzag attachment. Iron. Small embroidery hoop. Beam compass.

MATERIALS
44″-wide fabric: Heavyweight polyester double-knit, ½ yard brown; closely woven cotton, 1¼ yards white print. White vinyl, 8″ × 14″ piece. Black felt scrap. Sewing thread to match fabrics and vinyl. Double-fold bias tape ¼″ wide, 2 yards to match print fabric. Flat elastic ⅛″ wide, 1¼ yards. Two tiny snaps. Two clear round buttons, ⅜″. Pre-ruffled white lace trim ⅞″ wide, ¾ yard. Satin ribbon ⅜″ wide, ½ yard to match print fabric; for hair, 28 pieces 11″ long in assorted colors. Dark brown pompon, ⅝″. Six-strand cotton embroidery floss: black, white, red. Black sport-weight yarn. Polyester fiberfill for stuffing. White craft glue. Stretch socks, size 1 year.

GENERAL DIRECTIONS
Enlarge patterns for doll and clothes by copying onto paper ruled in 1″ squares; complete half-patterns indicated by long dash lines. Use dressmaker's carbon and dry ball-point pen to transfer patterns to wrong side of brown knit fabric, placing them ½″ apart. Reverse asymmetrical patterns for each second and fourth piece. Cut pieces ¼″ beyond marked lines for seam allowance. From brown knit fabric, cut out two heads, one head center, two bodies, two arms, four legs, and two soles. Zigzag-stitch edges to prevent raveling.

DIRECTIONS FOR DOLL
Face: On felt scrap, mark two pupils, including irises; cut out, but do not add seam allowance. Glue pupils in place on face.

Insert face area in hoop. Referring to Embroidery Stitch Details, page 185, work embroidery as follows: Using two strands of black floss in needle, work eye outlines in outline stitch, lashes in straight stitch. Using three strands of floss, work irises in satin stitch with white, mouth in outline stitch with red.

When embroidery is complete, remove fabric from hoop. Press gently wrong side up. Glue pompon in place for nose.

Head: Pin head center to head front and back, right sides facing, with bottom edges even. Stitch around sides and top, leaving neck edge open. Fold neck ¼" to wrong side. Clip into seam allowance at curves. Turn head to right side. Stuff firmly with fiberfill.

Body: Fold arms in half lengthwise, right side in. Stitch raw arm and hand edges, leaving straight edges open. Turn and use knitting needle to poke out corners; stuff firmly. Baste each arm closed ⅛" from raw edges, enclosing stuffing. Stitch legs together in pairs at front and back, leaving top and bottom edges open. Stitch soles to bottom openings, matching dots; turn and stuff. Baste each leg top as for arm, but with seams centered. On right side of one body (front), pin arms ½" down from shoulders, so that arms cross, hands point down, and side edges are even; stitch. Pin and stitch legs to body bottom in similar manner, so that toes point toward shoulders. Place body front on work surface with limbs on top, now extending outward. Fold left arm across body, so that hand extends above right shoulder and seam allowance faces out. Pin left side of body back, wrong side up, to body front; stitch. Pin and stitch right side of body in same manner (body will look like a tube with hands extending above and legs below). Push legs up through tube, so that only seam allowance extends at bottom; pin and stitch body bottom. Turn and stuff. Turn raw edges ¼" to inside; slipstitch opening closed. Slipstitch head, centered, over shoulders.

1 sq. = 1 in.

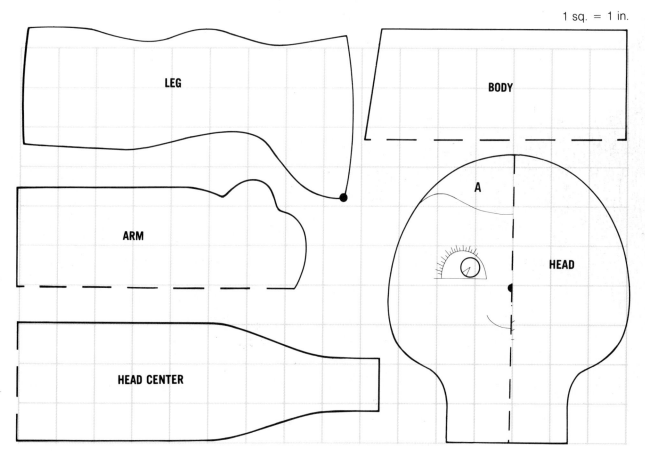

LEG

BODY

ARM

A

HEAD CENTER

HEAD

Hair: *Curls* Referring to Embroidery Stitch Details, page 185, use yarn to make ½"-long turkey work loops as follows: Start at front head seam on left side and work along marked forehead line to right side. Work loops down right side of front head seam to cheek, then around back of head and up left side to starting point. Work loops in closely spaced spiral rows all around, following contours, until entire head is covered. Do not clip loops. *Braids* Cut 12 pieces of yarn 6" long. Bundle strands together with ends even; secure one end with matching floss. Divide strands into three equal sections and braid for 2"; secure with another length of floss. Make 27 more braids in same manner, varying lengths from 1" to 3". Use floss to tack braids in place around head *(see photograph for placement)*. Tie assorted 11" ribbons around braid ends as shown.

DIRECTIONS FOR CLOTHES

Bloomers: From print fabric, cut two bloomers, omitting seam allowance at each leg bottom. Press waist edges ¼" to wrong side. Cut two 7½" lengths of elastic. Pin elastic across wrong side of each waist ⅛" from fold; stitch, using wide zigzag stitches. Reset machine for straight stitch. Encase leg bottoms with bias tape cut to size; topstitch. Cut two 7" lengths of elastic. Zigzag-stitch elastic across leg bottoms on wrong side 1" above tape. Reset machine for straight stitch. Stitch bloomers together at center front and back from waist to crotch. Stitch each inseam from leg bottom to crotch.

Dress: On wrong side of print fabric, mark skirt: Mark two concentric circles with diameters of 5" and 15¾"; mark a line from center circle to outer circle for slit (center back opening). Cut on marked lines. Cut bodice front using complete pattern, two bodice backs using half-pattern, and two sleeves,

omitting seam allowance at each sleeve bottom; also cut two 22" × 3⅜" sash ties and 125" × 2" ruffle, piecing for length. Stitch bodice front and backs together at shoulders. *Each sleeve* Finish sleeve bottom and attach elastic as for bloomer leg. Baste upper curved edge of sleeve between X's. Pin lower curved edges of sleeve to front and back armhole of bodice below X's. Gather upper curved edge to fit armhole; pin and stitch. Press long edges and one short edge of a tie ⅛" to wrong side twice; topstitch. Pleat raw tie end to fit side of bodice front; topstitch. Pin tie between bodice front and back so that right side of tie faces bodice front and all raw edges are even at sides. Stitch underarm and side in a continuous seam. Turn assembled bodice to right side. *Skirt* Press one long (bottom) edge of ruffle ⅛" to wrong side twice; topstitch. Gather top edge of ruffle to fit outer curved edge (bottom) of skirt; stitch in place, press seam toward waist, and topstitch around edge of skirt. Gather waist edge of skirt to fit bodice waist; stitch in place. Starting at ruffle bottom, stitch center backs together to 1½" below waist; press seam open. Above seam, press edges ⅛" to wrong side twice; topstitch. **To finish:** Cut lace trim to fit neck edge, plus ½". Press ends ¼" to wrong side; topstitch. Pin trim in place with right sides facing; stitch. Press seam to inside; trim will extend above neck. Sew snaps to neck opening and center back. Tie ½-yard length of matching ribbon into bow; tack to bodice front as shown.

Shoes: On wrong side of vinyl, mark two soles and two uppers. Cut out, omitting seam allowance on each upper at top and strap edges. On each upper, stitch ends together at back edge. Stitch soles to uppers, matching dots; turn. Test-fit shoes on doll; mark placement for snaps on strap ends and uppers, then remove. Sew snaps in place; sew a clear button over snap on each strap.

1 sq. = 1 in.

UPPER

STRAP

BLOOMERS

SOLE

BODICE

SLEEVE

Bo-Peep

SIZE
About 20" high.

EQUIPMENT
Pencil. Ruler. Tracing paper. Scissors. Tape measure. Dressmaker's tracing (carbon) paper. Dry ball-point pen. Straight pins. Sewing needle. Knitting needle. Sewing machine with zigzag attachment. Iron. Small embroidery hoop. Tapestry and embroidery needles. Tailor's chalk. Pinking shears. Wire cutters.

MATERIALS
Zweigart Ainring (Art. 3793), 18 threads-to-the-inch, 9" × 10" piece cream #264 (available by mail order from Art Needlework Treasure Trove, Box 2440 Grand Central Station, New York, NY 10163). Fabric 44" wide: closely woven cotton, ½ yard cream, ⅓ yard white; light, semisheer cotton, ½ yard each lavender-on-white dotted print and reverse white-on-lavender print. (**Note:** Choose fabrics with evenly spaced dots, which can be used as a smocking guide. We used a dotted bow print with dots spaced ¼" apart horizontally.) Nylon net 72" wide, ¾ yard lavender. Ribbed white nylon knit fabric, 9" × 12" piece. "Patent leather" vinyl, 8" × 12" piece white. Sewing thread to match fabrics and vinyl. Flat elastic ⅛" wide, ⅓ yard. Two tiny snaps. Flat lace trim 1" wide, ¾ yard white. Pre-ruffled scalloped lace trim 3" wide, 1⅓ yards white. Lavender satin ribbon: ⅛" wide, 2⅔ yards; ¼" wide, 1 yard; 2" wide, 1⅓ yards. Cream-color satin ribbon ⅜" wide, 1" piece. Embroidered flower appliqués 1" high, about 15. Six-strand cotton embroidery floss, two small skeins white; one small skein each color in color key (*see face chart*). Small lavender fabric flowers with stems. White plastic-covered wire coat hanger. Polyester fiberfill for stuffing. Cardboard. White craft glue. *For*

necklace Six-strand embroidery floss, 1 skein purple. Steel crochet hook No. 3. Baby beads to spell LITTLE BO PEEP. *For lamb* Pompadour yarn, 2 ozs. white, small amount pink. Steel crochet hook No. 1. Stuffing. Six-strand embroidery floss, 1 skein each of purple and pink. Scrap of pink felt. Pink satin ribbon ⅜" wide, ½ yard. Lavender satin ribbon: ¼" wide, ½ yard; ⅛" wide, ⅝ yard. Jingle bell.

GENERAL DIRECTIONS
Enlarge patterns for doll and clothes by copying onto paper ruled in 1" squares; complete half-patterns indicated by long dash lines. Use dressmaker's carbon and dry ball-point pen to transfer patterns to wrong side of cream-color cotton fabric, placing them ½" apart. Reverse asymmetrical patterns for each second and fourth piece. Cut pieces ¼" beyond marked lines for seam allowance. From cream-color cotton fabric, cut out one head (back), one head center, two bodies, two arms, four legs, and two soles. Omit thumb. Zigzag-stitch edges to prevent raveling.

Glue tracing of hem scallops to cardboard; cut on marked lines for template; set aside.

DIRECTIONS FOR DOLL
Face: Zigzag-stitch Ainring piece to prevent raveling. With 9" edges of piece at top and bottom, mark vertical center with a line of basting, working through a row of holes on fabric. On right side, mark one head (face), lining up center markings and leaving equal margins at top and bottom; do not cut out yet. *To stitch* Measure 3½" down from center of head top along basting for placement of first stitch; mark with straight pin. Insert face area in hoop. Work stitching as directed below, following chart, color key, page 20,

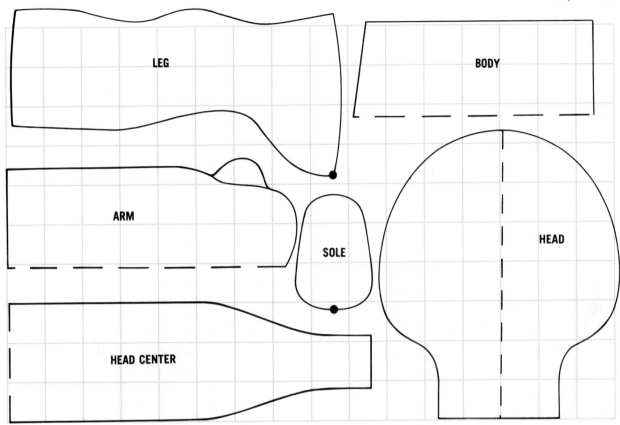

LEG

BODY

ARM

SOLE

HEAD

HEAD CENTER

and Embroidery Stitch Details, page 185. Chart is given for right half of face; reverse for left half. Each symbol on chart represents one cross-stitch, heavy lines embroidery; different symbols and letters represent different colors *(see key)*. Work cross-stitches first, then embroidery, using two strands of floss in needle, unless otherwise specified. *For cross-stitch* Beginning at stitch indicated by arrow on chart, work cross-stitches over one horizontal and one vertical fabric thread or "square." When working cross-stitches, work all underneath stitches in one direction and all top stitches in opposite direction. Make crosses touch by inserting needle in same hole used for adjacent stitch *(see detail)*. *For embroidery* Referring to key for colors, work each eyebrow with two rows of outline stitch. Work jawline, upper nose, and outline of

each eye and pupil in backstitch, taking each stitch over one square. Using chocolate floss, work backstitch to define bottom of mouth and to separate front teeth *(see photograph for placement)*; work straight-stitch lashes and fill in irises with satin stitch. Use one strand of honey floss to work straight stitches over each filled iris as shown.

When all embroidery is complete, remove fabric from hoop; remove basting. Press gently, wrong side up. Cut out face, adding ¼" seam allowance all around.

Head: Pin head center to head front and back with bottom edges even. Stitch around sides and top, leaving neck edge open. Fold neck ¼" to wrong side. Turn head to right side. Stuff firmly with fiberfill.

Body: Fold arms in half lengthwise, right side

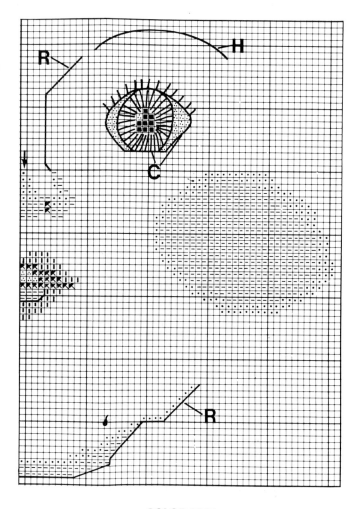

COLOR KEY

	⊡	**Bright White**
	⊡	**Pale Pink Pearl**
R	⊟	**Pale Rose**
	⊞	**Dusty Rose**
	⬔	**Dark Rose**
C	◼	**Chocolate**
H		**Honey**

in. Stitch raw arm and hand edges, leaving straight edges open. Turn; stuff firmly. Baste each arm closed ⅛″ from raw edges, enclosing stuffing. Stitch legs together in pairs at front and back, leaving top and bottom edges open. Stitch soles to bottom openings, matching dots; turn and stuff. Baste each leg top as for arm, but with seams centered. On right side of one body (front), pin arms ½″ down from shoulders, so that arms cross, hands point down, and side edges are even; stitch. Pin and stitch legs to body bottom in similar manner, so that toes point toward shoulders. Place body front on work surface with limbs on top, now extending outward. Fold left arm across body, so that hand extends above right shoulder and seam allowance faces out. Pin left side of body back, wrong side up, to body front; stitch. Pin and stitch right side of body in same manner (body will look like a tube with hands extending above and legs below). Push legs up through tube, so that only seam allowance extends at bottom; pin and stitch body bottom. Turn and stuff. Turn raw edges ¼″ to inside; slipstitch opening closed. Slipstitch head, centered, over shoulders.

DIRECTIONS FOR HAIR

MATERIALS
2 ozs. lightweight dress yarn, light brown. Steel crochet hook No. 1. Matching sewing thread.

GAUGE
5 dc = 1″; 1 row = ½″.

Side hair (make 10 strips): Ch 60, 2 dc in 4th ch from hook, 3 dc in each of next 30 ch, dc in each remaining ch. End off. (**Note:** First half of each strip will spiral into doll's curls; second half will lie flat and will be sewn to sides of head.) Vary length of curls, if desired.

Plain strips (make 4): Ch 30; sc in 2nd ch

from hook, hdc in next ch, dc in each remaining ch. End off.

Sew 5 strips with curls and 2 plain strips to each side of head, edges touching.

Back and top hair (make 11 strips): Ch 85; 2 dc in 4th ch from hook, 3 dc in each of next 40 ch, dc in each remaining ch. End off, leaving 2″ end.

Having curls hanging down back, sew flat sections from back of head across top of head to forehead, covering top edges of side hair. If necessary, to cover head, fill in any spaces with plain strips of crochet. Knot 4″ lengths of yarn across front ends of strips for 2″ bangs.

DIRECTIONS FOR CLOTHES

Pantalets: From white cotton fabric, cut two pantalets. Press waist edges ¼″ to wrong side. Cut two 4¼″ lengths of elastic. Pin elastic across wrong side of each waist ⅛″ from fold; stitch, using wide zigzag stitches. Reset machine for straight stitch. Press leg bottoms ¼″ to wrong side. Cut two pieces of 1″-wide lace to fit leg bottoms. On the right side of each leg, pin lace so that bottom edge extends ¾″ below fold; topstitch. Stitch pantalets together at center front and back from waist to crotch. Stitch each inseam from lace to crotch.

Dress: From dotted lavender fabric, cut the following pieces, lining up straight bottom edge of each piece with a horizontal (cross-grain) line of dots on fabric: Cut two sleeves, adding extra ¼″ at each sleeve bottom; cut bodice front, using complete pattern, and two bodice backs, using half-pattern and adding extra ¼″ at each center back. Also cut 44″ × 8″ skirt and 44″ × 2½″ skirt facing, lining up straight edges with lines of dots. From netting, cut four 44″ × 7″ pieces for underskirt. Stitch bodice front and backs together at shoulders. Press sleeve bottoms ¼″ to wrong side twice; slipstitch.

Smocking (for each sleeve): Place sleeve right side up on work surface with bottom folded edge at top. Using ruler and tailor's chalk, mark horizontal lines along dots on fabric for 3″-deep area, starting ⅜″ below top and ¾″ in from side edges. Starting at top left corner of rectangle, work smocking across lines of dots from left to right as directed, following diagram on page 190 for the two pattern stitches; each dot on diagram represents one dot on fabric. Use three strands of white floss in embroidery needle, knotting at beginning and end of strand. Keep needle pointing from right to left at all times as shown, but change position of thread to above or below point of needle as directed. As you insert needle through dot, pick up about ⅛″ of fabric and pull gently to gather fabric into folds. At end of each row, smocking should measure 5¼″; before ending off, adjust work if necessary by pulling up completed stitches with needle.

Row 1: Work outline stitch on first line. Keep thread below needle throughout.

Row 2: Work honeycomb stitch between third and fifth lines. Starting at third line, bring needle up on left side of first dot, then, with thread above needle, take stitch through second dot and pull; take another stitch through both dots to anchor. For next stitch, insert needle on right side of second dot again, then pass under fabric to bring needle up on left side of second dot in fifth line; take stitch through third dot, pull and anchor, then move back up to third row under fabric. Continue across between lines.

Row 3: Repeat row 2 between seventh and ninth lines.

Row 4 to end: Continue working honeycomb stitch down to two lines above bottom, skipping a line between rows of stitches. To end, repeat row 1 on last line. *To construct each sleeve* Baste upper curved edge of sleeve between X's. Pin lower curved edges of sleeve to front and back armhole of bodice below X's. Gather upper curved edge to fit armhole;

pin and stitch. Stitch underarm and side in a continuous seam. Turn assembled bodice to right side.

Skirt Using ruler and tailor's chalk, mark a line on wrong side of facing piece ¼" up from one long (bottom) edge; mark center of line. Starting at center and working outward to both ends, use template to mark scalloped edge, so that bottom of each scallop is even with marked line on fabric. Place skirt face up on work surface with long edges at top and bottom. Pin facing, marked side up, to skirt with bottom and side edges even; stitch scallops. Working through both thicknesses, trim excess fabric below scallops to ⅛"; turn facing to wrong side of skirt and press. Press top edge of facing under ¼"; slipstitch. Stack net underskirt pieces on work surface with long edges at top and bottom. Pin skirt, right side up, to underskirt, matching top (waist) and side edges. Machine-baste close to waist through all thicknesses. Gather waist to fit bodice waist. Stitch assembled skirt to bodice. Starting at hem, stitch center backs together to 1" below waist, making ½" seam; press seam open. Above seam, press edges ¼" to wrong side twice; slipstitch. **To finish:** Cut flat lace trim to fit neck edge, plus ½". Press ends ¼" to wrong side; topstitch. Pin trim in place with right sides facing; stitch. Press seam to inside; trim will extend above neck. Sew snaps to neck opening and center back. Cut scalloped lace to fit hem, plus ½". Pin lace to facing so that top edges are even; overlap ends and slipstitch in place, being careful not to catch skirt fabric with stitches. Pin appliqués to alternate scallops on skirt as shown in photograph; slipstitch in place.

Overdress: From dotted white fabric, cut one top back and two top fronts. Also mark 29" × 6¼" rectangle for skirt; do not cut out yet. At each end of one long marked edge, mark rounded corners, using bowl or plate. Cut on marked lines, discarding corners. Cut match-ing lining for each overdress piece. Stitch back and fronts together at shoulders, for outer top. Cut six 1" lengths of elastic for loops. Press loops in half widthwise and pin to right side of each outer front at open dots (*see pattern*), with raw edges even. Stitch lining pieces together at shoulders. Pin lining to outer top, right sides facing; stitch front, neck, and armhole edges. Turn to right side, pulling fronts through shoulders to back; press. Stitch sides of top. Stitch skirt pieces together, leaving long straight edge (waist) open; turn and press. Working through both thicknesses, gather skirt waist to fit top waist. Stitch skirt to top. Cut 31" length from ⅛"-wide ribbon; use to lace overdress front as shown.

Stockings: On nylon knit fabric, mark two stockings, lining up arrow with ribbing; cut out. Fold top straight edges ¼" to wrong side; zigzag-stitch close to folds. Fold each stocking in half lengthwise with right side in and edges even; zigzag-stitch ¼" in from raw edges, leaving top edge open; turn.

Shoes: On wrong side of vinyl, mark two soles, two uppers, and two tongues. Cut out soles and uppers, adding seam allowance to soles and to uppers at sole and back edges; cut out lacing holes on uppers. Cut out tongues on marked lines, pinking top straight edges. Glue tongue at bottom to inside of each upper, matching dots. Cut two 31" lengths of ⅛"-wide ribbon; use to lace shoes.

Bow: From 2"-wide ribbon, cut three lengths, one 12", one 11", and one 3". Overlap ends of 12" length ¼", forming a ring; glue to secure. Form second ring with 11" length. Referring to photograph, wrap 3" length around loops to form hair bow as shown; glue ends. Notch ends of remaining 2"-wide ribbon. Fold ribbon in half to form streamers; slipstitch folded end to back of bow. Make hair (as explained above) and tack bow to hair as shown.

1 sq. = 1 in.

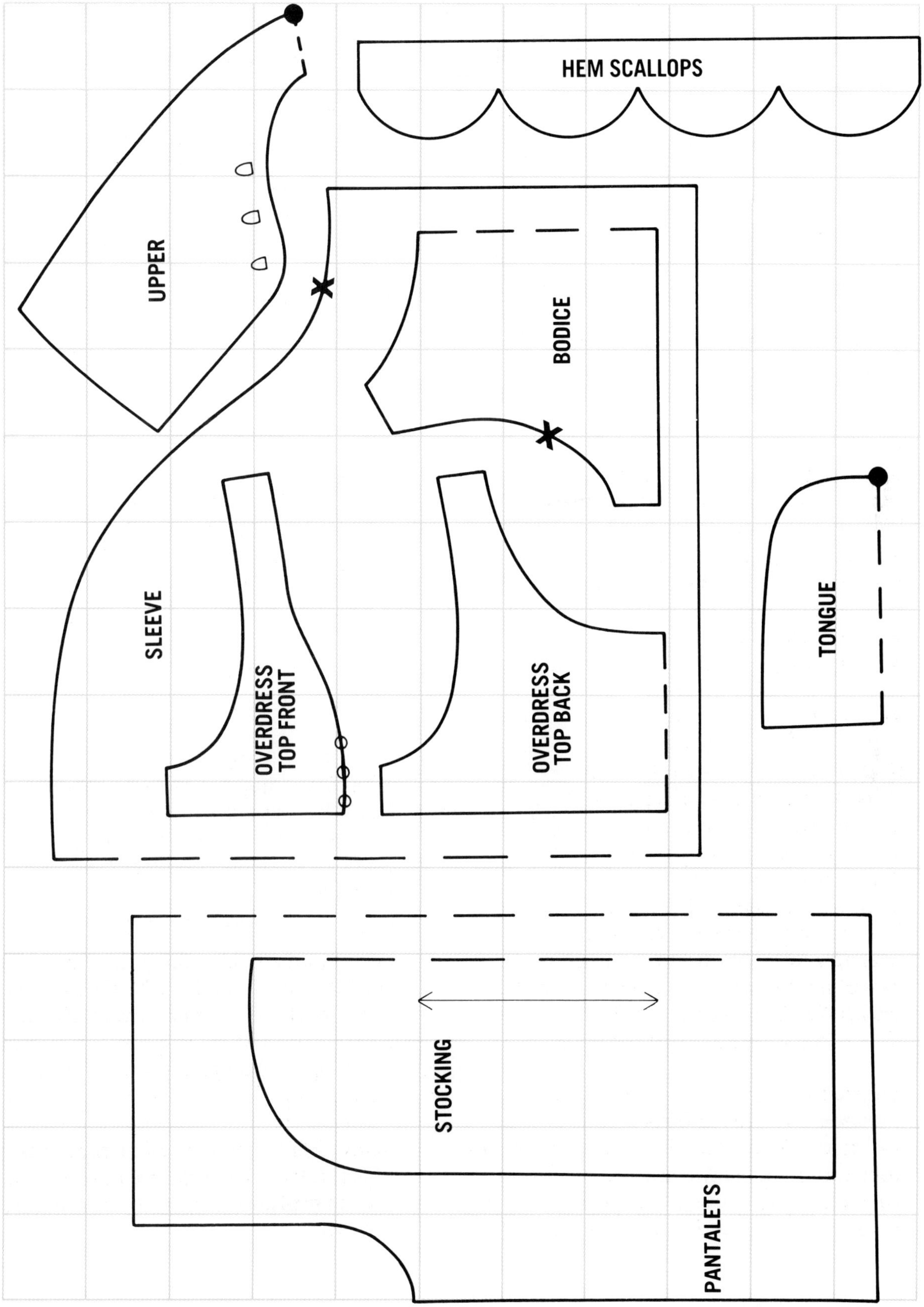

HEM SCALLOPS

UPPER

BODICE

SLEEVE

OVERDRESS TOP FRONT

OVERDRESS TOP BACK

TONGUE

STOCKING

PANTALETS

Crook: Clip one side of wire coat hanger at base of hook. Measuring from tip of hook, clip wire to 21½". Bend into crook shape, following photograph. Cut remaining ⅛"-wide ribbon into two equal lengths. Place ribbons together and tie into bow around crook as shown, inserting flower stems between crook and ribbon before securing. Form a loop from cream-color ribbon and slipstitch to doll's hand to support crook as shown.

DIRECTIONS FOR NECKLACE

First Chain: String beads spelling LITTLE in reverse order on embroidery floss. Beg 4" from end of floss, make a loop on hook, work a chain for 3½". Push "L" up, make a ch st to secure bead, ch 1, push "I" up, make a ch st to secure bead, ch 1; repeat this procedure until all beads are secured, work ch for 3½". Cut floss 4" from last ch, pull end through last ch.

Second Chain: String beads spelling BO PEEP in reverse order on embroidery floss. Work as for first chain, working ch for 4½" before first bead and after last bead, and making 4 ch between BO and PEEP.

Knot chains tog at beg and end of chain st and at ends of floss. Tie around doll's neck.

DIRECTIONS FOR LAMB

Head and body: Beg at front of head, with white, ch 2.

Rnd 1: 6 sc in 2nd ch from hook.

Rnd 2: Working in back lps, 2 sc in each sc around.

Rnd 3: Working in back lps, (sc in next sc, 2 sc in next sc) 6 times—18 sc.

Rnds 4-8: Sc in back lp of each sc, inc 3 sc evenly spaced each rnd—33 sc. Sl st in next st. Ch 1, turn.

Rnd 9: Loop st in each sc around. To make loop st, insert hook in st, wrap yarn back over right index finger, catch yarn with hook and draw through st, drop loop from finger, yo and through 2 lps on hook.

Rnd 10: Sc in each st around.

Rnds 11-22: Repeat rnds 9 and 10.

Rnds 23-26: Sc around, dec 3 sc each rnd—21 sc (end of head and neck).

Rnd 27: Loop st in each sc around.

Rnd 28: Sc around, inc 5 sc in rnd—26 sc.

Rnds 29-32: Repeat rnds 27 and 28 twice—36 sts.

Rnd 33: Loop st in each sc around.

Rnd 34: Sc in each st around.

Rnds 35-38: Repeat rnds 33 and 34 twice.

Rnd 39: Loop st in each sc around.

Rnd 40: Sc in each st around, dec 3 sc in rnd—33 sc.

Rnd 41: Loop st in each sc around.

Rnds 42-45: Repeat rnds 40 and 41 twice—27 sc. Sl st in next st. Ch 1, turn. Stuff lamb firmly. Sc 2 sts tog around until opening is closed.

Leg (make 4): Beg at foot, with pink, ch 2.

Rnd 1: 6 sc in 2nd ch from hook.

Rnd 2: Working in back lps, 2 sc in each sc around.

Rnd 3: Working in back lps, sc in each sc around—12 sc.

Rnd 4: Sc in each sc around, inc 3 sc in rnd—15 sc.

Rnd 5: Working in back lps, sc in each sc around, inc 3 sc in rnd—18 sc. Sl st in next sc. End off.

Rnd 6: Working around wrong side (inside) of leg, with white, loop st in each sc.

Rnd 7: Sc in each st around.

Repeat rnds 6 and 7, 3 times. End off. Place a flat button or heavy cardboard circle in bottom of leg, then stuff leg firmly. Sew legs to body.

Tail: With white, ch 2.

Rnd 1: 4 sc in 2nd ch from hook.

Rnd 2: 2 sc in back lp of each sc—8 sc.

Rnds 3-5: Sc in back lp of each sc. End off. Flatten tail. Sew to back of lamb at top.

To finish: With purple floss, embroider eyes in satin stitch. With pink floss, embroider nose in satin stitch, mouth in straight stitch.

From pink felt, cut 2 oval ears 1½" long, 1" wide. Fold oval in half lengthwise and cut small piece from end of oval to make a straight edge. Sew this straight folded edge to head with fold toward back. Place ¼"-wide lavender ribbon over pink ribbon. Tie around neck with bow at top of neck. Sew ends of ⅛"-wide ribbon under bow for "leash." Sew bell to neck ribbon under head.

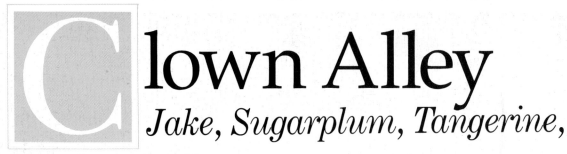

Clown Alley
Jake, Sugarplum, Tangerine, Patches, Balloon—5 crazy clowns.

Jake

SIZE
About 20″ tall.

MATERIALS
Knitting worsted-weight yarn, 2 ozs. each of white, light turquoise, bright coral, and navy blue. Crochet hook size G (4¼ mm). Polyester stuffing.

GAUGE
4 sc = 1″.

DIRECTIONS FOR CLOWN AND CLOTHES

Head: With white, ch 2.

Rnd 1: 6 sc in 2nd ch from hook.

Rnd 2: 2 sc in each sc around—12 sc.

Rnd 3: (2 sc in next sc, sc in next sc) 6 times—18 sc.

Rnd 4: (2 sc in next sc, sc in 2 sc) 6 times—24 sc.

Rnd 5: (2 sc in next sc, sc in 2 sc) 8 times—32 sc.

Rnd 6: (2 sc in next sc, sc in 3 sc) 8 times—40 sc.

Rnds 7-10: Work even on 40 sc.

Rnd 11: (Work 2 sc tog, sc in 8 sc) 4 times—36 sc.

Rnds 12-20: Work even on 36 sc.

Rnd 21: (Work 2 sc tog, sc in next sc) 12 times—24 sc.

Rnd 22: Work even on 24 sc.

Rnd 23: (Work 2 sc tog, sc in 2 sc) 6 times—18 sc.

Rnds 24 and 25: Work even on 18 sc. Sl st in next sc. End off.

Body: Join turquoise to neck edge of head.

Rnd 1: 2 sc in each sc around—36 sc.

Rnd 2: Sc in 8 sc, 2 sc in each of 2 sc, sc in 16 sc, 2 sc in each of 2 sc, sc in 8 sc—40 sc.

Rnds 3 and 4: Work even on 40 sc. Sl st in first sc. End off turquoise.

Rnd 5: With coral, sc in each sc around. Sl st in first sc. End off coral.

Rnd 6: With turquoise, working in back lps only, sc in each sc around.

Rnds 7-9: Working in both lps, sc in each sc around. Sl st in first sc. End off turquoise.

Rnds 10-19: Repeat rows 5-9 twice.

Rnds 20-27: With navy, work even on 40 sc.

Rnd 28: (Work 2 sc tog, sc in 8 sc) 4 times—36 sc. Sl st in first sc. End off navy. Stuff head and body firmly. Sew a seam at bottom from side to side to close opening.

Nose: With coral, ch 2.

Rnd 1: 4 sc in 2nd ch from hook.

Rnd 2: 2 sc in each sc around—8 sc.

Rnd 3: (2 sc in next sc, sc in next sc) 4 times—12 sc.

Rnd 4: Work even on 12 sc. End off. Stuff nose and sew to center of face.

Mouth: With coral, embroider a wide smile on face.

Eyes: With navy, embroider 1″ cross-stitches above and to sides of nose.

Ear (make 2): With white, ch 2.

Row 1: 4 sc in 2nd ch from hook. Ch 1, turn.

Row 2: 2 sc in each sc. Ch 1, turn.

Row 3: 2 sc in each sc—16 sc. End off. Sew ears to sides of head.

Hair: With coral, stitch 1½″ loops in front of ears and across back of head from rnd 10 to rnd 19. Make a backstitch after each loop so that loops will not pull out. Cut each loop and trim evenly.

Hat: With navy, ch 2.

Rnd 1: 6 sc in 2nd ch from hook.

Rnd 2: 2 sc in each sc around—12 sc.

Rnd 3: 2 sc in each sc around—24 sc.

Rnd 4: (2 sc in next sc, sc in 2 sc) 8 times—32 sc.

Rnd 5: (2 sc in next sc, sc in 3 sc) 8 times—40 sc.

Rnds 6-10: Work even on 40 sc.

Rnd 11: (2 sc in next sc, sc in 9 sc) 4 times—44 sc.

Rnd 12: (2 sc in next sc, sc in 10 sc) 4 times—48 sc.

Rnd 13: (2 sc in next sc, sc in 7 sc) 6 times—54 sc.

Rnd 14: Work even on 54 sc.

Rnd 15: (2 sc in next sc, sc in 8 sc) 6 times—60 sc.

Rnd 16: Work even on 60 sc. Sl st in next sc. End off. Stuff hat lightly. Sew hat to top of head to cover bald area. Fold up brim in front.

Tie: With navy, ch 15.

Row 1: Sc in 2nd ch from hook and in each ch. Ch 1, turn.

Rows 2-4: Sc in each sc. Ch 1, turn each row. End off. Wrap yarn around center to form bow tie. Sew to neck.

Suspenders (make 2): With navy, ch 50.

Row 1: Sc in 2nd ch from hook and in each ch. Ch 1, turn.

Row 2: Sc in each sc. End off. Sew suspenders to front at start of navy section, cross them in back and sew to navy section in back.

Hand (make 2): With white, ch 2.

Rnd 1: 4 sc in 2nd ch from hook.

Rnd 2: 2 sc in each sc around—8 sc.

Rnd 3: 2 sc in each sc around—16 sc.

Rnd 4: Work even on 16 sc.

Rnd 5: (Work 2 sc tog, sc in 2 sc) 4 times—12 sc.

Rnd 6: Work even on 12 sc. End off. Do not stuff hands.

Arm (make 2): With turquoise, ch 12. Join with sl st in first ch to form ring.

Rnd 1: Sc in each ch around.

Rnds 2-4: Sc in each sc around. Drop turquoise.

Rnd 5: With coral, sc in each sc around. Cut coral.

Rnd 6: With turquoise, sc in back lp of each sc around.

Rnds 7-9: Sc in each sc around. Drop turquoise.

Rnds 10-19: Repeat rows 5-9 twice. End off. Stuff arms lightly. Sew hands to one end of arms. Flatten other end and sew it closed. Sew this end to shoulder so arm swings freely.

Leg (make 2): *Upper section* With navy, ch 16. Join with sl st in first ch to form ring.

Rnd 1: Sc in each ch around.

Rnds 2-18: Sc in each sc around. Sl st in first sc. End off. Stuff lightly. Flatten both ends and stitch closed. Sew top edge to bottom seam of body.

Lower section With navy, ch 14. Join with sl st in first ch to form ring.

Rnd 1: Sc in each ch around.

Rnds 2-14: Sc in each sc around. Sl st in first sc. End off. Stuff lightly. Flatten both ends and stitch closed. Sew top edge to upper section of leg.

Shoe (make 2): With white, ch 2.

Rnd 1: 6 sc in 2nd ch from hook.

Rnd 2: 2 sc in each sc around—12 sc.

Rnd 3: 2 sc in each sc around—24 sc.

Rnds 4-7: Work even on 24 sc.

Rnd 8: (Work 2 sc tog, sc in 4 sc) 4 times—20 sc.

Rnd 9: (Work 2 sc tog, sc in 3 sc) 4 times—16 sc.

Rnd 10: Work even on 16 sc.

Rnd 11: (Work 2 sc tog, sc in 2 sc) 4 times—12 sc.

Rnd 12: Work even on 12 sc. Sl st in next sc. End off. Stuff shoes and stitch a seam for back of shoe. Sew shoes to lower legs.

Sugarplum

SIZE
10″ high, seated.

MATERIALS
Knitting worsted-weight yarn, 2 ozs. each of yellow, gray, and hot pink, 1 oz. white, few yards black. Crochet hook size G (4¼ mm). Polyester stuffing. Empty roll of bathroom tissue.

GAUGE
4 sc = 1″.

DIRECTIONS FOR CLOWN AND CLOTHES
Body: With yellow, ch 26.

Row 1: Sc in 2nd ch from hook and in each ch—25 sc. Ch 1, turn.

Rows 2-5: Sc in back lp of each sc. Ch 1, turn each row. At end of row 5, drop yellow. With gray, ch 1, turn.

Rows 6 and 7: With gray, sc in back lp of each sc. Cut gray.

Rows 8-12: With yellow, sc in back lp of each sc. Work 2 rows of gray, 5 rows of yellow until there are 56 rows, ending with 2 rows of gray. Sew last row to first row for back seam.

With yellow, work 1 row sc around one edge of body. Run a strand of yarn through all rows on other edge and pull rows tog to form neck. Slip body over roll of bathroom tissue.

Head: With white, ch 2.

Rnd 1: 6 sc in 2nd ch from hook.

Rnd 2: 2 sc in each sc around.

Rnd 3: Work even on 12 sc.

Rnd 4: (2 sc in next sc, sc in next sc) 6 times.

Rnd 5: Work even on 18 sc.

Rnd 6: (2 sc in next sc, sc in 2 sc) 6 times.

Rnd 7: Work even on 24 sc.

Rnd 8: (2 sc in next sc, sc in 3 sc) 6 times.

Rnd 9: Work even on 30 sc.

Rnd 10: (2 sc in next sc, sc in 4 sc) 6 times.

Rnds 11-17: Work even on 36 sc.

Rnd 18: (Work 2 sc tog, sc in 4 sc) 6 times—30 sc.

Rnd 19: (Work 2 sc tog, sc in 3 sc) 6 times—24 sc.

Rnd 20: (Work 2 sc tog, sc in 2 sc) 6 times—18 sc.

Rnd 21: Work even on 18 sc. Sl st in next sc. End off. Stuff head firmly and sew to neck edge of body.

Collar: With gray, ch 8.

Row 1: Sc in 2nd ch from hook and in each ch—7 sc. Ch 1, turn.

Rows 2-36: Working in back lps only, sc in each sc. Ch 1, turn each row. End off. Run yarn through one long edge of collar. Gather edge to fit around neck of clown. Sew back seam. Turn up collar slightly.

Nose: With hot pink, ch 2.

Rnd 1: 5 sc in 2nd ch from hook.

Rnd 2: 2 sc in each sc around—10 sc.

Rnd 3: (2 sc in next sc, sc in next sc) 5 times—15 sc.

Rnds 4 and 5: Sc in each sc around. Sl st in next sc. End off. Stuff nose and sew to center of face.

Eyes: With double strand of black, take 1½" vertical stitch crossed by ½" horizontal stitch each side of nose.

Mouth: With pink, embroider smile on face in outline stitch.

Hair: With double strand of pink, sew 1" loops all over back, top, and sides of head, taking backstitch after forming each loop to secure loop. Cut each loop and brush yarn for a fuzzy look. Trim ends. Cut 2 strands of yellow about 8" long. Tie a bow in hair on each side of head.

Arm (make 2): With yellow, ch 20.

Row 1: Sc in 2nd ch from hook and in each ch. Ch 1, turn each row.

Rows 2 and 3: Working in back lps only, sc in each sc. Cut yellow.

Row 4: With gray, sc in back lp of each sc. Cut gray.

Rows 5-7: With yellow, sc in back lp of each sc.

Row 8: Repeat row 4. Sew last row to starting ch. Stuff arms lightly.

Hand (make 2): With gray, ch 6.

Row 1: Sc in 2nd ch from hook and in each ch. Ch 1, turn.

Row 2: Sc in each sc. Ch 1, turn.

Row 3: Sc in each sc, ch 4 for thumb.

Row 4: Sl st in 2nd ch from hook and in next 2 ch, sl st in first sc, sc in 4 sc, ch 4 for little finger.

Row 5: Sl st in 2nd ch from hook and in next 2 ch, sl st in next sc, ch 5 for ring finger; sl st in 2nd ch from hook and in next 3 ch, sl st in next sc, ch 6 for middle finger; sl st in 2nd ch from hook and in next 4 ch, sl st in next sc, ch 5 for index finger; sl st in 2nd ch from hook and in next 3 ch, sl st in beg of thumb. Cut yarn. Make another piece the same. Sew 2 pieces tog for each hand. Do not stuff hands. Sew hand to end of arm. Sew arms in place on sides of body.

Leg (make 2): With yellow, ch 26.

Row 1: Sc in 2nd ch from hook and in each ch. Ch 1, turn.

Rows 2-5: Working in back lps only, sc in each sc. Ch 1, turn each row. Drop yellow.

Rows 6 and 7: With gray, sc in back lp of each sc. Cut gray.

Rows 8-12: With yellow, work as for row 2.

Rows 13 and 14: Work as for row 6. End off. Sew last row to starting ch. Stuff legs lightly. Seam both ends of leg flat across with gray stripe at center. Sew top of legs to bottom of body, matching gray stripes.

Shoe (make 4 pieces): With gray, ch 6.

Row 1: Sc in 2nd ch from hook and in next 3 ch, 3 sc in last ch; working on opposite side of starting ch, sc in 4 ch. Ch 1, turn.

Row 2: Sc in 2 sc, hdc in 2 sc, 2 dc in each of 3 sc, hdc in 2 sc, sc in 2 sc. Ch 1, turn.

Row 3: Sc in 2 sc, hdc in 2 hdc, 2 dc in each of 6 dc, hdc in 2 hdc, sc in 2 sc. Ch 1, turn.

Row 4: Sc in 2 sc, hdc in 2 hdc, 2 dc in each

of 12 dc, hdc in 2 hdc, sc in 2 sc. End off. Sew 2 pieces tog for each shoe, sewing through back lps, leaving straight edge open. Stuff shoes. Close straight edge (back of shoe). Sew shoes to ends of legs.

Tangerine

SIZE
About 18″ tall.

MATERIALS
Knitting worsted-weight yarn, 3 ozs. variegated orange (A), 2 ozs. bright orange (B), 1 oz. white (C), few yards brown. Crochet hook size G (4¼ mm). Polyester stuffing. Large-eyed tapestry needle.

GAUGE
4 sts = 1″.

DIRECTIONS FOR CLOWN AND CLOTHES
Head: Beg at top of head, with C, ch 2.

Rnd 1: 6 sc in 2nd ch from hook.

Rnd 2: 2 sc in each sc around.

Rnd 3: 2 sc in each sc around—24 sc.

Rnd 4: Work even in sc.

Rnd 5: (2 sc in next sc, sc in next sc) 12 times—36 sc.

Rnds 6-18: Work even in sc.

Rnd 19: (Work next 2 sc tog, sc in 4 sc) 6 times—30 sc.

Rnd 20: (Work next 2 sc tog, sc in 3 sc) 6 times—24 sc.

Rnd 21: (Work next 2 sc tog, sc in 4 sc) 4 times—20 sc.

Rnd 22: (Work next 2 sc tog, sc in 3 sc) 4 times—16 sc.

Rnds 23 and 24: Work even in sc. Sl st in next sc. End.

Body: With A, 2 sc in each sc around neck edge of head—32 sc.

Rnd 2: Sc in each sc around.

Rnd 3: (2 sc in next sc, sc in 3 sc) 8 times—40 sc.

Rnds 4-24: Work even in sc. Sl st in next sc. End off. Stuff head and body.

Bottom: With A, ch 6.

Rnd 1: 3 sc in 2nd ch from hook, sc in next 3 ch, 3 sc in last ch; working on opposite side of starting ch, sc in 4 ch, 2 sc in first sc—14 sc.

Rnd 2: (2 sc in next 2 sc, sc in 5 sc) twice—18 sc.

Rnd 3: (2 sc in next sc, sc in 2 sc) 6 times—24 sc.

Rnd 4: (2 sc in next sc, sc in 3 sc) 6 times—30 sc.

Rnd 5: (2 sc in next sc, sc in 5 sc) 5 times—35 sc.

Rnd 6: (2 sc in next sc, sc in 6 sc) 5 times—40 sc. Sl st in next sc. End off, leaving end for sewing. Sew bottom to opening at lower edge of clown.

Nose: With B, ch 2.

Rnd 1: 6 sc in 2nd ch from hook.

Rnd 2: 2 sc in each sc around—12 sc.

Rnd 3: (2 sc in next sc, sc in next sc) 6 times—18 sc.

Rnd 4: Work even on 18 sc. Sl st in next sc. End off. Stuff nose and sew to center of face.

Features: With B, embroider wide grin on face in outline stitch. With double strand of brown, embroider 1" cross-stitches above and to each side of nose for eyes. With double strand of B, sew 2" loops all over head for hair: Bring yarn out to right side, leave loop 2" high, take small backstitch in head to secure loop, bringing yarn out in position to make next loop.

Hand (make 2): With B, ch 2.

Rnd 1: 6 sc in 2nd ch from hook.

Rnd 2: 2 sc in each sc—12 sc.

Rnd 3: (2 sc in next sc, sc in 3 sc) 3 times—15 sc.

Rnd 4: Sc in each sc.

Rnd 5: (Work 2 sc tog, sc in 3 sc) 3 times—12 sc.

Rnd 6: Sc in each sc. Sl st in next sc. End off. Stuff hands.

Arm (make 2): With A, ch 12. Join with sl st in first ch to form ring.

Rnd 1: Sc in each ch around.

Rnd 2: Sc in each sc around.

Rnd 3: (2 sc in next sc, sc in 3 sc) 3 times—15 sc.

Rnds 4-20: Work even on 15 sc. Sl st in next sc. End off. Stuff arms. Sew hands to narrow end of arms. Sew arms to sides of body.

Leg (make 2): Work as for arm through rnd 4—15 sc.

Rnd 5: (2 sc in next sc, sc in 4 sc) 3 times—18 sc.

Rnd 6: Work even on 18 sc.

Rnd 7: (2 sc in next sc, sc in 5 sc) 3 times—21 sc.

Rnds 8-24: Work even on 21 sc. Sl st in next sc. End off. Stuff legs.

Shoe (make 2): With B, ch 14.

Rnd 1: 3 sc in 2nd ch from hook, sc in next 11 ch, 3 sc in last ch; working on opposite side of ch, sc in 12 ch, 2 sc in first sc—30 sc.

Rnd 2: 2 sc in next sc, sc in 12 sc, 2 sc in each of next 3 sc, sc in next 13 sc.

Rnd 3: 2 sc in each of 3 sc, sc in 6 sc, (2 hdc in next sc, hdc in next sc) 9 times, hdc in next sc, sc in 6 sc.

Rnd 4: Sl st in 12 sc, sc in 28 hdc, sl st in 6 sc. End off. Make another piece the same. Sew two pieces tog for each shoe, sewing through back lps of sts and stuffing wider section of shoe before closing seam. Narrow section is back of shoe. Sew shoes to narrow end of legs. Sew legs to front of clown in sitting position.

Ruff: With A, ch 18.

Row 1: 3 sc in 2nd ch from hook and in each ch. Ch 1, turn.

Row 2: Sc in each sc. Ch 1, turn.

Row 3: 2 sc in each sc. Ch 1, turn.

Row 4: Sc in each sc. End off. Place ruff around neck with opening at back. Sew ruff to neck; sew back opening tog.

Patches

SIZE
20″ tall.

EQUIPMENT
Pencil. Ruler. Paper for patterns. Scissors. Dressmaker's tracing (carbon) paper. Dry ball-point pen. Sewing machine with zigzag attachment. Embroidery and sewing needles. Pinking shears. Knitting needle. Wire hanger. Wire cutters.

MATERIALS
Cotton fabrics, ½ yard each of the following: red, 36″ wide; print, 45″ wide. Unbleached muslin, 36″ wide, ½ yard. Black velour, 7″ × 19″ piece. Scrap of red six-strand embroidery floss. Two red 1½″ pompons. One red ½″ shank button. Scraps of red, black, white felt. One skein yellow worsted-weight yarn. Sewing threads to match fabrics, felt, and yarn. Heavy-duty sewing thread to match muslin. Polyester fiberfill. One snap fastener.

DIRECTIONS FOR CLOWN AND CLOTHES
Enlarge patterns by copying on paper ruled in 1″ squares; complete half-patterns indicated by dash lines. Use dressmaker's carbon and dry ball-point pen to transfer patterns to wrong side of fabrics as directed below, placing them ½″ apart and ½″ from fabric edges. Except for felt and where otherwise indicated, cut out pieces ¼″ beyond marked lines for seam allowance. Stitch pieces together on marked lines or as directed with right sides facing, raw edges even, and using matching thread. Clip into seams at curves and corners; turn piece to right side and poke out corners with knitting needle.

Body: From muslin, cut four heads, two bodies, four arms, and four legs, reversing patterns for second and fourth pieces.

Stitch two head pieces together along center seam, to make head front. Using dressmaker's carbon and dry ball-point pen, transfer face to right side of head front. Using six strands of floss in embroidery needle, outline mouth with outline stitch, then fill in with satin stitch (*see Embroidery Stitch Details, page 185*). Set sewing machine for narrow zigzag stitch (¹⁄₁₆″ wide); using black thread, embroider eyebrows and straight lines radiating from eyes.

From felt, cut two white eyes and two black pupils, using patterns. Using pinking shears, cut two cheeks from red felt. Straight-stitch cheeks and eyes to face. Sew on button for nose.

Stitch remaining head pieces together, to make head back. Stitch head front to back along curve, leaving bottom open. Turn head to right side; stuff firmly with fiberfill.

Stitch arms together in pairs, leaving straight edge open. Turn; stuff firmly with fiberfill. Baste each arm closed ⅛″ from top, enclosing stuffing. Matching dots and raw edges, pin arms to right side of one body (front). Place body front, right side up, on work surface. Fold left arm across body, so that hand extends above right shoulder. Pin left side of body back to body front; stitch. Pin and stitch right side of body in same manner (body will look like a tube with hands extending above). Stitch bottom and shoulders, leaving neck open. Turn and stuff body. Turn neck edges of body and head ¼″ to inside and slipstitch head to body all around, using heavy-duty thread. Stitch legs in pairs, leaving top open; turn and stuff. Turn under ¼″ at top and stitch across close to fold, with seams centered. Slipstitch legs to body, between dots.

Hair: Using wire cutters, cut off hook portion of hanger and shape into rectangle about 3″

× 10″. Closely wrap yarn widthwise down length of rectangle, leaving 6″ at each end for tying. Machine-stitch lengthwise down center of yarn, making sure to catch every strand; clip loop ends to make a two-sided fringe. Repeat four or five times, until you have enough yarn to cover head. Tie sections together, end to end, to make one long fringe; trim tie ends. Slipstitch hair to head along stitching, using matching thread; start at center back and work in a spiral toward crown.

Jumpsuit and hat: From print fabric, cut four jumpsuits and one hat, using patterns. Stitch two jumpsuit pieces together along center from leg cuff to neck edge for front; stitch remaining pieces together from cuff to dot for back. Stitch jumpsuit front and back together along sides and underarm, then stitch along top of sleeve. Turn all remaining raw edges ⅛″ to wrong side and stitch; turn to right side. Stitch straight edges of hat together; finish raw edge as for jumpsuit.

From red frabric, cut the following strips: two 3″ × 36″ for neck and hat ruffles; four 3″ × 30″ for cuff ruffles. Finish raw edges as directed above, using red thread. Baste lengthwise down center of each ruffle. Pull basting thread and gather neck and hat ruffles to 11″; gather cuff ruffles to 9″. Pin ruffles to suit and hat as shown, so that bottom edge of each ruffle is even with finished edge; stitch along basting. To finish jumpsuit, stitch snap fastener to inside neck edge at open circle (*see pattern*). Stitch one pompon to center front of suit as shown; stitch the other to top of hat. Place jumpsuit and hat on clown; slipstitch hat brim to head all around.

Boots: Cut four pieces from black velour. Turn each straight edge ⅛″ to wrong side and stitch. Stitch boots together in pairs around curved edge; turn; place on feet.

1 sq. = 1 in.

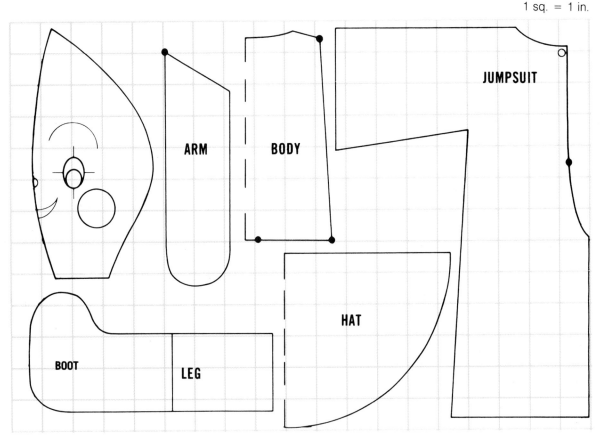

ARM

BODY

JUMPSUIT

HAT

BOOT

LEG

Balloon

SIZE
15″ tall.

EQUIPMENT
Pencil. Ruler. Scissors. Paper for patterns. Sewing machine with zigzag attachment. Sewing needle. Straight pins.

MATERIALS
Cotton print fabric, 12″ × 17″ piece. Felt: 9″ × 12″ sheet each of blue and light pink; scraps of red and medium pink. Three red pompons, 1½″ in diameter. White pre-gathered lace 1¼″ wide, 8″ piece. Red flat braid 1″ wide, 12″ piece. Sewing thread to match fabrics. Polyester fiberfill.

DIRECTIONS FOR CLOWN AND CLOTHES
Enlarge patterns by copying on paper ruled in 1″ squares; complete half-patterns indicated by dash lines; cut out patterns.

Use patterns to mark two suits and two sleeves on wrong side of fabric; cut out pieces ¼″ outside marked lines, for seam allowance. Mark the following on felt: two heads and two hands on light pink; two eyes, one hat, and two shoes on blue; two cheeks on medium pink; one mouth and nose on red. Cut out felt pieces on marked lines; do not add seam allowance.

Pin suits together, right sides facing, and stitch along curved edge and inseam, making ¼″ seams. With toes pointing up and out, insert a shoe between each suit "cuff," centered and with straight edge of shoe even with raw edge of cuff; baste across cuffs through all thicknesses, catching in shoe tops; pull basting thread tightly to gather. Machine-stitch over gathers to secure. Turn suit to right side and stuff with fiberfill until plump.

Fold each sleeve in half along dash line, wrong side out. Insert one hand inside sleeve

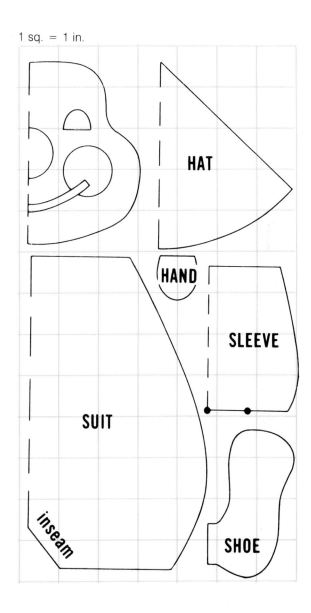

1 sq. = 1 in.

HAT

HAND

SLEEVE

SUIT

inseam

SHOE

between dots on pattern, with straight edge of hand even with raw edge of sleeve. Stitch around curved side and bottom of sleeve, catching in hand. Turn sleeve right side out and stuff with fiberfill.

Place a stuffed sleeve on either side of suit with folded edges of sleeves touching side seams of suit and top raw edges all in a line. Machine- or hand-baste across top edges of left sleeve, suit, and right sleeve, ¼" from raw edges. Baste across again, ⅛" from raw edges. Pull basting threads to gather until combined edges (neckline) measure 4" across; tie threads to hold gathers.

Following face pattern for placement, pin cheeks, nose, and eyes on one head piece. Carefully zigzag-stitch around edges, using matching thread and with machine set at eight stitches-to-the-inch. Zigzag-stitch mouth in place with one seam, overlapping cheeks as shown.

Place body over bottom edge of other head piece, pinning gathered neckline to follow curve of head; place face piece on top, concealing all gathering stitches. Baste, then machine-stitch head pieces together ⅛" from edges, stitching through sleeves and suit; leave a 2" opening at top of head for stuffing. Stuff head firmly with fiberfill, then stitch opening closed.

Machine-stitch top edge of lace along bottom of hat. Fold hat along dash line and stitch ⅛" from long edge. Stuff firmly with fiberfill; slipstitch hat to head all around brim. Stitch pompons to each side of head and to top of hat as shown. Tie flat braid into bow; stitch to neck.

ebbie Ann

She's a precious new arrival with a complete layette.

SIZE
Doll, about 15″ tall. Basket, about 16½″ long.

EQUIPMENT
Pencil. Ruler. Paper for patterns. Sewing, darning, embroidery, and tapestry needles. Dressmaker's tracing (carbon) paper. Dry ball-point pen. Straight pins. Knitting needle. Sewing machine with zigzag attachment. Iron. Pinking shears. Crochet hook size G (4¼ mm).

MATERIALS
For doll: Flesh-colored velour 45″ wide, ½ yard. Heavy-duty sewing thread to match velour. Sport-weight brushed acrylic yarn, 3 ozs. yellow. Six-strand embroidery floss, small amounts of brown, blue, white, and dark pink. Polyester fiberfill for stuffing. Coral crayon. **For clothes:** *Christening dress and bonnet* Closely woven white cotton fabric 45″ wide, ¾ yard. White galloon lace 2″ wide, ⅝ yard. White pre-gathered lace 1″ wide, 2½ yards. Baby blue satin ribbon ⅛″ wide, 1¾ yards. One round Velcro® fastener. *Nightgown* Closely woven cotton print fabric 45″ wide, ⅜ yard. Baby rickrack in contrasting color, 1¾ yards. Flat elastic ¼″ wide, ⅜ yard. One round Velcro® fastener. *Bib* White Ainring cloth, 18 mesh-to-the-inch, 6″ square. White cotton fabric 6″ square. White eyelet lace ½″ wide, ⅜ yard. White double-fold bias tape, ⅝ yard. Scraps of pearl cotton #8: light pink, dark pink, blue, green, orange. *Pillow, blanket, tote, diapers, bottle warmer, and basket* Closely woven cotton fabric in two coordinat-ing prints, 1½ yards print A, 2 yards print B. (**Note:** We used a dotted and a striped pink floral; see photograph.) Gingham in coordi-nating color, 12″ square. Pre-gathered eyelet lace 1″ wide in coordinating color, 4½ yards. Scrap of baby rickrack in coordinating color. Polyester fiberfill and quilt batting. Flexible lightweight and heavyweight cardboard. Purchased toy baby bottle, 1½″ in diameter. White cotton fabric 36″ wide, ¾ yard for diapers. Two diaper pins. Two Velcro® fas-tener strips. **For all items:** Sewing thread to match fabrics and trims.

GENERAL DIRECTIONS
Enlarge patterns by copying on paper ruled in 1″ squares. Complete half-patterns, indi-cated by heavy dash lines. Following individ-ual directions below, use dressmaker's carbon and dry ball-point pen to transfer patterns to wrong side of fabrics, unless otherwise di-rected, placing them ½″ from fabric edges and ½″ apart. Cut out pieces ¼″ beyond marked lines for seam allowance, unless otherwise indicated. When cutting additional pieces without patterns, do not add seam allowance. To assemble doll, clothes, and accessories, pin pieces together with right sides facing and raw edges even; stitch on marked lines, making ¼″ seams unless otherwise directed; use matching thread. Clip into seam allowance at curves and across corners; turn piece to right side and poke out corners with knitting needle. Referring to photograph, assemble and finish pieces as directed below.

DIRECTIONS FOR DOLL

Read General Directions. Prepare doll patterns as directed. From velour fabric, cut three heads (front, back, and lining), two bodies, four arms, two soles, and four legs, reversing patterns for second and fourth pieces; also cut 2¼" × 13½" strip for head center. Mark eyes and mouth on right side of one head (front). Using one strand of brown floss in an embroidery needle, straight-stitch eyelashes on head front (*see Embroidery Stitch Details, page 185*). With wrong sides facing, stitch head front and lining together, leaving neck edge open. Working through both thicknesses and using two strands of floss throughout, finish embroidery as follows: Using blue floss, satin-stitch eyes; add highlights with white floss and straight stitches; use pink floss to backstitch mouth. Do not turn; stuff piece evenly with fiberfill, using knitting needle, until face resembles a plump pancake; stitch neck opening closed. With right sides facing, pin long side edges of head center to head back and front with bottom straight edges even. Stitch, leaving neck edge open. Fold neck ¼" to wrong side; baste. Turn head to right side. Stuff firmly. Pair arm pieces, right sides facing, and stitch together, leaving top straight edges open. Turn and stuff. Baste each arm closed ⅛" from raw edges, enclosing stuffing. Stitch legs together in pairs, leaving top and bottom edges open.

1 sq. = 1 in.

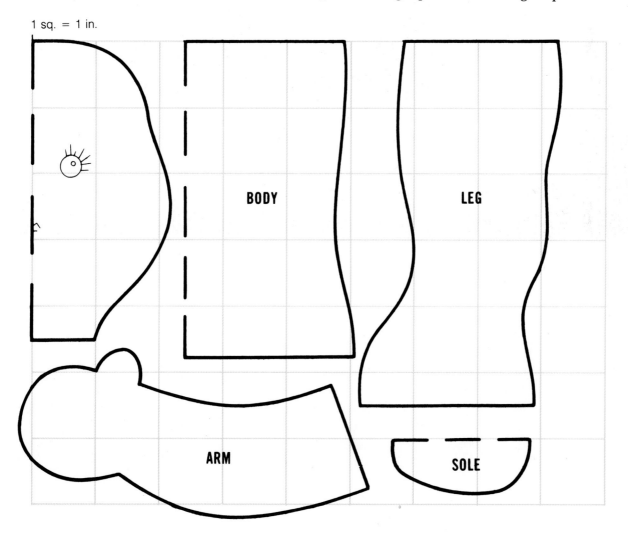

BODY

LEG

ARM

SOLE

Stitch soles to bottom openings; turn and stuff. Baste each leg top as for arm, but with seams centered at front and back. On right side of one body (front), pin arms even with shoulders, so that arms cross, thumbs point down, and side edges are even; stitch. Pin and stitch legs to body bottom in similar manner, so that toes point toward shoulders. Place body front on work surface with limbs on top. Fold left arm across body, so that hand extends above right shoulder and seam allowance faces out. Pin left side of body back, wrong side up, to body front; stitch. Pin and stitch right side of body in same manner (body will resemble a tube with hands extending above and legs below). Push legs up through body, so that only seam allowance extends at bottom; pin and stitch body bottom. Turn and stuff. Turn raw edges ¼″ to inside; slipstitch opening closed. Using heavy-duty thread, slipstitch head, centered, over shoulders.

Hair: Cut 100 36″ strands of brushed acrylic yarn. Make a set of curls with each strand: Wind yarn around two extended fingers of one hand; tie together at center with matching floss. Tack two sets of curls to center of front head seam. Working down toward cheeks, tack five sets of curls along seam on each side. Tack six sets across nape of neck between side curls. Tack one set to head center 1″ below front head seam for "bangs." Use remaining curls to fill in crown of head.

DIRECTIONS FOR CLOTHES

Read General Directions. Prepare patterns for clothes as directed. Make separate half- and whole patterns for dress front/back.

Additional directions: *To assemble* When assembling pieces, press seams open after stitching, unless otherwise directed; do not press felt.

To gather Hand- or machine-baste piece ⅛″ from raw edge. Pull basting to gather edge to fit as specified. Pin piece in place; adjust gathers evenly and stitch.

To finish edges with lace trim Press fabric edge ¼″ to wrong side. Cut lace trim to fit. Pin lace to fabric on wrong side, so that ruffle extends beyond fold. Topstitch close to fold.

To bind neck edges Cut a fabric strip same length as neck, plus ½″. Press short edges and one long edge ¼″ to wrong side, unless otherwise specified. Place strip on neck of garment, right sides facing and with raw edges even; pin and stitch. Fold strip to inside of garment, then slipstitch in place.

Christening dress: From white fabric, cut the following: one dress front (entire length to "bottom"), using whole pattern; two dress backs, using half-pattern but adding 1″ seam allowance to center edge only and reversing pattern to cut second piece; two collars and two sleeves, shortening sleeve pattern at dot/dash line. Stitch dress backs together along center from bottom to dot, making 1″ seam; press seam open; press raw edges above seam 1″ to wrong side. Stitch dress front to dress back along side seams. Turn bottom of dress ¼″ to wrong side and stitch all around. Cut galloon lace to fit dress bottom plus ½″. Fold lace in half widthwise and stitch ends together; press seam open. Matching seams on lace and dress back, pin lace to dress, so that bottom edge is even with dress bottom. Topstitch lace to dress ⅛″ in from each edge. Following Additional Directions, finish bottom edge of sleeves with 1″-wide lace. Cut two 4″ pieces flat elastic; pin each across wrong side of sleeve 1″ above bottom edge; stitch, using machine set for wide zigzag stitch. Fold each sleeve in half and stitch underarm edges together. Stitch sleeves to dress front and back along armholes (B); turn dress to right side. Place collar pieces together and stitch along outside edge (C); turn. Cut 1″-wide lace to fit plus ½″; fold ends under ¼″ and topstitch to outside edge of collar. Following

1 sq. = 1 in.

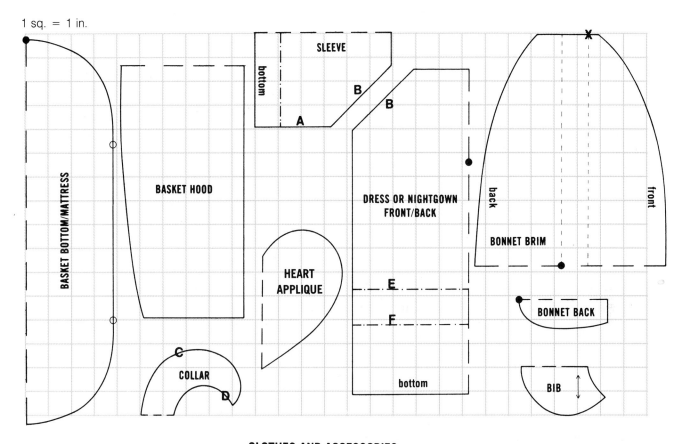

CLOTHES AND ACCESSORIES

Additional Directions, gather neck to fit inside edge of collar (D). On outside pin collar to neck; stitch ¼" in from neck edge. Bind neck with white fabric strip, following Additional Directions. Separate halves of Velcro® fastener. Stitch one half to each side of back opening at neck.

Bonnet: From white fabric, cut bonnet back and bonnet brim. Using light-colored dressmaker's carbon and dry ball-point pen, transfer fine dash lines on pattern to wrong side of brim. Following Additional Directions, gather back of brim to fit curved edge of bonnet back; stitch pieces together. Machine-baste along fine lines. Gather basting until width of piece is about 10½". Cut two 10½" pieces of ⅛"-wide baby blue ribbon. Set

machine for narrow zigzag and stitch ribbons to right side of brim over basting. Finish raw edges of bonnet with 1"-wide lace, following Additional Directions. To make ties, cut two 8" pieces ribbon. At one end of each, form 1" loop and tack to each side of bonnet brim at X. To shape bonnet, cut 1½" × 2" tab from white fabric; double-fold piece and zigzag lengthwise down center. On inside of bonnet, tack one end of tab to back at dot; tack other end to brim at dot.

Nightgown: From print fabric, cut the following: one nightgown front, using whole pattern; two nightgown backs, using half-pattern but adding 1" seam allowance to center edge only and reversing pattern to cut second piece; shorten patterns at line E. Also cut two sleeves. Construct nightgown as for Christening Dress, omitting collar and lace and edging sleeves and hem with baby rickrack. For decorative border, cut rickrack to fit and topstitch ½" above hem all around.

Bib: Using pattern and placing arrow along a row of threads on cloth, cut one bib (front) from Ainring cloth and one bib (lining) from white fabric. Zigzag-stitch around edges of bib front. (*Read How to Cross-Stitch, page 185.*) Fold front in half and mark center thread along neck edge with a pin. Measure 1⅛" down from pin for first stitch, indicated on chart by arrow. Each symbol on chart represents one cross-stitch, worked over one horizontal and one vertical group of threads or "square" of fabric. Different symbols represent different colors, as indicated by color key. Following chart and color key and using one strand of pearl cotton #8 in tapestry needle, work entire chart. Cut ½"-wide eyelet to fit outside edge of front; pin and baste in place. Place front and lining together and stitch around outside edge; turn; press. Cut 18" piece white bias tape and pin, centered, to neck edge of bib, enclosing raw edges. Press ends of tape ¼" to inside and stitch across ends and entire length of tape.

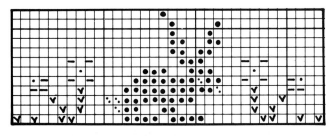

Color Key

● Dark Pink	▼ Green	⊡ Orange
⊡ Light Pink	⊟ Blue	

DIRECTIONS FOR ACCESSORIES

Read General Directions. Prepare patterns for basket bottom/mattress, hood, and heart appliqué as directed.

Pillow: Cut 4½" × 7½" piece each from print (B) and gingham fabric. Cut 24" piece ¾"-wide pre-gathered eyelet and pin around print piece, so that straight edge of lace is even with edge of fabric and ends overlap; baste ¼" in from edge all around. Place fabric pieces together, and stitch ¼" seam all around, leaving 3" opening; turn and stuff with fiberfill. Turn raw edges at opening ¼" to inside and slipstitch opening closed.

Bottle warmer: From print fabric (B), cut two 3" × 6" strips; cut one same-size piece batting. Stack fabric pieces together, with right sides facing and edges even; place batting on top. Stitch ¼" seam around three sides, leaving one short end open; turn. Cut two 6" pieces rickrack. On one side (outside), topstitch a rickrack piece to each long edge; begin and end stitching ¼" from short ends. Press raw edges ¼" to inside and slipstitch ends together all around. Place finished warmer over purchased baby bottle.

Tote: Cut one 9" × 15" piece each from prints A and B and two from batting. Place each fabric piece, right side up, on a batting piece; baste ⅛" from outside edges all around. With batting layer out, fold each piece in half widthwise and stitch sides together with ¼" seam to make two bags; trim bottom corners. Still wrong side out, turn each bag so a side seam is facing you. Spread and flatten corner; stitch across corner 1½" from end of seam to make triangle. Repeat on opposite corner, thus "boxing" bottom of each bag. Press top edge of each bag ¼" to wrong side. Turn one bag (tote) to right side. To make handles, cut four 1¼" × 12½" strips. Pair strips with right sides facing and stitch long sides together; turn and press. Topstitch 1/16" in from each long edge; press ends ¼" against one side. Referring to photograph, pin one strap to each side of tote in position shown, making two handles. Stitch handles to tote sides along topstitching and across ends. Still wrong side out, place lining inside tote and slipstitch top edges together all around.

Diapers: Using pinking shears, cut white cotton fabric into six 12″ squares. Fold and place diapers in tote bag along with two diaper pins.

Blanket: Cut one 12″ square each from print fabric (B), gingham, and batting. Using pattern, cut heart appliqué from print fabric (B), adding ¼″ seam allowance. Read How to Appliqué, page 179; machine-appliqué heart to center of gingham piece, using wide zigzag stitch. Cut 1″-wide pre-gathered eyelet to fit and pin around edge of gingham, so that straight edge of lace is even with edge of fabric and ends overlap; baste. Stack fabric pieces together, right sides facing and with batting on top, and stitch ¼″ seam all around, leaving 3″ opening; turn to right side. Turn raw edges at opening ¼″ to inside; slipstitch opening closed. Straight-stitch around appliqué, to quilt.

Basket: Using pattern, cut one basket bottom from print fabric (A) and one from batting. Also cut 5½″ × 46″ wall strip from A, 6½″ × 46″ wall strip from B, and 11½″ × 46″ strip from batting. Along one long edge of A strip on right side, pin 46″ piece pre-gathered eyelet lace, so that straight edge of lace is even with edge of fabric; baste. To same edge, pin one long edge of B strip, with right sides facing; stitch ¼″ seam; press seam open. Place wall and bottom pieces, right side up, on same-size batting piece and baste ¼″ in from edge all around. From lightweight cardboard, cut 5¼″ × 45½″ wall strip. Fold A/B piece in half widthwise, with right sides in, and stitch ends together to form tube. Fold tube in half lengthwise, with right sides

out, and insert cardboard between layers to make wall of basket; baste ¼″ in from raw edge all around. Pin raw edges of basket wall and basket bottom together, so that lace side of wall faces right side of bottom; stitch ¼″ seam all around. To make handles, cut two 4″ × 22″ strips from fabric A and two same-size pieces batting. With edges even, baste batting pieces to wrong sides of fabric pieces. With right side in, fold handles in half lengthwise and stitch long sides together; turn. Stitch one end of each to inside of basket bottom at open circles to make handles as shown. Turn basket to right side. From heavyweight cardboard, cut basket bottom; place in basket.

To make mattress, cut two mattress pieces from fabric B, using pattern. Place pieces together, right sides facing, and stitch edges all around, leaving 3″ opening. Turn, stuff with fiberfill; turn raw edges ¼″ to inside and slipstitch opening closed. Place mattress in basket.

For hood, cut one each from fabrics A and B and two from batting, using pattern. Baste batting pieces to wrong side of fabric pieces as for basket bottom and walls. To outside edge of one hood piece, pin 54″ piece of eyelet, so that straight edge of eyelet is even with edge of piece and ends overlap; baste. Place hood pieces together and stitch around three sides, leaving flat end open; turn. From lightweight cardboard, cut one basket hood. Insert cardboard into fabric hood between layers; turn raw edges at opening ¼″ to inside and slipstitch closed. Separate halves of two Velcro® strips. Place hood over basket in position shown in photograph; with pins, mark points where ends of hood touch basket. Using pins as a guide for placement, stitch half of each Velcro® strip to one end of hood and half to sides of basket. Attach hood to basket.

tthen-Oolah

This rosy-cheeked Eskimo even has his own pet seal pup.

SIZE
About 20" high.

EQUIPMENT
Pencil. Ruler. Tracing paper. Tape measure. Light and dark-colored dressmaker's tracing (carbon) paper. Dry ball-point pen. Small embroidery hoop. Embroidery and regular scissors. Embroidery and sewing needles. Knitting needle. Straight pins. Sewing machine with zipper foot attachment. Knitting needles No. 4. Yarn darning needle. Iron.

MATERIALS
Closely woven cotton fabric such as muslin or kettle cloth 44" wide, ½ yard off-white; ¼ yard navy; ¼ yard rough fabric in ecru. Short-piled navy fake fur 60" wide, ⅜ yard. Long-piled fake fur: beige, 20" × 30" piece; black, 20" square; dark gray, 8" × 24" piece. Scrap of beige corduroy. Sewing thread to match fabrics. Six-strand cotton embroidery floss: dark brown, black, navy, pink, red. Pink crayon. Heavyweight 6" separating zipper. Ribbon trim ½" wide with whale motifs, 1⅛ yards navy. Flat elastic ¼" wide, 10" piece. Knitting worsted: 2 ozs. dark gray or navy. Leather shoelace. Polyester fiberfill for stuffing.

GENERAL DIRECTIONS
Enlarge patterns by copying onto paper ruled in 1" squares. Complete half-patterns indicated by long dash lines. Use dressmaker's carbon and dry ball-point pen to transfer patterns to wrong side of fabrics, unless otherwise directed, placing them ½" from fabric edges and ½" apart; reverse asymmetrical patterns for each second and fourth piece. Cut out pieces ¼" beyond marked lines for seam allowance, unless otherwise directed. When cutting additional pieces without patterns, do not add seam allowance. To assemble dolls and clothes, pin pieces together with right sides facing and raw edges even. Stitch on marked lines, making ¼" seams, unless otherwise directed. When assembling clothes, press seams open after stitching, unless otherwise directed. Clip into seam allowance at curves, corners; turn to right side, poke out corners with knitting needle.

DIRECTIONS FOR DOLL
From off-white fabric, cut two heads, one head center, two bodies, two arms, four legs, and two soles. Transfer facial features to right side of one head piece (front).

Head: Insert face area of head front in hoop. Work embroidery as follows (*see Embroidery Stitch Details, page 185*): Using two strands of floss in a needle, work outline stitch for mouth, using red, and for nose, using pink; satin-stitch eyes and eyebrows, using brown. Use crayon to lightly "rouge" cheeks with pink.

Body: Fold arm in half lengthwise, right side in. Stitch raw arm and hand edges, leaving top straight edges open. Turn; stuff firmly.

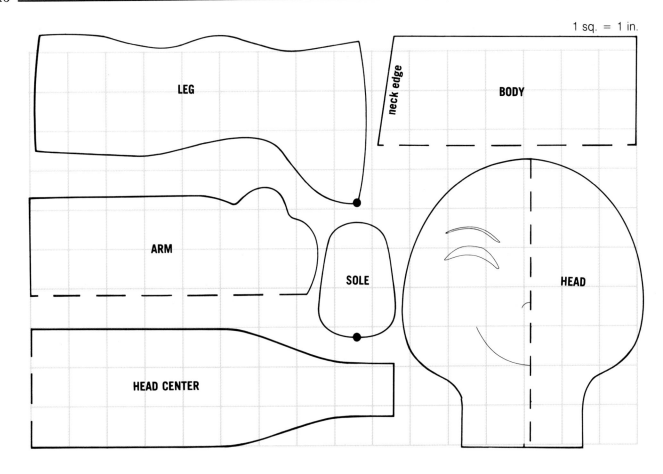

1 sq. = 1 in.

Baste each arm closed ⅛″ in from raw edges, enclosing stuffing. Stitch legs together in pairs at front and back, leaving top and bottom edges open. Stitch soles to bottom openings, matching dots; turn and stuff. Baste each leg top as for arm, but with seams centered. On right side of one body (front), pin arms ½″ down from shoulders, so that arms cross, thumbs point down, and side edges are even; stitch. Pin and stitch legs to body bottom in similar manner, so that toes point toward shoulders. Place body front on work surface with limbs on top, now extending outward. Fold left arm across body so that hand extends above right shoulder and seam allowance faces out. Pin left side of body back, wrong side up, to body front; stitch left side. Pin and stitch right side of body in same manner (body will look like a tube with hands extending above and legs below). Push legs up through tube, so that only seam allowance extends at bottom; pin and stitch body bottom. Turn and stuff body. Turn raw edges ¼″ to inside; slipstitch opening closed. Using matching thread, slipstitch head, centered, over shoulders.

Hair: Mark a line 1¼″ above each neck edge on patterns for head and head center. Place black fake fur wrong side up on work surface with nap running toward you. Using new lines for bottom edge, transfer one head (back) and head center to fake fur with neck edges across nap; cut out, adding ¼″ seam allowance. Stitch pieces together as for doll's head, forming hair. Place hair on head, matching seams. Fold raw edges under ¼″ and slipstitch in place all around. Finger-comb hair as desired.

DIRECTIONS FOR CLOTHES AND SEAL PUP

Tunic (not shown): From rough ecru fabric, cut one tunic front, one tunic back, two sleeves, one front facing, and one back facing; do not add seam allowance to Z edges of facings. Stitch tunic front to back at shoulder seams; also stitch facings together at shoulder seams (S). Set sewing machine for ⅛"-wide zigzag stitch and stitch along Z edges. From navy fabric, cut two whale appliqués (*see pattern for tunic front*). Baste one to each side of tunic front in position shown on pattern. Set sewing machine for ⅛"-wide zigzag stitch and zigzag around appliqués, covering fabric edges. Using two strands of navy floss in needle, embroider whale's "spout" along fine lines, using outline stitch (*see pattern*). On right side, pin facings to tunic along neck edge; stitch. Turn bottom edge of each sleeve ¼" to wrong side; stitch. Pin sleeves to armholes, matching dots to shoulder seams, and stitch; stitch underarms and sides in one continuous seam. Turn bottom edge of tunic ¼" to wrong side and stitch all around.

Trousers: From navy fabric, cut two trousers pieces. Stitch pieces together at center front and back from waist to crotch. Stitch each inseam from leg bottom to waist. For waistline casing, press waist edges ¼" then ½" to wrong side; stitch close to folds, leaving 1" opening in bottom edge of one side seam. Use safety pin to work elastic through casing; stitch ends to secure. Stitch casing closed. Turn leg bottoms ¼" to wrong side and stitch all around.

Boots: From beige fake fur, cut four boots so that nap of fur aligns with arrow on pattern; also cut two soles from beige corduroy. Pair boot pieces and stitch together along front and back seams from dots to boot top. Stitch soles to boots, matching dots at toe. Turn top edge of boots ½" to wrong side and slipstitch all around.

Mittens: Using gray or navy yarn and knitting needles, work each mitten as follows. **Gauge:** 11 sts = 2". Beg at lower edge, cast on 32 sts. Work in garter st (k each row) for 1". Work in stockinette st (k 1 row, p 1 row) for 1", end p row.

Eyelet row (right side): K 2, (yo, k 2 tog, k 1) 10 times. Beg with p row, continue in stockinette st for 2" more, end p row.

Shape top: K 2 tog, k 12, (k 2 tog) twice, k 12, k 2 tog—28 sts. P 1 row.

Next row: K 2 tog, k 10, (k 2 tog) twice, k 10, k 2 tog—24 sts. Bind off.

To finish: Sew side and top seam. Make a twisted cord or crocheted chain 18" long for each mitten. Run through eyelet row to tie at seam edge.

Jacket: From navy fake fur, cut two jacket fronts (using half-pattern), one jacket back (using whole pattern), two sleeves, and two hoods, with nap running in direction of arrows on patterns. Cut same pieces from lining fabric; set linings aside. On jacket fronts, turn front opening ¼" to inside; baste edges together. Using zipper foot and following manufacturer's directions, insert zipper along front opening. Remove basting; open zipper. From dark gray fake fur, cut two 2½" × 8" strips with nap running parallel to short sides. Pin one long edge of each to sleeve bottoms; stitch ¼" seam. Stitch jacket fronts to back at shoulder seams. Pin top of each sleeve to armhole, matching dot to shoulder seam; stitch. Stitch underarms and sides in one continuous seam. Fold edge of fur trim ¼" then 1" to wrong side; slipstitch all around. Stitch hood pieces together along curved edge. Trim front edge of hood with a 2½" × 10" piece dark gray fake fur, in same manner as for sleeves. Fold long edge of trim ¼" then 1" to wrong side; slipstitch. Pin bottom edge of hood to neck edge of jacket; stitch. Trim bottom edge of jacket with a 2½"

× 18″ piece gray fake fur, but allow ends to extend ½″ beyond zipper on either side. Fold ends ½″ to inside; baste. Fold bottom edge of fur trim ¼″ then 1″ to wrong side; slipstitch. Stitch hood lining pieces together along curved edge. Stitch front jacket linings to back at shoulder seams. Pin sleeve linings to armholes, matching dots to shoulder seams; stitch. Stitch underarm and side seams together in one continuous motion. Pin hood lining to neck edge of jacket lining; stitch. Press raw edges of lining ¼″ to inside. With jacket wrong side out, pin lining in place, pulling sleeve linings over sleeves. Slipstitch lining to jacket along cuffs, hood front, and jacket bottom so that lining overlaps fur trim about ⅛″. Slipstitch lining to front opening about ¼″ in from zipper. Tack hood lining to hood along neck seam to secure.

Baby seal: From beige fake fur, cut two bodies, two underbodies, and one gusset, so that nap lies in direction of arrow on patterns. Pin edges of gusset to T edge of bodies between dots; stitch. Pin underbodies together along Y edges and stitch. Pin V edges of bodies to V edges of underbodies, matching open circles; stitch. Stitch raw edges along head together from dot to open circle. Turn seal right side out; stuff firmly with fiberfill.

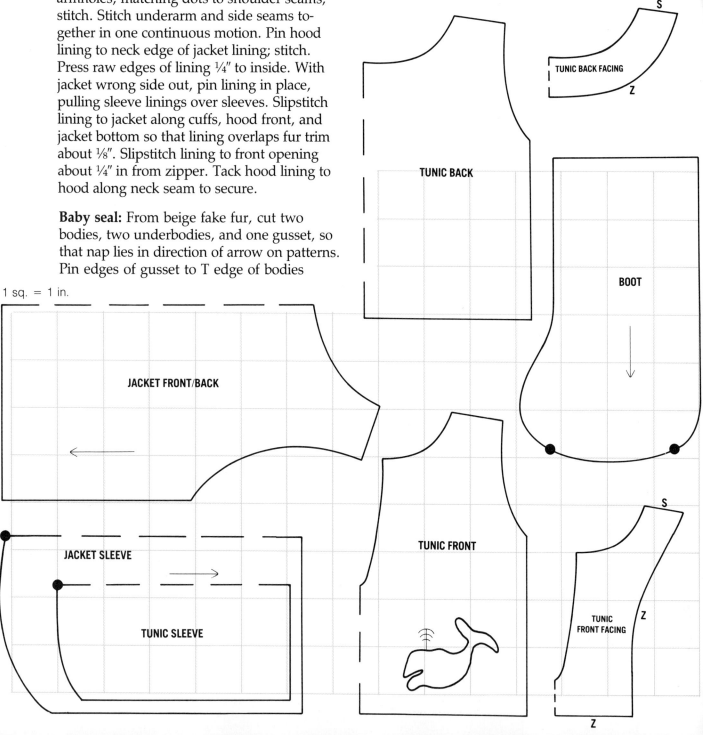

1 sq. = 1 in.

TUNIC BACK FACING

TUNIC BACK

BOOT

JACKET FRONT/BACK

JACKET SLEEVE

TUNIC SLEEVE

TUNIC FRONT

TUNIC FRONT FACING

1 sq. = 1 in.

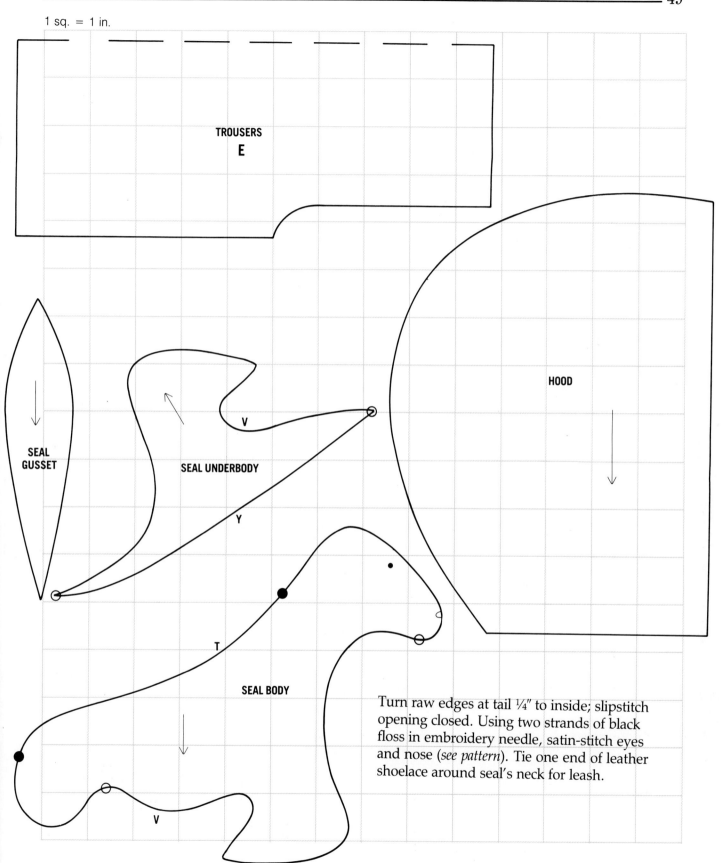

TROUSERS
E

SEAL
GUSSET

SEAL UNDERBODY

V

Y

HOOD

SEAL BODY

T

V

Turn raw edges at tail ¼" to inside; slipstitch opening closed. Using two strands of black floss in embroidery needle, satin-stitch eyes and nose (*see pattern*). Tie one end of leather shoelace around seal's neck for leash.

Fred Camel & Frank Giraffe

Crochet these two exotic animals for your own little zookeeper.

Fred Camel

SIZE
16" tall.

MATERIALS
Worsted-weight yarn, 3½ ozs. blue, small amounts of yellow, white, and black. Polyester fiberfill. Crochet hook size H (5 mm). Yarn needle.

GAUGE
4 sc = 1".

DIRECTIONS FOR CAMEL
Body, Side 1: With blue, ch 36.

Row 1: Sc in 2nd ch from hook and in each ch across—35 sc. Ch 1, turn each row.

Rows 2–18: Work even.

Row 19: *Start neck* Sc in 10 sc, ch 1, turn.

Rows 20–32: Work even on 10 sc. At end of row 32, ch 11, then turn work.

Row 33: *Start head* Working through back of ch 11, sc in 2nd ch from hook and in each ch across; then sc in each sc of row 32—20 sc. Ch 1, turn.

Rows 34–44: Work even on 20 sc. End off. Do not turn work.

Hump **Row 1:** With head facing to right, join yarn in 3rd st from neck on row 18. Sc in

same st and in next 14 sc of row 18—15 sc. Ch 1, turn.

Row 2: Work even.

Row 3: Dec 1 sc each side—13 sc.

Row 4: Work even.

Rows 5–12: Repeat rows 3 and 4, 4 times—5 sc.

Row 13: Repeat row 3—3 sc. End off.

Body, Side 2: (Side 2 is worked differently to insure that rows will match when head and neck are reversed.) Work same as Side 1 through row 18. End off. Turn work.

Row 19: *Start neck* Join yarn in 26th st from right on row 18; sc in same st and in remaining 9 sts to end—10 sc. Ch 1, turn.

Rows 20–31: Work even on 10 sc. End off. Turn work.

Row 32: Before beginning row, make a ch of 10. Then pick up work and sc in each sc of row 31.

Row 33: *Start head* Sc in each sc across, then sc in each ch—20 sc. Ch 1, turn.

Rows 34–44: Work even. End off. Do not turn work.

Hump **Row 1:** With head facing to left, join yarn in 9th st from right on row 18. Sc in same st and in next 14 sc of row 18—15 sc. Ch 1, turn.

Rows 2–13: Work as for Side 1 hump. End off. Sew body together and stuff as follows: Place the 2 pieces together, matching rows. Begin sewing at tip of nose, continue down front neck seam and across bottom. Sew up back edge and halfway around hump. Stuff body and hump; sew hump closed. Sew up other neck edge, stuffing neck firmly as you go. Finally, stuff head and sew closed across top.

Legs, Side 1 (make 4 pieces): With blue, ch 8.

Row 1: Sc in 2nd ch from hook and in each ch across—7 sc. Ch 1, turn each row.

Rows 2–4: Work even.

Row 5: Sc in 4 sc, ch 1, turn.

Rows 6-24: Work even on 4 sc. End off.

Legs, Side 2 (make 4 pieces): Work as for legs Side 1 through row 4. End off. Turn work.

Row 5: Rejoin yarn in 4th st from right on row 4; sc in same st and in next 3 sc—4 sc. Ch 1, turn.

Rows 6–24: Work even on 4 sc. End off. Place a Side 1 and a Side 2 leg piece together, matching rows. Starting with one long side, sew together all around, stuffing leg firmly as you sew up last long side. Repeat for other 3 legs. Sew to bottom of body as shown in photograph.

Ears (make 4 pieces): With blue, ch 2.

Rnd 1: 6 sc in 2nd ch from hook. Do not join rnds. Mark beg of rnds.

Rnd 2: 2 sc in each sc—12 sc.

Rnd 3: * Sc in 1 sc, 2 sc in next sc, repeat from * around—18 sc. End off. Sew 2 pieces together through back lps all around, stuffing lightly before closing completely. Repeat for 2nd ear. Sew ears to top of head about 3 sts in from back edge.

Eyes (make 2): With black, ch 2.

Rnd 1: 4 sc in 2nd ch from hook. Drop black, join white.

Rnd 2: 2 sc in each sc—8 sc. End off. Sew eyes to head, slightly in front of and below ears.

Nostrils (make 2): With white, ch 2. Work 6 sc in 2nd ch from hook, join with sl st and end off. Sew 1 nostril to each side of face near front tip.

Mouth: Using yellow yarn and chain stitch, embroider mouth around both sides of face as shown in photograph.

Tail: With blue, ch 15.

Row 1: Sc in 2nd ch from hook and in each ch across—14 sc.

Rows 2–4: Work even. End off. Fold tail lengthwise and sew up. Make tassel for end of tail: Cut 20 5″ strands of blue. Tie tightly in center with separate piece of yarn, leaving ends long enough for sewing. Fold strands in half at tie. Tie tightly about ½″ below fold with another piece of yarn. Trim tassel. Sew to bottom of tail, then sew tail to back of camel even with top edge.

DIRECTIONS FOR RUG

With yellow, ch 31 for first tie. Sl st in 2nd ch from hook and in each ch. Ch 46. Sl st in 2nd ch from hook and in next 29 ch for 2nd tie, sc in each remaining ch—15 sc. Ch 1, turn. Work even in sc on 15 sts for 12 rows. End off.

Cut 15 strands of yarn 3″ long. Knot a strand in each st across lower edge. Make 2 yellow tassels about 2″ long. Sew a tassel to end of ties.

Frank Giraffe

SIZE
19″ tall.

MATERIALS
Worsted-weight yarn, 4½ ozs. yellow, ¾ oz. orange, small amounts white and black. Polyester fiberfill. Crochet hook size H (5 mm). Yarn needle.

GAUGE
4 sc. = 1″.

DIRECTIONS FOR GIRAFFE
Body, Side 1: With yellow, ch 36.

Row 1: Sc in 2nd ch from hook and in each ch across—35 sc. Ch 1, turn each row.

Rows 2–22: Work even.

Row 23: *Start neck* Sc in 12 sc, ch 1, turn.

Rows 24–42: Work even on 12 sc. At end of row 42, ch 11, then turn work.

Row 43: *Start head* Working through back of ch 11, sc in 2nd ch from hook and in each ch across; then sc in each sc of row 42—22 sc. Ch 1, turn.

Rows 44–56: Work even on 22 sc. End.

Body, Side 2: (Side 2 is worked differently to insure that rows will match when neck and head are reversed.) Work same as Side 1 through row 22. End off. Turn work.

Row 23: *Start neck* Join yarn in 24th st from right on row 22, sc in same st and in remaining 11 sc to end—12 sc. Ch 1, turn.

Rows 24–41: Work even. End off. Turn work.

Row 42: Before beginning row, make a ch of 10. Then pick up work and sc in each sc of row 41. Ch 1, turn.

Row 43: *Start head* Sc in each sc, then sc in each ch—22 sc. Ch 1, turn.

Rows 44–56: Work even. End off.
Place the 2 pieces together, matching rows.

Begin sewing at tip of nose; continue down front neck seam and across bottom, then up back edge. Stuff body, then sew closed along top of back. Sew up remaining neck seam, stuffing firmly as you go. Finally, stuff head and sew closed across top.

Legs (make 8 pieces): With orange, ch 6.

Row 1: Sc in 2nd ch from hook and in each ch across—5 sc. Ch 1, turn each row.

Rows 2–4: Work even. Drop orange, join yellow.

Rows 5–30: Work even. End off. Place 2 leg pieces together, matching rows. With yellow yarn, sew down 1 long side to hoof; change to orange yarn and sew around hoof. Change back to yellow yarn and sew up other long side, stuffing leg as you go. Sew top closed. Repeat for other 3 legs. Sew 1 leg to bottom of body even with front edge, and another leg immediately behind it. Sew another leg to body even with back edge, and the last leg immediately in front of it.

Ears (make 4 pieces): With yellow, ch 6.

Row 1: Sc in 2nd ch from hook and in each ch across—5 sc. Ch 1, turn each row.

Rows 2–8: Work even. End off. Sew 2 pieces together all around, stuffing lightly before closing completely. Repeat for other ear. Sew ears to top of head, about 3 sts in from back edge.

Horns (make 2): With yellow, ch 8.

Row 1: Sc in 2nd ch from hook and in each ch across—7 sc. Ch 1, turn each row.

Rows 2–4: Work even. End off. Fold horn lengthwise and sew up, stuffing lightly as you go. Repeat for other horn. Sew horns to top of head, slightly in front of ears.

Eyes (make 2): With black, ch 2.

Rnd 1: 4 sc in 2nd ch from hook. Drop black, join white.

Rnd 2: 2 sc in each sc—8 sc. End off. Sew eyes to head slightly in front of and below horns.

Nostrils (make 2): With orange, ch 2. Work 6 sc into 2nd ch from hook, join with sl st and end off. Sew 1 nostril to each side of face at front tip.

Mouth: Using orange yarn and a chain stitch, embroider mouth around both sides of face as shown in photograph.

Tail: With yellow, ch 11.

Row 1: Sc in 2nd ch from hook and in each ch across—10 sc.

Rows 2–4: Work even. End off. Fold tail lengthwise and sew up. Make tassel for tail: Cut 20 10″ strands of yellow. Tie tightly in center with separate piece of yarn, leaving ends long enough for sewing. Fold strands in half at tie. Tie tightly about ½″ below fold with another piece of yarn. Trim tassel. Sew to bottom of tail, then sew tail to back of giraffe even with top edge.

Mane: Cut 66 4″ strands of yellow. Using 2 strands together each time, knot mane down entire back neck seam. To knot, fold 2 strands of yarn in half. Insert hook under back neck seam, catch yarn at fold and pull through, then pull ends through loop. Tighten knot. When mane is completely knotted, trim at a slight angle, from about ¾″ long at top to about 1¼″ long at bottom.

Large spots (make 20): With orange, ch 2.

Rnd 1: 6 sc in 2nd ch from hook. Do not join rnds.

Rnd 2: 2 sc in each sc—12 sc. End off.

Small spots (make 12): Work same as for large spots through rnd 1. Join with sl st and end off. Sew large spots randomly over body. Sew small spots randomly over neck.

ingham Girls & the Giant Car

Greta, Gale, and Grace are straight from covered-wagon days.

Gingham Girls

SIZE
About 20" high.

EQUIPMENT
Pencil. Ruler. Paper for patterns. Tape measure. Dressmaker's tracing (carbon) paper. Dry ball-point pen. Embroidery and regular scissors. Straight pins. Embroidery and sewing needles. Knitting needle. Sewing machine with zigzag attachment. Steam iron.

MATERIALS
For each doll: Sewing thread to match fabrics, felt, and trims. White heavy-duty sewing thread. Sport-weight yarn: 3 ozs. desired color for hair; small amount same or coordinating color for bows. Six-strand cotton embroidery floss, one skein to match hair; small amount red. Two tiny hook-and-eye fasteners. Polyester fiberfill for stuffing.
For Gale: Gingham fabric 36" wide, ½ yard tan. Homespun fabric 36" wide: ⅜ yard print in desired color for dress; ⅛ yard coordinating color for panties. Felt: 9" × 12" sheet coordinating color for moccasins; scraps of black, orange. Trims to match dress fabric: fringe 1" wide, 2 yards; baby rickrack, 4 yards; jumbo rickrack, ½ yard; grosgrain ribbon 1" wide, ½ yard; assorted threading beads ⅛"-³⁄₁₆" diameter, about three dozen. White flat elastic ¼" wide, piece 11". **For Greta:** Cotton fabric

36" wide: white, ¼ yard; pink gingham, ½ yard; green calico, 1 yard. Felt: 9" × 12" sheet green for shoes; scraps of navy blue, pink. Nylon net 36" wide, ¼ yard white. Medium-weight fusible interfacing 18" wide, ¼ yard white. White flat elastic ¼" wide, piece 12". White flat lace trim: ¾" wide, piece 19"; 1" wide, 1 yard; 1⅝" wide, 1 yard. White satin ribbon ½" wide, ¾ yard. Two round white buttons ½" diameter. Miniature artificial flowers. **For Grace:** Cotton fabric 36" wide: white, ¼ yard; brown gingham, ½ yard; red calico, ⅝ yard. Felt: 9" × 12" sheet red for shoes; scraps of black, pink. Nylon net 36" wide, ¼ yard white. White flat elastic ¼" wide, piece 12". White flat lace trim: 1" wide, ¾ yard; 1⅝" wide, 2 yards. Two round white buttons ½" diameter. Miniature artificial flowers.

GENERAL DIRECTIONS
Enlarge patterns by copying on paper ruled in 1" squares. Complete half-patterns indicated by heavy dash lines. Make separate patterns for eyes and cheeks. Use dressmaker's carbon and dry ball-point pen to transfer patterns to wrong side of fabrics, unless otherwise directed, placing them ½" from fabric edges and ½" apart; reverse for each second piece. Cut out ¼" beyond marked lines for seam allowance, unless otherwise directed. When cutting pieces from felt or additional pieces without

patterns, do not add seam allowance. To assemble dolls and clothes, pin fabric pieces together with right sides facing and raw edges even; stitch on marked lines, making ¼" seams. Stitch felt pieces to right side of fabric, using wide zigzag stitch. Clip into seam allowance at curves and across corners; turn piece to right side and poke out corners with knitting needle. Referring to color photograph, assemble and finish pieces as directed below.

DIRECTIONS FOR DOLLS

For each: Read General Directions. From gingham fabric, cut two heads, one head center, two arms, and two bodies. For Gale, cut two rectangles for legs, each 5⅝" × 9¾". For Greta and Grace, cut two gingham lower legs, each 5⅝" × 5", and two white upper legs, each 5⅝" × 5¼". From felt, cut the following pieces: For Gale, cut two black eyes, two orange cheeks, and two blue moccasins, transferring dots to one (right) side of moccasins. For Greta, cut two blue eyes, two pink cheeks, and two green shoes. For Grace, cut two black eyes, two pink cheeks, and two red shoes. Cut away toned area on each shoe.

Following original pattern for placement, stitch eyes and cheeks to one head piece (head front). Work red satin-stitch mouth, using two strands of floss in needle (*see Embroidery Stitch Details, page 185*). Pin head center to head front and back with bottom straight edges even. Stitch around sides and top, leaving neck edge open. Fold neck ¼" to wrong side; baste. Turn head to right side. Stuff firmly with fiberfill. **Each arm:** Fold arm in half lengthwise, right side in. Stitch raw arm and hand edges, leaving top straight edge open. Turn; stuff firmly. Baste arm together ⅛" from raw edges, enclosing stuffing. **Each leg:** For Greta and Grace, pin shoe to one 5⅝" edge (bottom) of lower leg, matching bottom and side edges. Stitch all around shoe, including opening. Cut 10" length from 1"-wide lace. Baste across top of lace, close to edge. Pull basting threads gently to gather lace to 5⅝". Place lower leg face up

on work surface with shoe pointing toward you. Place upper leg over lower leg, right sides facing, matching top and side edges. Sandwich lace between leg pieces with gathers at top, matching straight edges; pin. Stitch through all thicknesses. Open out leg; press lace toward shoe; press seam toward leg top. For Gale, pin and stitch moccasin, marked side up, to leg bottom as for shoe. For each doll, fold leg in half lengthwise, right side in; stitch long raw edges. Flatten leg so that seam is at center back; stitch across leg bottom. Turn and stuff. Baste leg top as for arm. For Greta and Grace, sew a button to outer side of shoe opening. For Gale, sew a large bead to moccasin at each large dot; sew on small beads at small dots.

On right side of fabric, pin arms to sides of one body piece ½" down from shoulders, so that hands face in, thumbs point in same direction, and side edges are even; baste. Baste legs to body bottom in similar manner, so that shoes point toward shoulders and legs face up. Pin second body piece to first, sandwiching arms and legs between. Stitch around sides and bottom, leaving shoulder edges open. Turn and stuff. Turn raw edges ¼" to inside; slipstitch opening closed. Using heavy-duty thread, slipstitch head, centered, over shoulders. **Hair:** For Greta and Gale, mark center part from front head seam to nape of neck. For braids, cut 120 30" lengths of yarn. Working with groups of 10 strands at a time and all six strands of matching embroidery floss, stitch center of each group to part, working from front seam back. Divide yarn on each side into three sections and braid; tie each braid with 8" length of yarn in same or coordinating color. Tack top of braids to head near cheeks to secure. For Grace, mark center part on head center only. For long braids, cut 72 18" lengths of black yarn. Working with groups of 12 strands at a time, stitch groups to center part, working from front seam back. Divide yarn on each side into six sections. Divide each section into thirds and braid; tie each braid with 6" length of red yarn. Arrange braids evenly around head;

tack bows to head to secure. For braided bangs, cut nine 5″ lengths of black yarn. Stitch to front of part. Divide yarn into three sections and divide and braid each section; tie with red yarn. Do not tack down.

DIRECTIONS FOR CLOTHES

Read General Directions. When transferring patterns for clothes, mark X's on wrong side of fabric; mark fine lines (placement lines) on right side. When assembling all clothes except Greta's bonnet, press seams open after stitching, unless otherwise directed.

Additional directions: *To bind neck* From dress fabric, cut 2″-wide bias strip to size plus ½″, piecing together as necessary. Press short edges and one long edge of strip ¼″ to wrong side. With right sides facing, stitch strip to neck, matching raw edges. Do not press seam open. Fold strip to inside of neck and slipstitch in place.

Gale's panties: From solid color homespun fabric, cut two panties for front and back. Press waist edges ¼″ to wrong side. Cut elastic in half to form two 5½″ lengths. Starting at one side edge of waist on each fabric piece with one end of elastic, pin length of elastic to wrong side of waist ⅛″ from fold; stitch, using wide zigzag stitches. Reset machine for straight stitch. Following markings for placement, stitch baby rickrack cut to size across top and bottom markings; stitch jumbo rickrack between. Stitch panties front and back together at sides and crotch. Fringe leg bottoms by pulling crosswise threads for ½″. **Gale's dress:** From print homespun

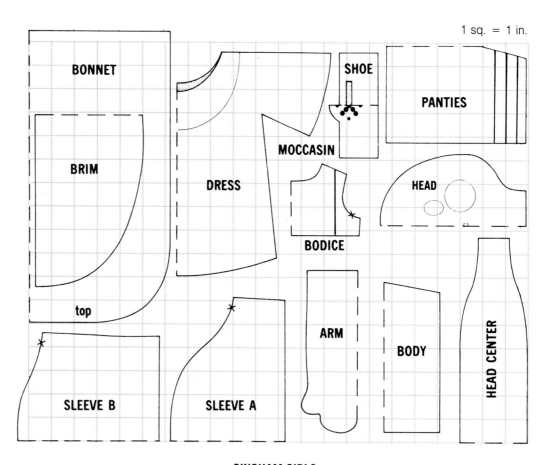

GINGHAM GIRLS

fabric, cut one dress front using complete pattern; cut away toned area. Also cut two backs, using half-pattern; transfer X to backs only. Stitch backs together at center back below X; press seam open. Above X, press edges under ⅛" twice; topstitch. Press sleeve bottoms ⅛" to inside twice; topstitch. Cut fringe to fit stitched edges. Cut two pieces baby rickrack same length as fringe. Pin fringe to each sleeve bottom on right side so it extends ½" beyond fold; stitch. Stitch baby rickrack to fringe along topstitching. For bodice trim, cut 21" length each of fringe and baby rickrack. Starting at center front of bodice with center of fringe, pin fringe in place along marked lines; stitch. Attach rickrack as for sleeves. Bind neck, following directions above. Stitch each underarm and side in a continuous seam. For hem, press under ⅛" twice; stitch. Cut fringe and baby rickrack to fit hem, plus 1". Trim hem, overlapping ends at center back. Sew hook-and-eye fasteners to opening at neck and center back. **Headband:** Cut two pieces baby rickrack same length as grosgrain ribbon. Stitch to ribbon ¼" from long edges. Test-fit band around doll's head; pin ends. Remove band and stitch ends together; press seam open. Turn ends under ¼" twice; stitch. Sew beads around band, following photograph.

Grace's dress: From calico fabric, cut one bodice front using complete pattern, two backs using half-pattern, and two A sleeves; cut one 34" × 9" rectangle for skirt. From nylon net, cut two 34" × 7½" rectangles for underskirt. Stitch bodice front and backs together at shoulders. *Each sleeve* Fold under bottom edge of sleeve ⅛" twice; topstitch. Cut 12½" length of 1⅝"-wide lace. On right side of sleeve, pin lace over stitching, so that bottom edge extends 1¼" beyond fold; stitch. Cut elastic in half to form two 6" lengths. Starting at one side edge of sleeve with one end of elastic, pin elastic to sleeve bottom on wrong side ⅞" above top fold; stitch, using wide zigzag stitches. Reset machine for straight stitch. Machine-baste upper curved

edge of sleeve between X's. Pin lower curved edges of sleeve to front and back armhole of dress below X's. Pull basting threads, gathering upper curved edge of sleeve to fit upper armhole; pin and stitch. Stitch underarm and side in a continuous seam; turn to right side. **Grace's pinafore:** From white fabric, cut one 15½" apron, one 3" × 4" bib, and two 2¼" × 6½" straps. Mark a line on one (wrong) side of bib halfway between 3" edges. With 3" edges at top and bottom, center bib on bodice front, right sides facing, with waist edges even; pin. Topstitch on marked line. Press bib top down over bottom, matching edges; baste ⅛" from waist. Cut two 11" lengths from 1⅝"-wide lace. Baste and gather top edge of each to 6½". Pin lace to bodice front and back, gathers facing, following lines for placement (lace will extend beyond shoulders); baste. Press fabric straps in half lengthwise; baste over lace, matching raw edges; stitch. Press fabric straps toward center front, covering bib sides. Press under short side edges and one long (bottom) edge of apron ⅛" twice; stitch. Cut 15½" length of 1⅝"-wide lace and trim apron bottom as for sleeves, except turning under lace ends before stitching. Stack net underskirt pieces on flat work surface with long edges at top and bottom. Place skirt, right side up, over underskirt, matching top (waist) and side edges. Center apron, right side up, on skirt with waist edges even; pin. Machine-baste waist close to edge through all thicknesses. Pull threads to gather waist of skirt and underskirt to fit bodice waist. Stitch assembled apron/skirt to bodice. *To finish dress* Press center back edges ⅛" to wrong side; topstitch. Starting at hem, stitch center backs together to 1" below waist; press seam open. Above seam, press edges under ⅛"; stitch. Turn dress to right side. Bind neck, following directions above, and hem skirt. Sew hook-and-eye fasteners to opening at neck and center back. Tack miniature flowers to waist front.

Greta's dress: From calico fabric, cut one

bodice front using complete pattern, two backs using half-pattern, and two B sleeves; cut one 34″ × 9″ rectangle for skirt. Assemble bodice and sleeves as for Grace, trimming each sleeve with 9½″ length of ¾″-wide lace. *Skirt and apron* From white fabric, cut one 15½″ × 6½″ apron. From nylon net, cut two 34″ × 7½″ rectangles for underskirt. Cut 15½″ length from 1⅝″-wide lace. Assemble as for Grace's pinafore bottom; gather at waist and stitch to bodice. *To finish dress* Finish back and neck as for Grace. Tack miniature flowers to center of white ribbon. Place dress on doll; tie ribbon around waist with bow at center back. **Bonnet:** From calico fabric, cut one bonnet, two brims, and two 2″ × 12″ ties. Cut two brims from fusible interfacing, omitting seam allowance. Fuse interfacing, centered, to wrong side of each brim, following manufacturer's directions. Baste and gather

1″-wide lace to fit curved edge of brim. Place brims together, right sides facing; sandwich lace between, so that gathers are even with straight edges; pin and stitch. Turn to right side (lace will extend beyond brim). Press raw edges ¼″ to inside. Baste curved edge of bonnet and gather to fit straight edge of brim. Insert gathered edge ¼″ into brim between layers and slipstitch in place on each side. Press straight edge ⅛″ to wrong side twice; hem. Baste ⅛″ from hem; do not end off. Test-fit bonnet on doll and pull basting, gathering to fit head. Secure thread; end off. Remove bonnet from doll. Fold each tie in half lengthwise, right side in. Stitch raw edges, leaving opening in each long edge for turning; turn. Fold raw edges ¼″ to inside on each; slipstitch openings closed; press. Tack ties to back edges of brim.

Giant Car

SIZE
23″ long, 14″ tall.

EQUIPMENT
Pencil. Ruler. Paper for patterns. Scissors. Compass. Dressmaker's tracing (carbon) paper. Dry ball-point pen. Sewing needle. Sewing machine. Iron.

MATERIALS
Closely woven cotton fabric 45″ wide in compatible colors: solid, 1¾ yards; print, ½ yard; check, ⅜ yard; scrap of yellow. Sewing thread to match fabrics. Medium-weight fusible interfacing 18″ wide, 2 yards. Polyester fiberfill.

DIRECTIONS FOR CAR
Enlarge patterns by copying on paper ruled in 3″ squares. Solid outlines indicate stitching lines, heavy dash lines indicate appliqués, fine dash lines indicate placement lines, and fine solid lines indicate embroidery. Using compass, mark circles for additional patterns: 6½″ dia. for wheel, 3¼″ dia. for hubcap,

and 2″ dia. for headlights.

Cut out the following pieces, using patterns and adding ¼″ seam allowance all around: From solid fabric, cut two sides, one rear/top, one windshield, one hood, one bottom, two axle bottoms, four axle sides, four axle ends, and two headlights. Cut one grill and 10 wheels from print fabric. Cut two headlights from yellow fabric. For each piece, cut a same-size piece of interfacing, omitting seam allowance, and press to wrong sides of fabric pieces.

Using dressmaker's carbon and dry ball-point pen, transfer embroidery and appliqué lines to fabric pieces. Using patterns and following directions in How to Appliqué, page 179, cut windows from checked fabric and machine-appliqué to sides of car, windshield, and rear/top, setting sewing machine for close zigzag stitch (about ⅛″ wide); also, stitch embroidery lines on sides. Cut five hubcaps from solid fabric and appliqué to five wheels.

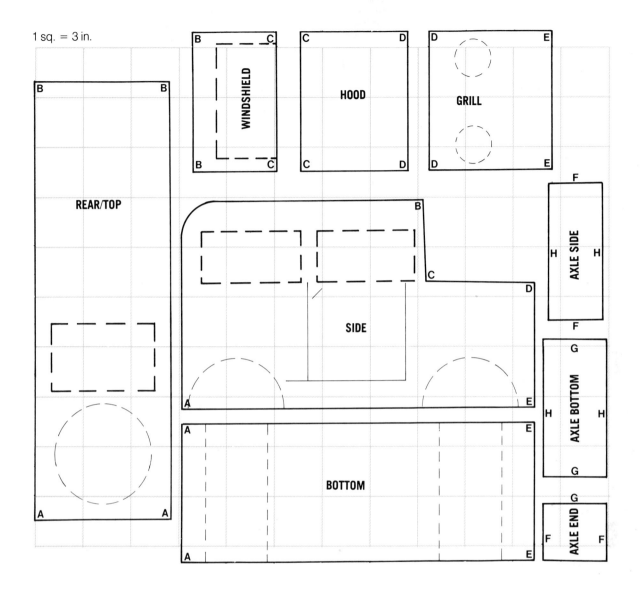

1 sq. = 3 in.

WINDSHIELD

HOOD

GRILL

REAR/TOP

SIDE

BOTTOM

AXLE SIDE

AXLE BOTTOM

AXLE END

With right sides facing and edges even, and making ¼″ seams, pin and stitch pieces together as follows: Matching letters, pin and stitch hood to windshield, windshield to rear/top, rear/top to bottom, bottom to grill, and grill to hood. Pin and stitch sides of car, matching corners carefully; leave 6″ opening along bottom for turning. Clip into seam allowance at corners and turn. Stuff car with fiberfill; turn edge of opening ¼″ to inside; slipstitch opening closed.

Make two axles: For each, stitch one bottom, two sides, and two ends together to form a rectangular box; turn and stuff. Place car with bottom up. Fold open edges of axle ¼″ to inside and slipstitch to bottom of car along placement lines (*see pattern*). Pair appliquéd wheels with remaining wheels and stitch together ¼″ from edge; leave 2″ opening for turning. Clip into seam allowance all around; turn. Loosely stuff wheels; turn openings ¼″ to inside and slipstitch closed. Following placement lines on pattern, tack center of one wheel to rear of car; tack others to axle ends so that wheels rest on surface. Stitch headlights together as for wheels; tack to front of car, following placement lines (*see pattern*), with yellow side facing out.

 oney Bee *has an appliquéd face and wings made of felt. She wears bumblebee sneakers.*

SIZE
About 20″ high.

EQUIPMENT
Pencil. Ruler. Tracing paper. Tape measure. Light and dark-colored dressmaker's tracing (carbon) paper. Dry ball-point pen. Small embroidery hoop. Embroidery and regular scissors. Embroidery and sewing needles. Knitting needle. Straight pins. Silk pins. Sewing machine and buttonhole attachment. Iron. Wire cutters. Safety pin.

MATERIALS
Closely woven cotton fabric such as kettle cloth 44″ wide, ½ yard yellow, ¼ yard black. Black satin 48″ wide, ⅜ yard. Felt: white 36″ wide, ⅜ yard; scraps of peach, yellow, and black. Yellow satin ribbon ⅝″ wide, 3 yards. Sewing thread to match fabrics and felt. Six-strand cotton embroidery floss: black, red. White eyelet lace: flat 1″ wide, 22″ piece; pre-gathered ¾″ wide, ⅝ yard. Flat elastic ¼″ wide, 12″ piece. White 20″ shoelaces. White nylon stretch anklet socks, size 1 year. White Velcro® fastener strip. Heavy-gauge wire or wire coat hanger. Polyester fiberfill for stuffing. Batting.

DIRECTIONS FOR BEE
Enlarge patterns by copying onto paper ruled in 1″ squares. Complete half-patterns indicated by long dash lines. Use dressmaker's carbon and dry ball-point pen to transfer patterns to wrong side of fabrics, placing them ½″ from fabric edges and ½″ part. Reverse asymmetrical patterns for each second and fourth piece. Cut pieces ¼″ beyond marked lines for seam allowance. From yellow fabric, cut one head, two bodies, and four arms. From black cotton fabric, cut four legs and two soles. From black satin, cut three heads, one head center, and four antennae. Transfer eyes and mouth to right side of yellow head piece.

When cutting additional pieces without patterns, do not add seam allowance. To assemble doll and clothes, pin pieces together with right sides facing and raw edges even; use silk pins for satin pieces. Stitch on marked lines, making ¼″ seams. When assembling clothes, press seams open after stitching. Clip into seam allowance at curves and corners; turn piece to right side and poke out corners with knitting needle.

Head: Insert face area of yellow head in hoop. Work embroidery as follows (*see Embroidery Stitch Details, page 185*): Using two strands of black floss in needle, work lashes with straight stitch; outline eyes with outline stitch; fill in eyes with satin stitch. Use two strands of red floss to outline-stitch mouth. Use pattern to cut two cheeks from peach felt; do not add seam allowance. Pin cheeks to face and slipstitch all around.

To wrong side of two satin head pieces, transfer dot-dash line. Place pieces together and stitch along dot-dash line; trim away

center from piece to within ¼" of stitching. Turn piece right side out; press. Place face piece right side up, with black piece on top. Using ⅛" zigzag, stitch outside edges together; also finish edges of remaining satin pieces to prevent raveling. Using single strand of black thread in needle, invisibly slipstitch inside edge of black piece to yellow all around. Set sewing machine for buttonhole stitch and make ¾" buttonhole at each slash mark on head center (*see pattern*); cut buttonholes open with scissors. Pin head center to face and remaining head piece (back) with bottom edges even. Stitch around sides and top, leaving neck edge open. Fold neck ¼" to wrong side; baste. Turn head to right side. Stuff firmly with fiberfill. Pair antennae and stitch together, leaving flat ends open; turn. Use wire cutters to cut two 10" pieces from

heavy wire or coat hanger. Bend each wire in half to form a narrow loop. Place one loop in each antenna, curved end first; stuff antennae firmly with fiberfill; baste across ends to close. Push antennae through buttonholes in crown of head for 2"; slipstitch buttonholes to antennae all around, closing opening.

Body: Pair arms and stitch together, leaving straight ends open. Turn; stuff firmly. Baste each arm closed ⅛" in from raw edges, enclosing stuffing. Stitch legs together in pairs at front and back, leaving top and bottom edges open. Stitch soles to bottom openings, matching dots; turn and stuff. Baste each leg top as for arm, but with seams centered. On right side of one body (front), pin arms ½" down from shoulders, so that arms cross, thumbs point up, and side edges

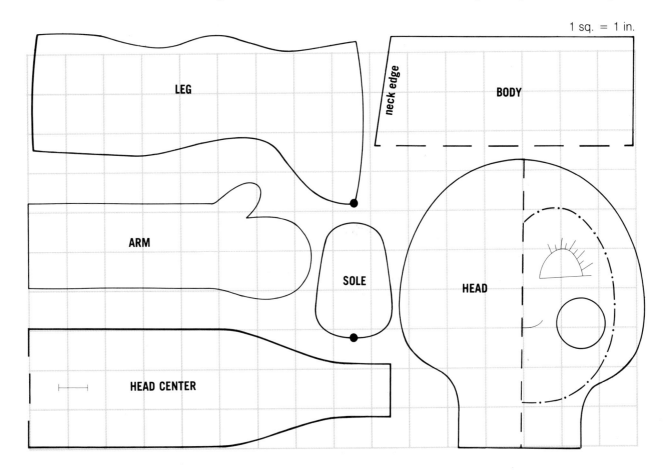

1 sq. = 1 in.

are even; stitch. Pin and stitch legs to body bottom in similar manner, so that toes point toward shoulders. Place body front on work surface with limbs on top, now extending outward. Fold left arm across body so that hand extends above right shoulder and seam allowance faces out. Pin left side of body back, wrong side up, to body front; stitch left side. Pin and stitch right side of body in same manner (body will look like a tube with hands extending above and legs below). Push legs up through tube, so that only seam allowance extends at bottom; pin and stitch body bottom. Turn and stuff body. Turn raw edges ¼" to inside; slipstitch opening closed. Using matching thread, slipstitch head, centered, over shoulders.

Wings: Using pattern, cut two wings from white felt and one from batting, omitting seam allowance. Transfer dotted lines to one (back) piece using light-colored dressmaker's carbon. Stack wings with batting between and back piece on top; topstitch along marked lines; also stitch ⅛" in from edges all around. Cut two 1½" Velcro® strips; slipstitch half of each to front of wings, about 1" on either side of center. In corresponding position, stitch remaining halves to back of rompers about 1" on either side of back opening.

DIRECTIONS FOR CLOTHES

Rompers: From black satin, cut two romper backs, using half-pattern, and one romper front, using complete pattern. Transfer stripe lines to right side of romper pieces. To make stripes, cut yellow ribbons to fit and pin in place; topstitch ¹⁄₁₆" in from ribbon edges. Stitch romper backs together from closed dot to crotch; stitch front to back at shoulders, side seams, and along inseam. Press leg bottoms ¼", then ¾" to inside; stitch close to fold for casings, leaving 1" opening in seam. Cut flat eyelet into two equal pieces. Pin raw edges of lace to casing on wrong side, so that lace extends ¾" beyond legs. On right

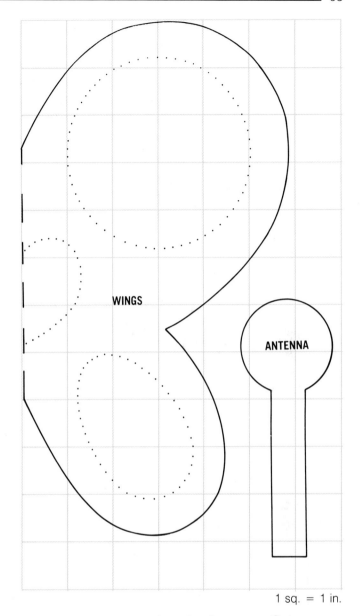

WINGS

ANTENNA

1 sq. = 1 in.

side, topstitch ⅛" in from leg bottoms. Cut elastic into two equal pieces. Use safety pin to work one length through casing; overlap and stitch ends to secure. Stitch casing closed. Turn rompers right side out. Cut pieces of pre-gathered lace to fit armholes and neck, plus ½". On right side, pin lace in place, right sides facing and with bound edge of lace even with raw edge of fabric; overlap ends of armhole lace at side seams; at neck opening, fold lace ends ¼" toward you. Baste lace in

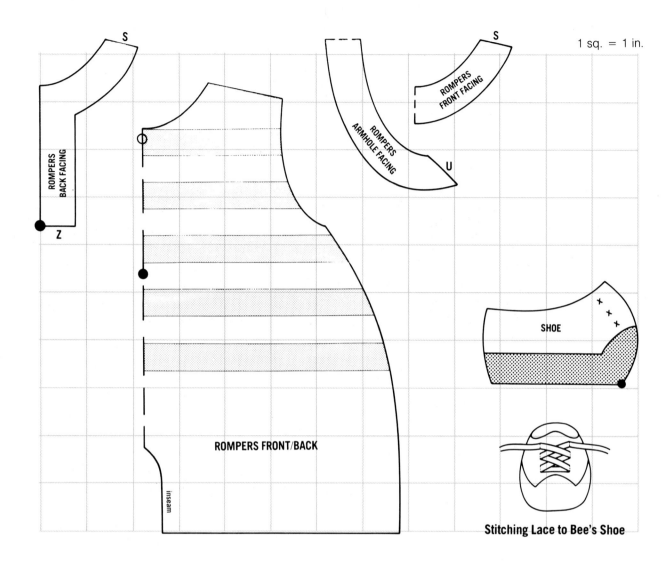

1 sq. = 1 in.

ROMPERS BACK FACING

ROMPERS FRONT FACING

ROMPERS ARMHOLE FACING

ROMPERS FRONT/BACK

inseam

SHOE

Stitching Lace to Bee's Shoe

place ⅜" in from fabric edges. Cut two 7" pieces yellow ribbon; pin one end of each to neck opening at open circles; baste.

From black satin, cut one front facing, two back facings, and two armhole facings; do not add seam allowance to edge Z of back facing. Stitch armhole facings together along under-arm seam (U). Stitch front facing to back facings along shoulder seams (S). On right side, pin armhole facings to armholes, match-ing underarm and side seams. Pin remaining facing to neck and back opening, matching dots and shoulder seams; stitch, turn, and press facings to wrong side.

Shoes (For each): Cut two shoes from yellow felt, using whole pattern; do not add seam allowance to top edge of shoe. From black felt, cut two pieces, using shaded portion of pattern only and adding seam allowance to toe and bottom edges only; also cut two soles. Pin black shoe pieces over yellow and stitch ¹⁄₁₆" in from edges of black pieces all around. Pair uppers and stitch together along toe and heel, then stitch sole to upper, matching dot. Using black thread, topstitch ⅛" in from top edge of shoe all around. Pin, fold, and stitch shoelace to shoe at X's to resemble lacing (*see diagram*). Tie laces in bow.

International Miniatures

Each little ambassador is dressed in her native costume, embroidered with a variety of colorful stitches.

SIZE
About 6″ high.

EQUIPMENT
Pencil. Tracing paper. Dressmaker's tracing (carbon) paper. Dry ball-point pen. Cotton swabs. Embroidery and regular scissors. Sewing and embroidery needles. Knitting needle.

MATERIALS
For each doll: White felt, 9″ × 12″. Clear sewing thread. Spray adhesive. Cardboard. Small flat stone or lead weight. Food coloring: red, yellow, brown. Polyester fiberfill or cotton balls for stuffing. Six-strand cotton embroidery floss and Persian yarn, one skein of each color listed below. Small amounts white floss and additional yarns and threads.
For African doll: Floss: salmon, lt. brown, black. Yarn: daffodil, lt. yellow-orange, lt. orange, red-orange, yellow-green, forest green, dk. brown, black. Gold metallic thread.
For Bavarian doll: Floss: lt. pink, pink, dk. pink, molasses, forest green. Yarn: white, forest green, chocolate, black. Pale yellow mohair fingering yarn. Silver metallic thread.
For Dutch doll: Floss: lt. pink, pink, dk. pink, lt. yellow, lt. green, delft blue, royal blue, navy, lt. chocolate. Yarn: white, pale yellow, fawn, lt. honey. Pearl cotton #8: royal blue.
For Eskimo doll: Floss: pale pink, copper, black. Yarn: white, pale honey, navy, chocolate, black. **For French doll:** Floss: lt. pink, pink, dk. pink, dusty rose, dk. sea green, forest green, silver-gray, black. Yarn: black. Pearl cotton #5: white. **For Japanese doll:** Floss: lt. yellow, pink, red, lt. purple, dk. purple, royal blue, forest green, black. Yarn: black. Gold metallic thread. **For Mexican doll:** Floss: salmon, coral, honey, black. Yarn: daffodil, orange, hot pink, red, fuchsia, olive drab, forest green, chocolate, black. **For Polynesian doll:** Floss: lt. pink, pink, dk. pink, black. Yarn: lemon, coral, black. Pearl cotton #5: daffodil, lime. Artificial raffia: brilliant lt. avocado. **For Scottish doll:** Floss: pale pink, red, chocolate. Yarn: white, bright yellow, red, royal blue, purple, forest green, chocolate, black. Gold metallic thread. **For USA doll:** Floss: pink, salmon, red, emerald, chocolate, black. Yarn: silver-gray, copper, gray-blue, dk. blue. White heavy-duty sewing thread.

GENERAL DIRECTIONS

Read all directions before beginning work. Enlarge patterns for dolls and bases by copying onto paper ruled in 1" squares. Complete half-patterns indicated by long dash lines. For each doll, mark two bodies and one base on felt, using dressmaker's carbon and dry ballpoint pen; mark embroidery lines on one body piece (front). Cut out pieces; do not add seam allowance. Cut one base from cardboard; trim ¹⁄₁₆" all around. Complete body front as directed below. To add skin tone, mix food coloring and water for desired shade; dilute red to make pink for cheeks; brush on skin areas with cotton swab.

DIRECTIONS FOR DOLLS

Cut floss, thread, or yarn into 18" lengths. Begin embroidery by leaving an end on back and working over it to secure; to end length or to begin a new one, weave under stitches on back; do not make knots. Work embroidery on each doll as follows (*see Embroidery Stitch Details, page 185*). **Face:** Use two strands of floss in needle, unless otherwise directed. Outline eyes in outline or fly stitch; work matching straight stitches at corners, using single strand of floss; use two strands to work pupils in satin stitch; work irises in seed stitch. Work eyebrows in straight stitch. Work freckles in seed stitch. Work nose and smile in fly or straight stitch; work a straight stitch at each end of smile where indicated. Work lips (French doll) in satin stitch. **Hair:** Read directions below and work hair on each doll as shown or as desired, using one strand of yarn in needle. For straight hair, work satin stitch. For short curls, work French knots. For "part," work satin stitch to cover left side, then right side of head. For long curls at sides of face, work bullion stitches. *Braids* Thread 6″ length of yarn and take a tiny stitch at side of face to anchor; remove needle and even ends; repeat twice more for three doubled strands. Working with each doubled strand as one, make braid. Secure bottom with 3½″ length of floss (six strands) or pearl cotton (one strand); tie into bow. Repeat for second side. *Looped braids* Make braids as directed above. Using matching yarn, secure bottom of each braid; tack bottom of braid to top. **Clothing and accessories:** Work embroidery following directions below; use one or more strands of floss, yarn, or thread in needle to work each area as directed or as desired; use single strand of pearl cotton. Work keyed areas as follows: For woven stitch (A's on original patterns), work with all six strands of floss or three strands of yarn in needle, unless otherwise directed. Lay vertical stitches side by side first (*see Embroidery Stitch Details, page 185*). To begin weaving, bring needle to front of work at side of an outermost stitch; weave needle over and under stitches as shown, then take needle through to back of work; bring to front below end of previous stitch to begin weaving next stitch in opposite direction. For laid filling stitch (B), use six strands desired color floss or one strand of yarn for underneath stitches, laid diagonally or vertically to form squares or diamonds; then couch intersections with small straight stitches or cross-stitches; when working crosses, work all underneath stitches in one direction and all top stitches in opposite

direction. For knotted buttonhole lace (C), prepare fabric edge to be trimmed by working tiny backstitches completely across; use six strands of floss or one strand of pearl cotton. Begin working knotted buttonhole lace by bringing needle to front of work at A (*see detail*). Work one or more rows of knots as follows: Work first row of knots from left to right, working through alternate backstitches as shown. Work second row of knots from right to left, working through each loop of previous row and reversing direction of knots. When last row is completed, take needle through to back of work; end off.

Outline areas such as arms, feet, and parts of clothing in couching, outline stitch, or backstitch; work fingers in straight or fly stitch. Work "star" flowers in straight stitch, double cross-stitch, or bullion stitch. Work other large flowers in satin stitch or raised rose; work a French knot center in each raised rose. Work medium flowers in woven stitch or double cross-stitch. Work small flowers in upright or diagonal cross-stitch, double cross-stitch, or French knot. Work leaves in lazy daisy, satin, or seed stitch; work stems in outline stitch. Work additional areas as follows:

African doll: Work heavy lines on skirt in chain stitch. For "checkerboard" (D), work shaded squares in satin stitch first; then work a couched cross-stitch over each worked and unworked square, alternating colors in adjoining areas. For "cross-and-double-cross" (E), and "pinwheel" (F), work dividers in upright laid filling stitch first; then work shaded areas in satin stitch. For E, work a cross-stitch over each worked square and a double cross over each unworked square. For "trellis" (G), work outer lines in straight stitch first, then large X's in cross-stitch, using dark brown; work upright laid filling over brown crosses, couching with cross-stitch and using red-orange; then work woven-stitch

1 sq. = 1 in.

AFRICAN

BAVARIAN

DUTCH

ESKIMO

flowers in light yellow-orange. Work blouse and jug in satin stitch. Work belt in couching. Work necklaces and bracelets in straight stitch, using gold metallic thread.

Bavarian doll: Work hat brim, crown, bodice, and basket in satin stitch. Work feather in turkey work; clip loops. Work basket handle in chain stitch. Work bodice detail in chain stitch and French knots, using silver metallic thread.

Dutch doll: Work hat, bodice, sleeves, and shoes in satin stitch. Work basket handle and skirt bottom in chain stitch. Work basket in Roman chain stitch. "Lace" the bodice in cross-stitch, using pearl cotton and tying ends in a bow.

Eskimo doll: Work hood in turkey work; clip loops. Work skirt in straight stitch. Fill in diamond spaces with double cross-stitch.

1 sq. = 1 in.

FRENCH

JAPANESE

MEXICAN

Work mittens and feet in satin stitch; work boot legs in chain stitch.

French doll: Work fine dash lines (*see pattern*) in backstitch. Work hair bow and bodice in satin stitch. For belt, cut 9″ length of floss. Using all six strands, take needle through one side of waist from front to back, then through opposite side from back to front, leaving ends on front; even ends, then knot to prevent raveling. Tie ends in bow at center waist; couch belt on each side of center.

Japanese doll: Work bow, sash, kimono edging, butterflies, and fan in satin stitch. Work fan "ribs" in straight stitch, using gold metallic thread. Work hair band in couching. Work chin in fly stitch.

Mexican doll: Work hat crown and maraca in satin stitch; work design on maraca in straight stitch. Work poncho in chain stitch; work bottom fringe in turkey work; do not clip loops. Work soles and ankle straps of sandals in outline stitch.

Polynesian doll: Work bodice in horizontal satin stitch. Work skirt in vertical satin stitch, using artificial raffia.

Scottish doll: Work woven stitch in each A area, using assorted colors of yarn for plaid effect. Work other large areas in satin stitch; use gold metallic thread for belt buckle. Work design on cuffs in straight stitch and French knots, using gold metallic thread. For sporran, work 1½″-long turkey work loops along dot/

1 sq. = 1 in.

POLYNESIAN

SCOTTISH

USA

dash line; clip loops; work horizontal satin stitch to cover top of stitches, using gold metallic thread.

USA doll: Work cat's fur and ears and girl's overalls and sneakers in satin stitch. Outline suspenders and pockets and "separate" legs with couching. Use three strands of floss to work woven-stitch shirt. Work French knot buttons. "Lace" sneakers in straight stitch and cross-stitch, using heavy-duty thread; tie ends into bows as shown. Work cat's eyes as for girl. Work whiskers in straight stitch; work mouth in outline or fly stitch; work French knot nose.

To assemble: Place bodies together, wrong sides facing; whipstitch edges with clear thread, starting at bottom of one side and working up and around; leave bottom edge open. Stuff firmly, using knitting needle where necessary. Apply spray adhesive to one (wrong) side of felt base; press cardboard in place with edges even. Slipstitch base to body bottom, leaving small opening. Insert flat stone or lead weight into bottom, then slipstitch opening closed.

To finish: To "separate" or define areas such as arms, use clear thread to work a line of backstitches through assembled body, taking stitches beneath previous stitching where necessary. "Separate" arms, head, and legs in this manner; define waistline or bodice as desired.

Jacques *This bearded trapper wears a beaded buckskin, fleecy boots, and a fur cap.*

SIZE
About 20" high.

EQUIPMENT
Pencil. Ruler. Paper for patterns. Tape measure. Dressmaker's tracing (carbon) paper. Dry ball-point pen. Small embroidery hoop. Embroidery and regular scissors. Embroidery and sewing needles. Knitting needle. Straight pins. Sewing machine. Iron. Safety pin. Compass. Awl or large darning needle.

MATERIALS
Closely woven cotton fabric such as weaver's or kettle cloth 44" wide, ½ yard off-white; scrap dark green. Suedecloth 44" wide, ½ yard tan, or use pieces of chamois (available in auto supply stores). Fake fur: For hair, long-pile piece 20" square rust color; for coonskin hat, 13" × 22" piece brown, or use collar from old coat; for "sheepskin" boots and trim, scrap of off-white "woolly" fabric. Scraps of brown leather or vinyl. Felt scraps, white, pink, green, brown, black. Sewing thread to match fabric, fur, and felt. Giant red rickrack. Three brown toggle buttons ½". Rough off-white wooden or plastic button for pouch clasp. (**Note:** We used a cross-section of an elk antler.) Large snap. Flat elastic ½" wide, 10" piece. Six-strand cotton embroidery floss, white, pink, red, orange, coral, tan, brown, black. Brown rug yarn. Brown silk cord, 22" piece. Two round wooden threading beads ½". Seed beads in assorted colors. Blue bugle beads. Polyester fiberfill for stuff-ing. Craft glue. Toy harmonica. Small comb. Small pencil. Small notebook, about 2¼" × 4". Piece of map, 3½" × 5". Small corncob pipe. Magnetic compass.

GENERAL DIRECTIONS
Enlarge patterns by copying on paper ruled in 1" squares, unless otherwise directed. Complete half-patterns indicated by long dash lines. Use dressmaker's carbon and dry ball-point pen to transfer patterns to wrong side of fabrics, unless otherwise directed, placing them ½" from fabric edges and ½" apart; reverse asymmetrical patterns for each second and fourth piece. Cut out pieces ¼" beyond marked lines for seam allowance, unless otherwise directed. When cutting additional pieces without patterns, do not add seam allowance. To assemble dolls and clothes, pin pieces together with right sides facing and raw edges even; stitch on marked lines, making ¼" seams unless otherwise directed. When assembling clothes, press seams open after stitching, unless otherwise directed. Clip into seam allowance at curves and across corners; turn piece to right side and poke out corners with knitting needle.

DIRECTIONS FOR DOLL
From off-white fabric, cut two heads (omitting hairline), one head center, two bodies, two arms, four legs, and two soles. From felt, cut following pieces, omitting seam allowance: two pink cheeks; two of each eye piece: #1, brown; #2, white; #3, green; #4, black.

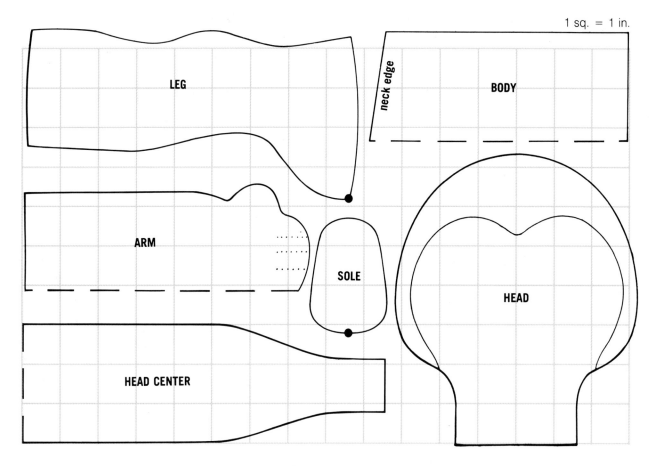

1 sq. = 1 in.

LEG

neck edge

BODY

ARM

SOLE

HEAD

HEAD CENTER

Referring to illustration for placement, transfer mouth lines and eye outline to right side of head front.

Insert mouth area in hoop. Work embroidery as follows, using three strands of floss in needle; see Embroidery Stitch Details, page 185. Work satin stitch in coral for tongue and black for remainder of mouth. Work brown outline stitch around entire mouth. When embroidery is complete, remove from hoop. Press gently, wrong side up. **Nose:** From off-white fabric, cut 1¼" circle. Baste around circle close to edges. Pull basting thread gently to gather, forming "pouch." Stuff with fiberfill, then pull thread to close opening. Stitch nose to face as shown. Pin cheeks in place, stuffing in bits of fiberfill; topstitch close to edges. **Each eye:** Glue #4 to #3, #3 to #2, then #2 to #1, following pattern for placement. Pin eye in place; topstitch #2

close to edges. Use three strands of white floss in needle to work a straight-stitch iris on #4.

Pin head center to face and head back with bottom edges even. Stitch around sides and top, leaving neck edge open. Fold neck ¼" to wrong side; baste. Turn head to right side. Stuff firmly with fiberfill.

Body: Fold arms in half lengthwise, right side in. Stitch raw arm and hand edges, leaving top straight edges open. Turn; stuff firmly. Baste each arm closed ⅛" from raw edges, enclosing stuffing. Stitch legs together in pairs at front and back, leaving top and bottom edges open. Stitch soles to bottom openings, matching dots; turn and stuff. Baste each leg top as for arm, but with seams centered. On right side of one body (front), pin arms ½" down from shoulders, so that arms cross, thumbs point down, and side edges are even; stitch. Pin and stitch legs to body bottom in similar manner, so that toes point toward shoulders. Place body front on work surface with limbs on top, extending outward. Fold left arm across body, so that hand extends above right shoulder and seam allowance faces out. Pin left side of body back, wrong side up, to body front; stitch. Pin and stitch right side of body in same manner (body will look like a tube with hands extending above and legs below). Push legs up through tube, so that only seam allowance extends at bottom; pin and stitch body bottom. Turn and stuff. Turn raw edges ¼" to inside; slipstitch opening closed. Using heavy-duty thread, slipstitch head, centered, over shoulders. Topstitch hand along dotted lines (*see pattern*), forming fingers.

Hair: Make pattern: Mark line 1¼" above each neck edge on patterns for head and head center. Place rust-color fake fur wrong side up on work surface with nap running toward you. Using new lines for bottom edge, transfer one head (back) and head center to fake fur with neck edges across nap; cut out, adding ¼" seam allowance. Stitch pieces together as for doll's head, forming hair. Place hair on head, matching seams. Fold raw edges under ¼" and slipstitch in place all around. Finger-comb hair as desired.

Beard and mustache: From rust-color fake fur, cut 7" × 4½" beard and 7½" × 1¼" mustache, cutting each so that short edges are parallel to nap. Fold each piece in half lengthwise with right side in; stitch ¼" from raw edges, leaving opening in each for turning; turn. Fold raw edges ¼" to inside; slipstitch openings closed. Following illustration for placement, pin beard to face with nap running downward, overlapping hair at sides; slipstitch in place. Center mustache above mouth and pin in place, curving ends downward over beard sides; slipstitch. Finger-comb beard and mustache downward.

DIRECTIONS FOR CLOTHES

Jacket: On right side of suedecloth, mark one jacket back, two jacket fronts, one placket (including fine lines), two sleeves, and fringe for jacket fronts and back; do not cut out. Transfer buffalo to center of jacket back. **To embroider:** Work embroidery as follows; see Embroidery Stitch Details, page 185. *Buffalo* Referring to pattern, use all six strands of floss in needle to work A in long and short stitch with tan. Using three strands of brown floss, fill in C's with French knots, E with straight stitch. Work satin stitch in black for B's, white for D's. Work black French-knot eye and nose. *Placket* Use all six strands of brown floss to work design in backstitch.

When embroidery is complete, cut out pieces; do not add seam allowance to neck edges, placket, sleeve and jacket bottoms, or center edges of jacket front. Pin a front fringe piece to each jacket front, following pattern for placement. Using two strands of brown floss in needle, sew top edge of fringe in place with running stitch (*see photograph*). In same manner, attach fringe to jacket back. From suedecloth, cut four strips, two 1½" × 3½" and two 1½" × 4¼". Fringe one long edge of each strip, making 1"-long slashes ⅛" apart. On right side, pin uncut long edge of each 3½" strip to side of jacket front, matching bottom edges; baste ⅛" in from edge. In same manner, baste 4¼" strips to one long edge of each sleeve. Slipstitch placket to right jacket front. Machine-stitch jacket fronts to back at shoulders. Stitch curved edge of sleeves to jacket armholes, matching dots with shoulder seams. Stitch each underarm and side, making continuous seams. Using two strands of brown floss in needle, work running stitch ¼" in from neck edge. From "sheepskin," cut three strips, two 1" × 6" and one 1" × 15". Fold strips in half lengthwise right side out. Pin short strips around sleeve bottoms and long strip around jacket bottom, enclosing edges; slipstitch raw edges in place on both sides of jacket. Using pattern, cut three button loops from leather. Pin right side of each loop against wrong side of right jacket front at center edge between marks, so that loops extend ⅝" beyond fabric (*see photograph*); stitch. Sew toggle buttons to left jacket front where indicated by open circles. Thread a needle with heavy-duty thread; knot ends together. String seed beads on thread to make 1½" strand; do not cut thread. Stitch strand to front jacket fringe at a dot; end off. Make seven more strands in same manner; stitch strands to remaining dots.

Trousers: From suedecloth, cut four trousers and two 1½" × 10¼" strips. Fringe one long edge of each strip as for jacket and baste to sides of two trouser pieces between dots. Pair trouser pieces and stitch together at center front and back from waist to crotch. Stitch side seams from leg bottoms to waist; stitch inseams. Press waist edges ¼" then ½" to wrong side; stitch close to folds, leaving 1" opening in bottom edge at one side seam. Use safety pin to work elastic through casing; stitch ends to secure. Stitch casing closed. Turn leg bottoms ¼" to wrong side and slipstitch all around. To finish, cut pieces of rickrack to fit and slipstitch to sides of legs just in front of side seams. Sew seed and bugle beads to rickrack for decoration.

Boots: From "sheepskin," cut four boots. Also cut two soles from black felt. Pair boot pieces and stitch together along toe and boot back between solid dots. Stitch soles to uppers, matching dots at toe; turn. Cut two ¾-yard pieces of brown rug yarn and tack center of each to back of boot at open circle, for thongs.

Pouch: Using pattern, cut two pouches and one pouch flap from suedecloth. Use compass to make patterns for 2½"- and 1½"-diameter circles. Use patterns to cut large circle from dark green fabric and small circle from leather. Press edges of fabric piece ¼" to wrong side and slipstitch to center of pouch flap. Using awl or large darning needle and thimble,

punch a ring of holes in leather circle, ⅛" in from edge and ⅛" apart. Thread embroidery needle with three strands of red floss and backstitch piece to center of fabric circle through punched holes (*see Embroidery Stitch Details, page 185*). Following diagram and photograph, finish embroidering medallion, using lazy daisy and straight stitches; punch additional holes as needed. Using two strands of pink or orange floss, work over design on leather piece as desired; also fill in centers of outermost row of lazy daisy stitches.

Stitch flap to a pouch, matching A edges. Place pouch pieces together and stitch along curved edge; turn. Knot silk cord 2" from each end. Sew one end to side of pouch as shown. At other end of cord, sew half of snap fastener to cord and half to side of pouch; fasten. Make three 2½" strands of seed beads as for jacket and sew to side of pouch just below cord. To make clasp, cut 8"-long strip of leather narrow enough to fit through hole in plastic or wooden button. Thread through two holes and tie in square knot on one side (front). Thread each end through a round wooden bead; knot end. Sew finished clasp to pouch front as shown.

Coonskin cap: (**Note:** If using old raccoon collar, remove any linings or padding before using. Cut skin carefully from back, so as not to cut fur.) Using compass, make pattern for 7"-diameter circle. Use pattern to cut circle from brown fake fur or raccoon skin for crown; also cut 3" × 20" strip for brim and 7" × 9" strip for tail. Fold brim in half widthwise and stitch short edges together to make tube. Stitch one edge of tube to outside of crown, easing fullness as needed to fit. Turn remaining edge ¼" to wrong side and slipstitch all around. Place 7" × 9" strip, wrong side up, on flat surface. Fold edges of strip ¼" to wrong side; baste. Fold long edges of strip to center; slipstitch invisibly together. Slipstitch one short edge of piece to brim of cap for tail.

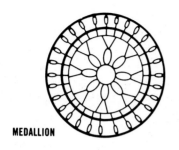

MEDALLION

1 sq. = 1 in.

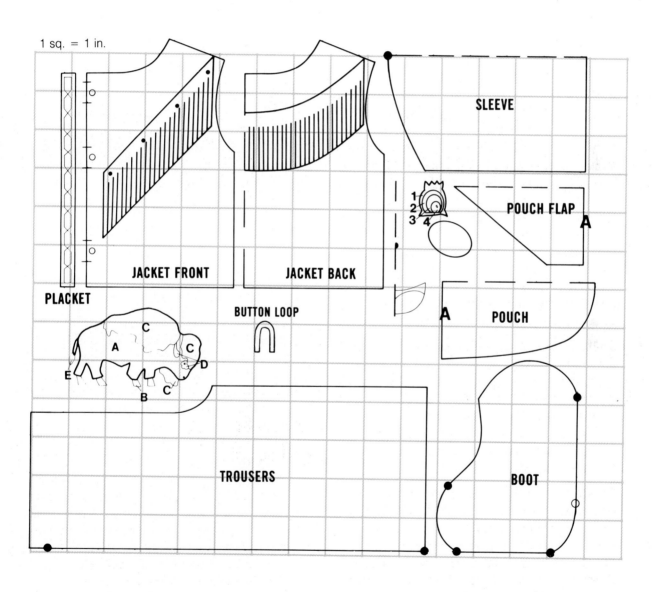

SLEEVE

PLACKET

JACKET FRONT

JACKET BACK

POUCH FLAP

A

A

POUCH

BUTTON LOOP

1
2
3   4

C

A

C

D

E

C

B

TROUSERS

BOOT

atie *is a charmer, with her red hair pulled into ponytails and tied with ribbon bows.*

SIZE
About 20″ tall.

EQUIPMENT
Pencil. Ruler. Paper for patterns. Tape measure. Dressmaker's tracing (carbon) paper. Dry ball-point pen. Small embroidery hoop. Embroidery and regular scissors. Embroidery and sewing needles. Knitting needle. Straight pins. Sewing machine with zigzag attachment. Iron. Compass.

MATERIALS
For doll: Closely woven cotton fabric such as muslin or kettle cloth 45″ wide, ½ yard flesh color. Flesh-color sewing thread and heavy-duty sewing thread. Sport-weight yarn, 3 ozs. light brown for hair. Six-strand embroidery floss, one skein to match hair; small amounts of white, blue, brown, pink, yellow, and green. Polyester fiberfill for stuffing. Blue grosgrain ribbon ⅜″ wide, 1 yard. **For clothes:** Closely woven cotton fabric at least 45″ wide: ½ yard blue calico for dress; 1 yard white for pinafore, underskirt, and bloomers. Small amount brown felt for shoes. Flat elastic ¼″ wide, 1 yard. Pre-gathered cotton eyelet trim 1″ wide, 2½ yards. Buttons, ⅜″-diameter: two each black and pearlescent. Sewing thread to match fabrics and felt. White stretch socks, size 1 year.

DIRECTIONS FOR DOLL
Enlarge patterns by copying on paper ruled in 1″ squares. Complete half- and quarter-patterns indicated by long dash lines; fine lines are for placement or embroidery.

Use dressmaker's carbon and dry ball-point pen to transfer patterns to wrong side of flesh-color fabric, placing them ½″ from fabric edges and ½″ apart; reverse leg and body patterns to make a front and a back for each. Cut out one head center, two bodies, two arms, two soles, and four legs, leaving ¼″ seam allowance around all pieces. Do not transfer dotted lines for fingers.

Mark one head on fabric, for face; center and transfer actual-size pattern for face to right side of fabric, including fine lines for embroidery. Do *not* cut out.

Insert face area into embroidery hoop. Using three strands of floss in needle, work pink mouth in outline stitch (*see Embroidery Stitch Details, page 185*); work eyes in vertical satin stitch with blue; work a white cross-stitch with an additional vertical stitch in center of each eye. Using two strands of floss in needle, outline eyes in backstitch with brown; work matching lashes in straight stitch. When embroidery is completed, remove fabric from hoop. Press gently, wrong side up. Cut out face; use as pattern to cut head back.

To assemble: Pin head center to face and head back with bottom straight edges even. Stitch around sides and top, leaving neck

edge open. Fold neck ¼" to wrong side; baste. Turn head to right side. Stuff firmly with fiberfill.

Fold arms in half lengthwise, right side in. Stitch raw arm and hand edges, leaving top straight edges open. Turn; stuff firmly. Baste each arm closed ⅛" from raw edges, enclosing stuffing. Stitch legs together in pairs at front and back, leaving top and bottom edges open. Stitch soles to bottom openings, matching dots; turn and stuff. Baste each leg top as for arm, but with seams centered. On right side of one body (front), pin arms ½" down from shoulders, so that arms cross, thumbs point down, and side edges are even; stitch. Pin and stitch legs to body bottom in similar manner, so that toes point toward shoulders. Place body front on work surface with limbs

on top, extending outward. Fold left arm across body, so that hand extends above right shoulder and seam allowance faces out. Pin left side of body back, wrong side up, to body front; stitch. Pin and stitch right side of body in same manner (body will look like a tube with hands extending above and legs below). Push legs up through tube, so that only seam allowance extends at bottom; pin and stitch body bottom. Turn and stuff. Turn raw edges ¼" to inside; slipstitch opening closed. Using heavy-duty thread, slipstitch head, centered, over shoulders.

Nose: From flesh-color fabric, cut 1¼"-diameter circle, using compass. Baste around circle ¼" in from edge. Pull basting to gather, forming "pouch." Stuff with fiberfill, then

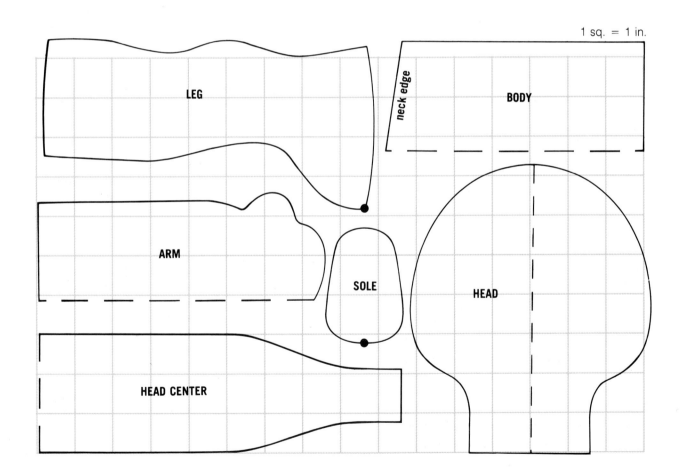

1 sq. = 1 in.

LEG

neck edge

BODY

ARM

SOLE

HEAD

HEAD CENTER

pull threads to close opening. Stitch nose to face as shown in color photograph.

Hair: Mark center part from front head seam to nape of neck. For ponytails, cut 120 24″ lengths of yarn. Working with groups of 10 strands at a time and all six strands of matching embroidery floss, stitch center of each group to part, working from front seam to back. For bangs, cut 100 12″ lengths of yarn. Working with groups of 10 strands at a time and all six strands of floss, stitch yarn across hairline, 1″ from ends; finger-comb 1″ ends over forehead. Cut grosgrain ribbon in half. Gather hair on each side of head into ponytail; secure with ribbon as shown.

DIRECTIONS FOR CLOTHES

Bloomers: On solid-color fabric, mark two bloomers, adding ¼″ to each waist edge; cut out, adding seam allowance all around. Press leg bottoms ¼″ to wrong side. Cut eyelet trim to fit leg bottoms. Pin eyelet in place on wrong side, so that ruffles extend below folds; topstitch on right side close to folds, using wide zigzag stitch. Cut four 5″ lengths of elastic. Starting at a side edge of each leg with one end, pin elastic to wrong side 1½″ above fold; zigzag-stitch in place. Press waist edges ½″ to wrong side. Pin and stitch elastic to wrong side of waist ¼″ below fold as for leg. Reset machine for straight stitch. Stitch bloomers together at center front and back from waist to crotch. Stitch each inseam from eyelet to crotch; turn to right side.

Dress: Cut 45″ × 7″ piece for skirt. Cut one bodice front, using complete pattern. Double fabric and mark bodice back, using half-pattern and adding 1″ to center back; also mark dress sleeve; cut two of each. From white fabric, cut two 45″ × 5″ pieces for underskirt; hem one long edge of each. Stitch bodice front and backs together at shoulders. *Each sleeve* Cut eyelet trim to fit sleeve bottom; attach as for bloomers. Stitch 4½″ length of elastic 1¼″ above fold. Reset machine for

straight stitch. Baste upper curved edge of sleeve between X's. Pin lower curved edges to front and back armhole of bodice below X's. Gather basted edge to fit armhole; pin and stitch. Stitch underarm and side in a continuous seam. *Skirt* Stack underskirt pieces on flat work surface with hemmed edges at bottom. Pin skirt, right side up, to underskirt, matching top (waist) and side edges. Machine-baste close to waist through all thicknesses. Gather waist to fit bodice waist. Stitch assembled skirt to bodice; turn. **To finish:** Finish neck edges as for sleeve bottom. Press center back edges ⅛″ to wrong side; stitch. Reset machine for straight stitch. Starting at hem, stitch center backs together to 2½″ below waist, making ¾″ seam; press seam open. Above seam, press edges under ¾″. On one side of center back, make ½″ button-holes ½″ and 1¾″ below neck edge. Sew buttons to corresponding positions on other side. Press hem ¼″ then ¾″ to wrong side; slipstitch.

Pinafore: From solid color fabric, cut two ruffles. Also cut the following pieces: bib, 4⅞″ × 4¾″; two straps, 2¼″ × 6¾″; skirt, 45″ × 6⅛″; two waistband/ties, 16″ × 2½″. Press curved edge of ruffles under ⅛″ twice; stitch. Baste straight ruffle edges; gather each to 6¼″; press. Press straps in half lengthwise, right side out. Pin straps, centered to right side of ruffles with 6¾″ length of eyelet trim sandwiched between and all long raw edges even; stitch. Press bib in half, right side out, to form 4⅞″ × 2⅜″ piece. With fold at top, embroider one side (front) of bib; use three strands of floss, refer to color photograph,

Embroidery Pattern For Pinatore

and place flowers 1″ in from side edges as follows: Work pink lazy daisy flowers with yellow French knot centers; work green lazy daisy leaves and straight-stitch stems (*see Embroidery Stitch Details, page 185*). Place bib right side up on work surface. Pin ruffles/straps to bib at sides, so that ruffles are on top with curved edges facing in, and bottom and side raw edges are even; stitch sides. Press under seam allowances; ruffles and eyelet will extend beyond sides. Press short edges of skirt ¼″ to wrong side; stitch ⅛″ from folds. Press one long (bottom) edge ¼″ then ¾″ to wrong side; stitch close to top fold.

Baste waist edge of skirt; gather to 10¼″; press. Center bib on skirt, right sides facing, with waist edges even; pin and baste. Overlap each side of waist and ruffle with one end of a waistband/tie for 3¼″, raw edges even; pin and stitch waist. Fold ties in half lengthwise, right side in; pin. Stitch long raw edge of each from short edge (back) of skirt to end; stitch ends; turn and press. Fold under long raw edges of waistbands ¼″; turn to wrong side of waist, covering stitching (bib will extend above waist); slipstitch. Starting at waist seam, topstitch inner edge of ruffles close to straps for 1″ to secure. Pin right side of strap ends against wrong side of waistbands, so that back edges are even and bottom edge of each ruffle is even with waistband top; zigzag-stitch.

Shoes: On wrong side of felt, mark two soles; also mark four uppers, marking strap on two pieces only. Cut out, omitting seam allowance on each upper at top and strap edges. Stitch together uppers in pairs at front and back. Stitch soles to uppers, matching dots; turn. Test-fit shoes on doll; mark placement for strap ends and remove shoes. Tack strap ends in place; sew a button over each tack.

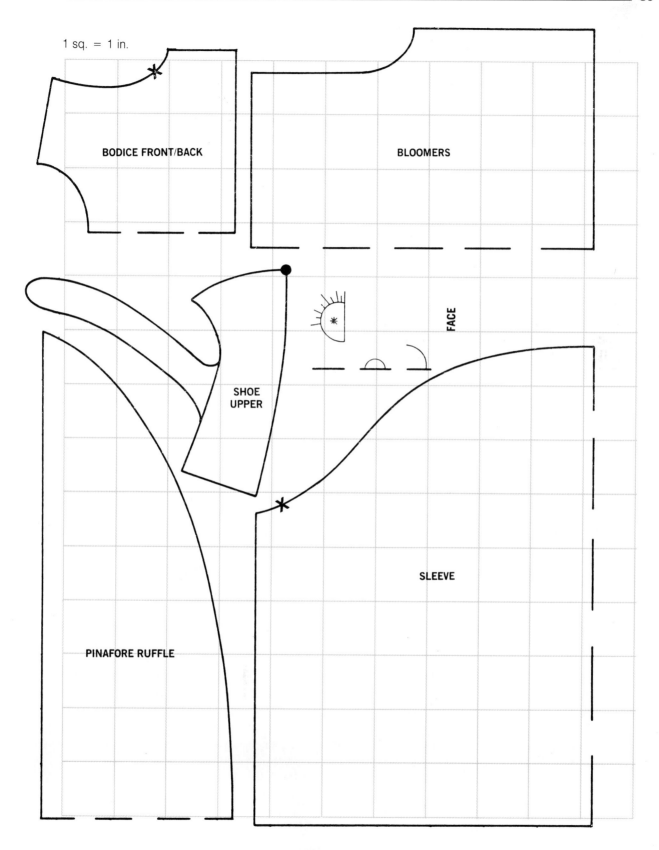

1 sq. = 1 in.

BODICE FRONT/BACK

BLOOMERS

FACE

SHOE
UPPER

SLEEVE

PINAFORE RUFFLE

ittle Mermaid

The Little Mermaid rides the waves along with her two shell pillows.

SIZE
Doll, 16″ tall. Scallop shell pillow, 12½″ tall. Conch shell pillow, 10½″ tall.

EQUIPMENT
Pencil. Ruler. Paper for patterns. Scissors. Dressmaker's tracing (carbon) paper. Tailor's chalk. Dry ball-point pen. Sewing and embroidery needles. Straight pins.

MATERIALS
Unbleached muslin 36″ wide, ⅜ yard. Closely woven dotted fabric 45″ wide: green, ½ yard; salmon, ⅜ yard; dark brown, ⅜ yard; scrap of tan. White pre-gathered lace ½″ wide, 2½ yards. Polyester fiberfill. Polyester quilt batting. Sewing thread to match fabrics. Yellow knitting worsted. Six-strand embroidery floss: green, black, and dark pink. Green satin ribbon ¼″ wide, 2 yards. Pink crayon. Six white plastic flowers, 1″ diameter. Small strand pre-strung seed pearls.

GENERAL DIRECTIONS
Enlarge patterns by copying on paper ruled in 1″ squares. Complete half-patterns, indicated by long dash lines; make separate patterns for large and small sections of conch shell, as well as complete shell. Heavy solid lines indicate seamlines; dotted lines indicate quilting lines; fine lines indicate placement lines and embroidery; dash lines indicate darts and tucks; dot-dash lines are alternate cutting lines. Cut out pieces as directed below, adding ½″ seam allowance all around. When assembling pieces, unless otherwise indicated, stitch together with right sides facing and edges even, making ½″ seams.

DIRECTIONS FOR DOLL
Using patterns, cut two heads and two upper body pieces from muslin; set body pieces aside. Transfer eyes and mouth to right side of one head piece (front), using dressmaker's carbon and dry ball-point pen. Using two strands of floss in embroidery needle, satin-stitch irises with green and pupils with black floss (see *Embroidery Stitch Details, page 185*). Finish eyes with black: use backstitch for eyelids and straight stitches for lashes and lines radiating out from pupils. Use pink floss and satin stitch to embroider mouth. Color cheeks as shown, using pink crayon. Pin front and back head pieces together and stitch around curved edge, leaving bottom (neck) open; clip curves and turn; stuff with fiberfill. To make hair, first lightly mark center part from front of head at X (see *pattern*) to nape of neck, using pencil. From yellow yarn, cut 120 25″ strands. Working in groups of 10 strands at a time and using yellow sewing thread, stitch center of each group along part, working from front to back. From top hair, pick up three nine-strand groups on each side of part and braid; trim each braid to 6″; tie end. Pull hair, including braids, to each side of head and tack at ear level, catching in ends

of braids. Divide hair into four groups on each side and braid each; tie ends. Curl each braid into a loop and tack end to head next to end of crown braids; trim braid ends to 1" long.

Stitch darts on upper body pieces; pin pieces together and stitch along edge, leaving bottom open; clip curves, turn, and stuff with fiberfill. Fold raw edges of neck opening ½" to inside and slipstitch head to center of shoulders; set piece aside.

Using pattern, cut two lower body pieces from green dotted fabric; reverse pattern for second piece (back), cutting top along heavy dot-dash line. From single layer of quilt batting, cut tail portion of body, shortening pattern along fine dot-dash line. Place front lower body, right side up, on flat surface and transfer quilting lines from pattern, using dressmaker's carbon and dry ball-point pen. Turn piece over. Place back lower body on flat surface with wrong side up. To wrong sides of both lower body pieces, transfer tuck markings: transfer entire dash line (from triangle to dot) to lower body back; transfer portion of line between triangles to lower body front. Pin batting piece to wrong side of lower body front, matching lower edges; baste. On right side, quilt marked lines, using white thread and following Quilting Stitch Detail, page 190. Machine-stitch four tucks on wrong side of each piece, following marked lines on bodice. Pin front to back and stitch edges together, leaving top edge of bodice open; clip curves and turn. Cut ½"-wide lace to fit top of bodice and pin to right side, so that top edge of lace is even with top edge of bodice; stitch. Fold top of lace and seam to wrong side, so that lace extends beyond bodice edge, as shown in photograph. Place bottom of upper body into opening at top of bodice and adjust, so that top of bodice aligns with placement lines on pattern. Slip-stitch top edge of bodice invisibly to body all around. To finish, cut two strands of

pearls to fit neck and wrist; slipstitch in place. Cut four 12" pieces green satin ribbon, tie into bows, and tack to sides of hair as shown. Tack white plastic flowers to bodice center and hair.

DIRECTIONS FOR SCALLOP PILLOW
Using pattern, cut two scallop pieces from salmon dotted fabric and one same-size piece batting. Place one fabric piece (front) right side up on flat surface, and transfer quilting lines, using dressmaker's carbon and dry ball-point pen. With edges even, pin batting piece to wrong side of scallop front; baste. On right side, quilt marked lines as for doll. Cut ½"-wide lace to fit scallop edge, omitting bottom. Pin lace around scallop front, so that curved edge of lace faces in and straight edge of lace overlaps seamline 1⁄16"; stitch. Pin front scallop to back and stitch pieces together, leaving bottom open; clip curves, turn, stuff with fiberfill. Turn raw edges at opening ½" to inside and slipstitch closed.

DIRECTIONS FOR CONCH PILLOW
Using pattern, cut small section of conch from tan dotted fabric. Cut large section and one whole conch (back) from brown dotted fabric. Cut large section from single layer of quilt batting. Cut ½"-wide lace to fit inner edge of small section; pin lace to edge in same manner as for scallop; stitch. Place large section on flat surface and transfer quilting lines to right side, using dressmaker's carbon and dry ball-point pen. Pin quilt batting to wrong side of large section with edges even; baste. On right side, quilt marked lines, using white thread. Pin conch sections together with right sides facing, and stitch inner edges together to make pillow front as shown. Pin pillow front to back and stitch together all around, leaving 4" opening for turning; clip curves, turn, stuff with fiberfill. Turn raw edges at opening ½" to inside; slipstitch opening closed.

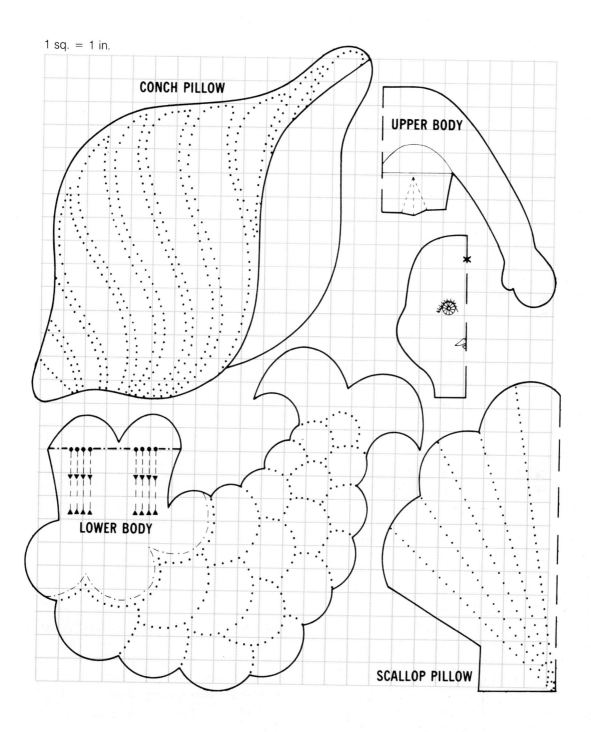

1 sq. = 1 in.

CONCH PILLOW

UPPER BODY

LOWER BODY

SCALLOP PILLOW

Mary Christmas *is*

wearing a fur-trimmed dress and cap.

SIZE
About 20″ tall.

EQUIPMENT
Pencil. Ruler. Paper for patterns. Tape measure. Dressmaker's tracing (carbon) paper. Dry ball-point pen. Small embroidery hoop. Embroidery and regular scissors. Embroidery and sewing needles. Knitting needle. Straight pins. Sewing machine with zigzag attachment. Iron. Cardboard, 7″ × 20″. Compass.

MATERIALS
For doll: Closely woven cotton fabric such as muslin or kettle cloth 45″ wide, ½ yard desired flesh color. Flesh-color sewing thread and heavy-duty sewing thread. Sport-weight yarn, about 3 ozs. brown for hair. Six-strand embroidery floss: one skein to match hair; small amounts of black, white, green, red, and beige. Pink crayon. Polyester fiberfill for stuffing. **For clothes:** Deep red velvet fabric 44″ wide, 1 yard. White short-pile fake fur 36″ wide, ⅜ yard. White cotton fabric 36″ wide, ¼ yard for bloomers. Small amounts black suedecloth and brown vinyl for boots; heavy-duty black thread for laces. Flat elastic ¼″ wide, 1 yard. White pre-gathered lace trim 1″ wide, ½ yard. Gold trim ⅜″ wide, 6″. Four gold ½″ shank-type buttons. Three snap fasteners. Florist's holly berries and leaves. Sewing thread to match fabrics, plus gold.

DIRECTIONS FOR DOLL
Enlarge patterns by copying on paper ruled in 1″ squares. Complete half- and quarter-patterns indicated by long dash lines; fine lines are for placement or embroidery.

Use dressmaker's carbon and dry ball-point pen to transfer patterns to wrong side of flesh-color fabric, placing them ½″ from fabric edges and ½″ apart; reverse leg and body patterns to make a front and a back for each. Cut out one head center, two bodies, two arms, two soles, and four legs leaving ¼″ seam allowance around all pieces. Do not transfer dotted lines for fingers.

Mark one head on fabric, for face; center and transfer actual-size pattern for face to right side of fabric, including fine lines for embroidery. Do *not* cut out.

Face: Insert face area in embroidery hoop. Embroider as follows, referring to Embroidery Stitch Details, page 185: Using two strands of floss in needle, work black pupils and green irises in vertical satin stitch; work white cornea in horizontal satin stitch; also with white, make a few short satin stitches in the center of each pupil; outline eye with brown backstitches; make beige backstitch nose and red satin stitch mouth. Using one strand brown floss in needle, work backstitch lashes and brows. When embroidery is completed, remove fabric from hoop. Press gently, wrong

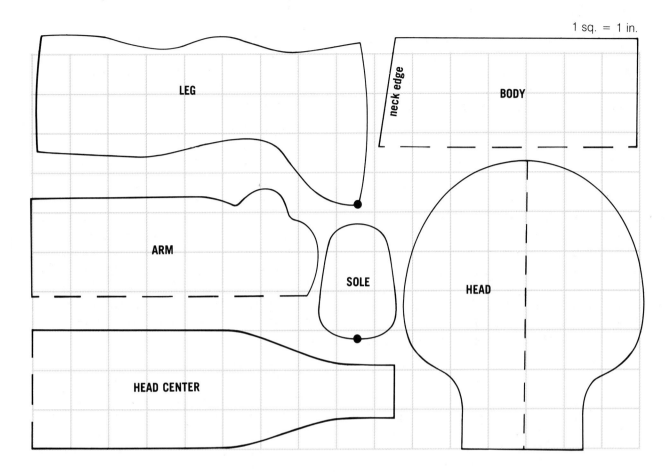

1 sq. = 1 in.

side up. Cut out face; use as pattern to cut head back.

To assemble: Pin head center to face and head back with bottom straight edges even. Stitch around sides and top, leaving neck edge open. Fold neck ¼" to wrong side; baste. Turn head to right side. Stuff firmly with fiberfill. "Rouge" cheeks with crayon.

Fold arms in half lengthwise, right side in. Stitch raw arm and hand edges, leaving top straight edges open. Turn; stuff firmly. Baste each arm closed ⅛" from raw edges, enclosing stuffing. Stitch legs together in pairs at front and back, leaving top and bottom edges open. Stitch soles to bottom openings, matching dots; turn and stuff. Baste each leg top as for arm, but with seams centered. On right

side of one body (front), pin arms ½" down from shoulders, so that arms cross, thumbs point down, and side edges are even; stitch. Pin and stitch legs to body bottom in similar manner, so that toes point toward shoulders. Place body front on work surface with limbs on top, extending outward. Fold left arm across body, so that hand extends above right shoulder and seam allowance faces out. Pin left side of body back, wrong side up, to body front; stitch. Pin and stitch right side of body in same manner (body will look like a tube with hands extending above and legs below). Push legs up through tube, so that only seam allowance extends at bottom; pin and stitch body bottom. Turn and stuff. Turn raw edges ¼" to inside; slipstitch opening closed. Using heavy-duty thread, slipstitch head, centered, over shoulders.

Hair: Wind yarn around cardboard about 200 times, making 7″ loops. Tie strands tightly together at one end (top), leaving 1¼″ loops free for "bun." Tack bun to crown of head, then finger-comb long looped ends around entire head; tack ends around face and neck to secure, 1″ from loops.

DIRECTIONS FOR CLOTHES

Bloomers: On white fabric, mark two bloomers, adding ¼″ to each waist edge; cut out, adding seam allowance all around. Press leg bottoms ¼″ to wrong side. Cut lace trim to fit leg bottoms. Pin lace trim in place on wrong side, so that ruffles extend below folds; topstitch on right side close to folds, using wide zigzag stitch. Cut four 5″ lengths of elastic. Starting at a side edge of each leg with one end, pin elastic to wrong side 1½″ above fold; zigzag-stitch in place. Press waist edges ½″ to wrong side. Pin and stitch elastic to wrong side of waist ¼″ below fold as for leg. Reset machine for straight stitch. Stitch bloomers together at center front and back from waist to crotch. Stitch each inseam from lace trim to crotch; turn to right side.

Dress: From red velvet, cut 44″ × 7″ piece for skirt. Cut one bodice front, using complete pattern, and two bodice backs, using half-pattern and adding 1″ to each center back; also cut two upper sleeves and two 2¼″ × 7½″ lower sleeves. Stitch bodice front and backs together at shoulders. *Each sleeve* Cut 2½″ × 7½″ piece of fake fur for cuff. Stitch a cuff to one 7½″ edge of lower sleeve; fold fur over sleeve edge to wrong side; turn fur edges under ¼″; slipstitch in place. Baste upper curved edge of upper sleeve between X's. Pin lower curved edges to front and back armhole of bodice below X's. Gather basted edge to fit armhole; pin and stitch. Baste lower edge of upper sleeve; gather to fit edge of lower sleeve opposite cuff; pin and stitch. Stitch underarm and side in a continuous seam. *Skirt* Gather one long (waist) edge to fit bodice waist; pin and stitch to bodice.

To finish: Trim neck edge with fur as for sleeve bottom. Press center back edges ⅛″ to wrong side; stitch. Starting at hem, stitch center backs together to 1″ below waist, making ¾″ seam; press seam open. Above seam, press edges under ¾″. Sew three snap fasteners to back, one at neck edges, one at waist, and one evenly spaced between. Cut fur strip 44″ × 4½″; finish hem with fur as for sleeve bottom. Cut gold trim in half widthwise; topstitch across bodice front as shown in color photograph. Tack a gold button to each end of trim.

Cap: From velvet, cut one cap. Fold in half with right sides facing; stitch; turn. Finish brim as for skirt hem. Cut two 2″-diameter circles of fake fur for pompon. Stitch circles together with right sides facing, leaving small opening for turning. Turn to right side; stuff with fiberfill; stitch opening closed. Tack pompon to tip of cap. Tack holly to brim as shown in color photograph.

Boots: On wrong side of vinyl, mark two soles; cut out. On suedecloth, mark four uppers and two tongues; cut out, omitting seam allowance on tongues and on each upper at top edges. Stitch together uppers in pairs at back and front from toe edge to X. Above seam, turn edges under ⅛″; topstitch. With right side of tongue facing wrong side of upper, stitch straight edge of tongue across upper ¼″ below front opening. Stitch soles to uppers, matching dots; turn. Thread needle with black heavy-duty thread; use to lace boots; cut thread, leaving long ends for tying.

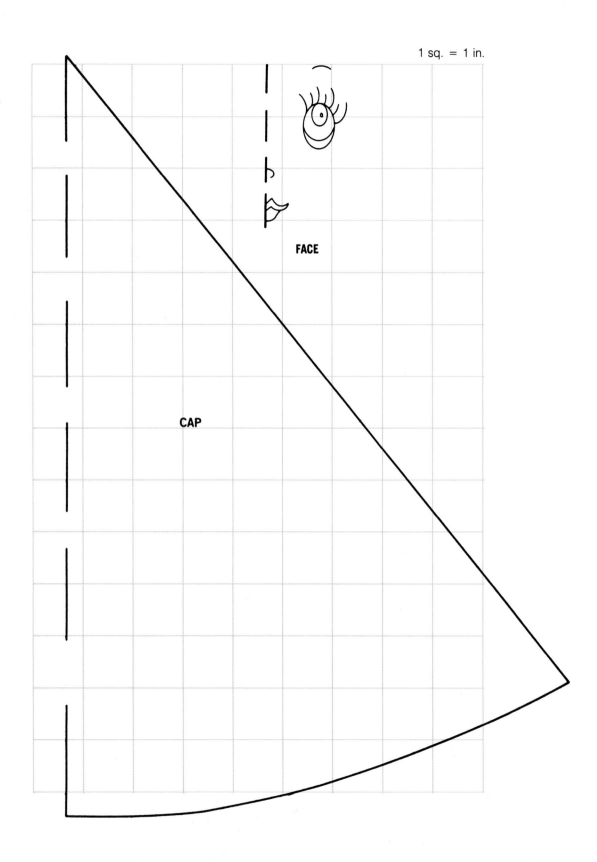

1 sq. = 1 in.

FACE

CAP

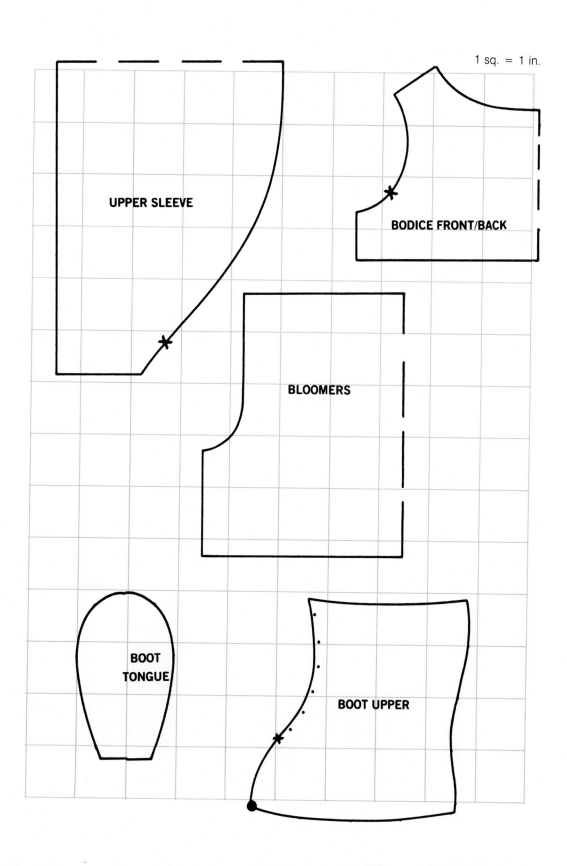

1 sq. = 1 in.

UPPER SLEEVE

BODICE FRONT/BACK

BLOOMERS

BOOT TONGUE

BOOT UPPER

oah's Ark

The animals march two-by-two from this colorful crocheted Noah's Ark.

SIZE
18″ × 14″.

MATERIALS
4-ply knitting-worsted weight 4-oz. skeins: 2 skeins tan, 1 skein each off-white and gray. Sport yarn 2-oz. skeins: 2 skeins each off-white and yellow; 1 skein each blue, green, pink, black, and rust. Stuffing. Masonite® and saw or foamcore board and mat knife: 24″ × 30″ piece. ½ yd. cotton muslin. Sewing

needle and thread. All-purpose glue. Tapestry needle. Crochet hooks sizes C and G (2¾ and 4¼ mm). ½″ button (doorknob).

GAUGE
3½ sc = 1″ (size G hook and knitting worsted).

DIRECTIONS FOR ARK

Cabin sides (make 2): With off-white 4-ply and G hook, ch 31.

Row 1: Sc in 2nd ch from hook and in each ch across—30 sc. Ch 1, turn each row.

Rows 2–24: Sc in each sc. At end of row 24, end off.

Cabin ends (make 2): With off-white 4-ply and G hook, ch 2.

Row 1: 3 sc in 2nd ch from hook. Ch 1, turn each row.

Row 2: Sc in each sc—3 sc.

Row 3: 2 sc in first st, sc to last st, 2 sc in last st—2 sts increased.

Row 4: Sc in each sc. Repeat last 2 rows 9 times—23 sc.

Rows 23–46: Sc in each sc. At end of row 46, end off.

Roof (make 2): With tan and G hook, ch 31.

Row 1: Sc in 2nd ch from hook and in each ch across—30 sc. Ch 1, turn each row.

Rows 2–22: Sc in each sc. At end of row 22, end off.

Base (make 2): With tan and G hook, ch 2.

Row 1: 3 sc in 2nd ch from hook. Ch 1, turn each row.

Row 2: 2 sc in first st, sc to last st, 2 sc in last st—5 sc.

Rows 3–15: Repeat row 2—31 sc.

Rows 16–54: Sc in each sc.

Row 55: Draw up a lp in first 2 sts, yo and through 3 lps on hook (1 dec); sc to last 2 sts, dec—29 sc.

Rows 56–68: Repeat row 55—3 sc.

Row 69: Draw up a lp in each st, yo and through 4 lps on hook. End off.

To assemble: Using crocheted pieces for patterns, cut pieces of Masonite® or foamcore board for each piece of cabin and 1 for base. Cut fabric to shape of crocheted pieces for cabin (not base) leaving a 1″ seam allowance. Cover 1 side of each piece of board for cabin, gluing seam allowances to wrong side of boards.

From right side, with off-white, sc cabin sides and ends tog. To join roof, attach tan in top point of one end; hold one roof piece in place along sloped end, sc roof to end along sloped edge, sc long edge of roof to side of cabin, sc roof to other end along sloped edge. Now sc 2nd roof piece to first piece across top of roof. Continue around 2nd roof piece with sc, but do not join to cabin, working 3 sc in each lower corner. When top of roof is reached, sc down sloped edge of cabin end, across long side and up 2nd sloped edge to top. Join; end off.

Insert covered boards for ends and sides into cabin. With needle and thread, using catch stitch, sew fabric to lower edges of cabin. Sew top edges of sides in place. Sew one roof piece to closed half of roof along top and bottom edges. Sew other roof piece to open half of roof around all four sides. Sew sloped edges at open ends of cabin in place.

Sandwich board for base between 2 crocheted base pieces. With tan, work 1 rnd sc, joining base pieces tog and stuffing on 1 side of board to round bottom before closing. Work 2 rnds more, inc at corners and ends to keep edge flat. End off.

Center cabin on base, rounded side down; sew cabin to base using tapestry needle and off-white sport.

Cabin trimming: *Gingerbread strip* With blue and C hook, ch 185.

Row 1: Dc in 4th ch from hook and in each ch across—183 dc (turning ch counts as 1 dc). Cut blue; join off-white sport, ch 5, turn.

Row 2: * Sk 2 dc in next st, ch 3, repeat from * across, end last repeat dc in turning ch. Ch 1, turn.

Row 3: * In next ch-3 sp work (sc, dc, ch 3, sl st in 3rd ch from hook, dc, sc), repeat from * across. End off. With blue, sew strip around cabin below roof.

Fans (make 6): With pink and C hook, ch 4.

Row 1 (right side): 2 dc in 4th ch from hook— 3 dc. End off. Do not turn each row; work all rows from right side.

Row 2: Join off-white sport in first dc, ch 3, dc in same dc, dc in next dc, 2 dc in last dc. End off.

Row 3: With pink, 2 sc in first st, sc in next 3 dc, 2 sc in last st—7 sc. End off.

Row 4: With off-white sport, sc in each st across. End off.

Row 5: With blue, 2 sc in first st, sc in next 5 sts, 2 sc in last st—9 sc. End off.

Row 6: Join off-white sport in first sc, * ch 4, sl st in 2nd ch from hook, ch 1, sk 1 st, sc in next st, repeat from * across. End off. With off-white sport, sew 1 fan to each corner on upper half of cabin ends.

Windowpanes (make 16): With off-white sport and C hook, ch 4. Sl st in first ch to form ring, ch 1.

Rnd 1: 12 sc in ring, sl st in first sc, ch 1.

Rnd 2: (Sc in next 2 sts, 2 sc in next st) 4 times—16 sc. Sl st in first sc, ch 1.

Rnd 3: Sc in 3 sts, (3 sc in next st, sc in 3 sts) 3 times, 3 sc in last st—24 sc. Sl st in first sc. End off.

6-pane window (make 2): With wrong sides tog, with blue and C hook, join 6 panes tog in 2 rows of 3 panes. Work 1 rnd sc around outer edge of 6-pane piece. With blue, sew a 6-pane window to each side of cabin.

Make a 4-pane window and sew to back of cabin.

Long window boxes (make 2): With blue and C hook, ch 28.

Row 1: Dc in 4th ch from hook and in each ch across—26 dc. Ch 3, turn.

Row 2: Dc in 2nd dc and in each dc across. End off. Sew a box below each 6-pane window, leaving top edge free.

Short window box: With blue and C hook, ch 20.

Row 1: Dc in 4th ch from hook and in each ch across—18 dc. Ch 3, turn.

Row 2: Dc in 2nd dc and each dc across. End off. Sew box below 4-pane window leaving top edge free.

Shutters (make 6): With pink and C hook, ch 9.

Row 1: Sc in 2nd ch from hook and in each ch to end—8 sc. Ch 1, turn each row.

Rows 2, 4, 6, 8, 10, and 12: Working in front lps only, sc in each sc across.

Rows 3, 5, 7, 9, 11, and 13: Working in back lps only, sc in each sc across. After row 13, end off. With pink, sew 1 shutter to either side of each window.

Vines (make as many as desired): With green and C hook, * ch 7, sl st in 4th ch from hook, repeat from * 4 to 7 times. End off. Tack vines growing out of window boxes and twining around windows.

Door: With pink and C hook, ch 22.

Row 1: Dc in 4th ch from hook and in each ch across—20 dc. Ch 3, turn every row.

Rows 2, 4, and 6: Working in front lps only, dc in each dc across. Ch 3, turn.

Rows 3 and 5: Working in back lps only, dc in each dc across. At end of row 6, cut pink; join green, ch 1, turn. Work sc around 3 sides of door, inc at corners to keep work flat. End off.

Door arch: (**Note:** Do not turn work at end of rows; always join yarn in first st made on previous row.) With off-white sport and C hook, ch 4.

Row 1: 5 dc in 4th ch from hook—6 dc. End off.

Row 2: Attach green to first dc, ch 3, dc in same st, 2 dc in each dc across. End off.

Row 3: With pink, 2 sc in first st, sc in next st, (2 sc in next st, sc in next st) 5 times. End off.

Row 4: With off-white sport, sc in each sc across. End off. With green, sew base of arch to top of door.

Door edging **Row 1:** From right side, attach blue in first green sc at base of door, ch 3, dc in each st to top of door; working along arch (dc in next 2 sts, 2 dc in next st) 6 times, dc in each st to bottom of door. End off.

Row 2: With off-white sport, sc in first st of row 1, * ch 4, sl st in 3rd ch from hook, ch 1, sk next dc, sc in next dc, repeat from * around 3 sides of door. End off. Sew door to cabin, end; sew button to door for knob.

Heart window: With pink and C hook, ch 2.

Row 1: 3 sc in 2nd ch from hook. Ch 1, turn each row.

Row 2: 2 sc in first st, sc in next st, 2 sc in last st.

Row 3: 2 sc in first st, sc in 3 sts, 2 sc in last st.

Row 4: 2 sc in first st, sc in 5 sts, 2 sc in last st.

Row 5: Sc in first st, dc in next st, tr in next st, dc in next st, sl st in next st, dc in next st, tr in next st, dc in next st, sc in last st. End off.

With green, work 1 rnd sc around heart. Sew heart to upper half of cabin above door.

Flowers: *Rose* (make 4): With yellow and C hook, ch 4, sl st in first ch to form ring.

Rnd 1: 12 sc in ring. End off.

Rnd 2: With pink, sc in any sc, (ch 4, 2 tr in next st, ch 4, sc in next st) 6 times, sl st in first st. End off.

Tulip (make 2): With yellow and C hook, ch 8.

Row 1: Sl st in 2nd ch from hook, sc in next ch, dc in each of next 3 ch, sc in next ch, sl st in last ch.

Rows 2 and 3: Ch 7, repeat row 1. After row 3, end off. *Tulip stem:* Sl st green to base of each tulip, ch 15. End off.

Bluebells (make 12): With blue and C hook, ch 4.

Row 1: 3 dc in 4th ch from hook. End off. * With green, sl st in base of 1 bluebell, ch 3, repeat from * twice, ch 12 for stem. End off. Make 3 more sprays in same manner.

Rosebud (make 2): With pink and C hook, ch 4.

Row 1: 3 dc in 4th ch from hook. Ch 3, turn.

Row 2: (Yo, insert hook in next st and draw up a lp, yo and through 2 lps) 3 times, yo and through all lps on hook. End off. *Rosebud leaves and stem:* With green and C hook, sl st in base of rosebud, (ch 5, sl st in 2nd ch from hook, sc in next ch, dc in next ch, sc in next ch, sl st in base of rosebud) 2 times, ch 45 for stem. End off.

Small leaves (make 6): With green and C hook, work same as for Rosebud.

Large leaves (make 4): With green and C hook, ch 10.

Rnd 1: Sl st in 2nd ch from hook, * sc in next ch, dc in each of next 2 ch, tr in next ch, dc in next 2 ch, sc in next ch, sl st in last ch; working along opposite side of ch repeat from *. End off.

Flower placement: Sew 1 bluebell spray to base in front of door. Sew small leaf to end of stem. Sew rose and large leaf to center of stem. Repeat at back of ark. On each side of roof sew 1 bluebell spray. Radiating from stem sew large leaf, tulip, rosebud, rose, and 2 small leaves.

Dove: With blue and C hook, ch 2.

Row 1: 3 sc in 2nd ch from hook. Ch 1, turn.

Row 2: 2 sc in first st, sc in next st, 2 sc in last

st—5 sc. Sl st in first sc. Continue working in rnds; do not join rnds; mark end of each rnd.

Rnd 3: 2 sc in each sc around—10 sc.

Rnd 4: Sc in each sc.

Rnd 5: (Sc in 4 sts, 2 sc in next st) twice—12 sc.

Rnds 6 and 7: Sc in each sc.

Rnd 8: (Sc in 2 sts, draw up a lp in next 2 sts, yo and through 3 lps) 3 times—9 sc.

Rnd 9: Sc in each sc.

Rnd 10: (2 sc in next st, sc in next 2 sts) 3 times.

Rnd 11: Sc in each sc—12 sc.

Rnd 12: (2 sc in next st, sc in 2 sts) 4 times—16 sc.

Rnd 13: (2 sc in next st, sc in 3 sts) 4 times—20 sc.

Rnds 14–19: Sc in each sc.

Rnd 20: (Sc in 2 sts, dec) 5 times—15 sc.

Rnd 21: (Sc in next sc, dec) 5 times—10 sc. Ch 1, turn.

Row 22: Sc in 5 sts. Ch 1, turn.

Row 23: 2 sc in first st, sc in 3 sts, 2 sc in last st. Ch 1, turn.

Row 24: 2 sc in first st, sc in 5 sts, 2 sc in last st. Do not turn.

Row 25: (Ch 5, sc in 2nd ch from hook and in next 3 ch, sl st in next sc) 8 times. End off.
Wings With blue and C hook, ch 6.

Row 1: Sc in 2nd ch from hook and in each ch across. Ch 1, turn.

Row 2: Sc in each sc—5 sc. Ch 1, turn.

Row 3: 2 sc in first st, sc in 3 sts, 2 sc in last st—7 sc. Ch 1, turn.

Row 4: 2 sc in first st, sc in 5 sts, 2 sc in last st—9 sc. Do not turn.

Row 5: Repeat row 25 of Dove. End off.
   Attach blue to opposite side of foundation ch; work 1 sc in each ch. Ch 1, turn. Repeat rows 2–5 for other wing. End off. Sew foundation row to center of dove's back. Stuff dove and sew tail opening closed. Close beak opening.

Olive branch With green and C hook, * ch 7, sl st in 4th ch from hook, repeat from * once, end off. Sew branch to beak. With yellow, embroider eyes. Sew dove to roof.

DIRECTIONS FOR ANIMALS
Rabbit (make 2): With off-white sport and C hook, ch 2.

Rnd 1: 6 sc in 2nd ch from hook. Do not join.

Rnd 2: 2 sc in each st—12 sc.

Rnds 3 and 4: Sc in each sc.

Rnd 5: (Ch 10, sl st in 2nd ch from hook, sc in next ch, dc in next ch, tr in next 3 ch, dc in next ch, sc in next 2 ch, sc in next sc) twice for ears, sc in 10 sc.

Rnd 6: Ch 1, sc in sc between ears, ch 1, sc in 11 sc.

Rnd 7: (Sc in ch-1 sp, sc in next st) twice, sc in 10 sts—14 sc.

Rnd 8: (2 sc in next st, sc in 6 sts) twice.

Rnds 9 and 10: Sc in each sc—16 sc.

Rnd 11: (Sc in 3 sts, 2 sc in next st) 4 times.

Rnd 12: Sc in 13 sts, (ch 6, sc in 2nd ch from hook and in next 4 ch, sc in next 2 sc) twice for paws, sc in last 3 sts.

Rnd 13: Sc in 13 sts, (sl st in ch and sc around paw, 2 sc in next 2 sts) twice, sc in 3 sts.

Rnd 14: Working behind paws, sc in each sc—20 sc.

Rnd 15: Dec 4 sts evenly spaced around.

Rnds 16 and 17: Sc in each sc. Stuff body.

Rnd 18: (Sc in 2 sts, dec) 4 times—12 sc.

Rnd 19: Dec 6 sc around. Finish stuffing; sew opening.

To finish Make a small pompon for tail, sew to end. Embroider black eyes, pink nose, rust mouth.

Zebra (make 2): Beg at nose, with rust and C hook, ch 2.

Rnd 1: 6 sc in 2nd ch from hook. End off.

Rnd 2: With off-white sport, work 2 sc in each sc.

Rnds 3-5: Sc in each sc—12 sc.

Rnd 6: (2 sc in next st, sc in next 5 sts) twice.

Rnd 7: Sc in each sc—14 sc.

Rnd 8: Sc in 3 sts, 2 sc in next st, sc in 6 sts, 2 sc in next st, sc in 3 sts.

Rnds 9 and 10: Sc in each sc—16 sc.

Rnd 11: (Ch 4, sl st in 2nd ch from hook, sc in next 2 ch, sc in 3 sc) twice for ears, sc in 10 sts.

Rnd 12: Working behind ears, (ch 1, sc in 3 sc) twice, sc in 10 sts. Drop off-white. Stuff head.

Note: When changing colors, complete last sc with new color.

Rnd 13: With black, sc in ch-1 sp, sc in 3 sts, sc in ch-1 sp, sc in 5 sts, sl st in 3 sts, sc in 5 sts. Drop black.

Rnd 14: With off-white, sc in 9 sts, sl st in 5 sts, sc in 4 sts. Drop off-white.

Rnd 15: With black, sc in 2 sts, dec over next 2 sc, sc in 4 sts, 2 sc in next st, (sc in next st, 2 sc in next st) twice, sc in 5 sts.

Rnd 16: With off-white, (sc in next st, dec) twice, sc in 14 sts—18 sts.

Rnd 17: With black, (dec, sc in next st) twice, sc in 4 sts, (2 sc in next st, sc in next st) twice, sc in 4 sts.

Rnd 18: With off-white, sc in 6 sts, 2 sc in next st, (sc in 2 sts, 2 sc in next st) twice, sc in 5 sts.

Rnd 19: With black, sc in each sc—21 sc.

Rnd 20: With black, inc 4 sc evenly around—25 sc.

Rnd 21: With off-white, sc in each sc.

Rnd 22: With black, sc in each sc. Stuff neck.

Note: From this point alternate 2 rnds off-white with 2 rnds black.

Rnd 23: Inc 5 sc evenly around.

Rnd 24: Sc in each sc—30 sc.

Rnd 25: (Dec, sc in next st) twice, sc in 6 sts, (2 sc in next st, sc in 2 sts) 4 times, sc in 6 sts—32 sc.

Rnds 26-28: Sc in each sc.

Rnd 29: Sl st in 5 sts, sc in 25 sts, sl st in 2 sts.

Rnds 30-33: Sc in each sc—32 sc.

Rnd 34: Dec 6 sc in rnd.

Rnds 35 and 36: Sc in each sc—26 sc.

Rnd 37: Dec 6 sc in rnd.

Rnds 38 and 39: Sc in each sc—20 sc. Stuff body.

Rnd 40: (Sc in 2 sts, dec) 5 times—15 sc.

Rnd 41: Sc in next sc, (dec) 7 times—8 sc.

Rnd 42: Sl st opening closed. End off.

Legs (make 4): With black and C hook, ch 2.

Row 1: 6 sc in 2nd ch from hook. Ch 1, turn.

Rows 2-4: Sc in each sc. Ch 1, turn.

Row 5: 2 sc in first st, sc in 4 sts, 2 sc in last st—8 sc. Do not turn.

Rnd 6: Sc in first sc of row 5 to form ring, sc in each st around—8 sc. Mark end of each rnd.

Rnd 7: Sc in each sc. From this point, alternate 1 rnd each off-white and black.

Rnd 8: With off-white, sc in each sc.

Rnds 9-12: Sc in each sc.

Rnd 13: (Sc in next st, 2 sc in next st) 4 times—12 sc.

Rnds 14 and 15: Sc in each sc.

Rnd 16: (Sc in 2 sts, 2 sc in next st) 4 times—16 sc.

Rnds 17-19: Sc in each sc. End off.

Tail With black and C hook, ch 10. Sl st in 2nd ch from hook and in each ch to end. End off.

To finish: With rust, embroider eyes. With black, on either side of head, work chain stitch from nose to below eyes, connect lines under head. Work chain stitch up center of head. Knot fringe along back of neck; clip short for mane. Attach tail; sew a small tassel to end. Stuff legs firmly; sew to body.

Lion: With yellow and C hook, ch 2.

Rnd 1: 6 sc in 2nd ch from hook. Do not join rnds.

Rnd 2: 2 sc in each st—12 sc.

Rnds 3 and 4: Sc in each sc.

Rnd 5: (Sc in next st, 2 sc in next st) 6 times—18 sc.

Rnds 6 and 7: Sc in each sc.

Rnd 8: (Sc in 2 sts, 2 sc in next st) 6 times—24 sc.

Rnd 9: Sc in each sc.

Rnd 10: (Ch 5, dc in 4th ch from hook and in next ch, sc in 6 sts) twice for ears, sl st in 6 sts, sc in 6 sts.

Rnd 11: Working behind ears, (ch 1, sc in 6 sts) twice, sl st in 6 sl sts, sc in 6 sc.

Rnd 12: Sc in ch-1 sp, dec, sc in 2 sts, dec, sc in ch-1 sp, sc in 6 sts, (2 sc in next st, sc in next st) 3 times, sc in 6 sts—27 sts.

Rnd 13: Sc in 13 sts, (2 sc in next st, sc in 2 sts) 3 times, sc in 5 sts—30 sc.

Rnd 14: Sc in 12 sts, (2 sc in next st, sc in 3 sts) 3 times, sc in 6 sts—33 sc.

Rnd 15: Dec, sc in 3 sts, dec, sc in 6 sts, 2 sc in next st, sc in 12 sts, 2 sc in next st, sc in 6 sts—33 sts.

Rnd 16: Repeat rnd 15.

Rnd 17: (Sc in 2 sts, dec) twice, sc in 23 sts, dec—30 sc.

Rnds 18-22: Sc in each sc. Stuff body.

Rnd 23: Sc in 15 sc, (dec, sc in 3 sc) twice, sc in 5 sc.

Rnd 24: Sc in each sc.

Rnd 25: Sc in 15 sc, dec, sc in 3 sc, dec, sc in 6 sc.

Rnds 26-30: Sc in each sc.

Rnd 31: Sc in 14 sc, dec, sc in 3 sc, dec, sc in 5 sc.

Rnd 32: Sc in each sc. Continue to stuff body.

Rnd 33: Sc in 12 sts, (dec, sc in next st) 4 times.

Rnds 34 and 35: Sc in each sc—20 sc.

Rnds 36 and 37: Dec in each 2 sts around—5 sc.

Rnd 38: Sl st in each st. End off.

Back legs (make 2): With yellow and C hook, ch 2. Sl st in first ch to form a ring.

Rnd 1: 12 sc in ring. Do not join; mark end of every rnd.

Rnd 2: Sc in each sc.

Rnd 3: (Sc in next st, dec) 4 times—8 sc.

Rnds 4-6: Sc in each sc.

Rnd 7: (Sc in next st, 2 sc in next st) 4 times.

Rnds 8-11: Sc in each sc—12 sc.

Rnd 12: (Sc in 2 sts, 2 sc in next st) 4 times—16 sc.

Rnds 13 and 14: Sc in each sc. End off.

Front legs (make 2): Work same as for back legs through rnd 11. End off.

Tail With yellow and C hook, ch 13, sl st in 2nd ch from hook and in next 4 ch, sc in next 7 ch. Sew to body. Knot 2 strands rust in end of tail.

To finish: With green, work eyes in straight stitch. Embroider brown mouth and nose and cross green eye stitches. Cut 4 strands of off-white 3" long for whiskers. Draw strands through head at rnd 3. Cut strands of rust 3½" long. Knot single strands around head for mane.

To assemble Stuff legs firmly and sew in place.

Lioness: Work same as for lion omitting

rnds 4, 7, and 18 on body, rnd 11 on legs, and mane.

Tiger (make 2): Work as for lioness, alternating 1 rnd black and 1 rnd yellow after rnd 3.

To finish: Embroider blue eyes, rust mouth. Draw 4 strands of off-white through head for whiskers. Attach black and yellow on back, ch 15 for tail. Stuff legs firmly and sew to body.

Giraffes (make 2): With rust and C hook, ch 2.

Row 1: 6 sc in 2nd ch from hook. Ch 1, turn.

Row 2: 2 sc in first st, sc in 4 sts, 2 sc in next st. Do not turn.

Rnd 3: Sc in first st on row 2 to join, sc in each st.

Rnd 4: (Sc in next st, 2 sc in next st) 4 times.

Rnds 5 and 6: Sc in each sc—12 sc.

Rnd 7 (Ears): Sl st in 4 sts, sc in 2 sts, * ch 4, sl st in 2nd ch from hook, sc in next 2 ch *, sc in 4 sts, repeat from * to *, sc in last 2 sts.

Rnd 8: Sl st in next 4 sl sts, sc in 2 sts, ch 1; working behind ears, sc in 4 sts, ch 1, sc in 2 sts.

Rnd 9: (2 sc in next st, sc in next st) twice, draw up a lp in next 2 sts, yo and through 3 lps on hook (1 dec), sc in ch-1 sp, sc in next st, dec, sc in next sc, sc in ch-1 sp, dec—13 sc.

Rnd 10: Sc in each sc.

Rnd 11: (Sc in next st, 2 sc in next st) twice, sc in 2 sts, dec, sc in 3 sts, dec—13 sc.

Rnd 12: Sc in each sc.

Rnd 13: Repeat rnd 11.

Rnd 14: Sc in each sc.

Rnd 15: (Sc in next st, 2 sc in next st) 3 times, sc in 3 sts, dec, sc in 2 sts—15 sc.

Rnd 16: Sc in 13 sts, dec—14 sc.

Rnds 17-21: Sc in each sc.

Rnd 22: (Sc in 6 sts, 2 sc in next st) twice—16 sc.

Rnd 23: Sc in each sc.

Rnd 24: (Sc in 3 sts, 2 sc in next st) 4 times—20 sc.

Rnd 25: Sc in each sc.

Rnd 26: (Sc in 4 sts, 2 sc in next st) 4 times—24 sc.

Rnds 27-33: Sc in each sc. Stuff giraffe.

Rnd 34: (Sc in 2 sts, dec) 6 times—18 sc.

Rnd 35: (Sc in next st, dec) 6 times—12 sc.

Rnd 36: Dec each 2 sts around—6 sc. Add stuffing. Sl st in each st around to close. End off.

Front legs (make 2): With rust and C hook, ch 5.

Row 1: Sc in 2nd ch from hook and in each ch to end—4 sc. Ch 1, turn.

Rows 2-7: Sc in each sc. Ch 1, turn.

Row 8: 2 sc in first st, sc in 2 sts, 2 sc in last st—6 sc. Ch 1, turn.

Rows 9-13: Sc in each sc. Ch 1, turn.

Row 14: 2 sc in first st, sc in 4 sts, 2 sc in last st—8 sc. Do not turn.

Rnd 15: Sc in first st of row 14, sc in each st around—8 sc. Do not join.

Rnds 16 and 17: Sc in each sc.

Rnd 18: (Sc in next st, 2 sc in next st) 4 times—12 sc.

Rnds 19-21: Sc in each sc. After rnd 21, ch 1, turn.

Row 22: Sc in 6 sts. Ch 1, turn.

Row 23: Dec, sc in 2 sts, dec—4 sc. Ch 1, turn.

Row 24: Dec twice. Ch 1, turn.

Row 25: Draw up a lp in remaining 2 sts, yo and through all lps. End off.

Back legs Work as for front legs through rnd 20.

Tail Attach rust to body, ch 14. Sl st in each ch. Sew a small rust tassel to end.

To finish: Embroider black eyes and mouth.

Horns (make 2): Attach yellow to head next to ear, ch 5, sl st in 3rd ch from hook and in next 2 ch.

Sew beg rows of legs tog; stuff firmly. Sew front legs to body with points to front. Sew back legs to body. With double strand yellow, embroider irregular grid over back, neck, and upper half of legs.

Elephant (make 2): With gray and G hook, beg at trunk, ch 8.

Rnd 1: Sc in first ch to form ring, sc in each remaining ch—8 sc.

Rnds 2-11: Sc in each sc. Mark end of rnds.

Rnd 12: (Sc in next sc, 2 sc in next st) 4 times.

Rnd 13: Sc in each sc—12 sc.

Rnds 14 and 15: Sl st in 4 sts, sc in 8 sts.

Rnd 16: (2 sc in next st, sc in 2 sts) twice, sc in 6 sc—14 sc.

Rnd 17: (Sc in 2 sts, 2 sc in next st) 4 times, sc in next st, 2 sc in next st—19 sc.

Rnd 18: Sc in each sc.

Rnd 19: (Sc in 3 sts, 2 sc in next st) 4 times, sc in 2 sts, 2 sc in next st—24 sc.

Rnds 20-23: Sc in each sc.

Rnd 24: Sc in 2 sts, sl st in 6 sts, sc in 16 sts.

Rnd 25: Sc in 2 sts, sl st in 6 sl sts, sc in 6 sts, dec, sc in 2 sts, dc, sc in 4 sts. Stuff head.

Rnd 26: Sc in 2 sts, (2 sc in next st, sc in next st) 3 times, sc in 6 sts, (dec) twice, sc in 4 sts—23 sts.

Rnd 27: Sc in each sc.

Rnd 28: Sc in 2 sts, (2 sc in next st, sc in 3 sts) 3 times, sc in 2 sts, (dec) twice, sc in 3 sts—24 sc.

Rnd 29: Sc in each sc.

Rnd 30: (2 sc in next st, sc in 5 sts) 4 times—28 sc.

Rnd 31: Sc in each sc.

Rnd 32: Sc in 3 sts, (2 sc in next st, sc in 6 sts) 3 times, 2 sc in next st, sc in 3 sts—32 sc.

Rnd 33: (Sc in 7 sts, 2 sc in next st) 4 times—36 sc.

Rnds 34-45: Sc in each sc. Stuff body.

Rnd 46: (Sc in 2 sc, dec) 9 times—27 sc.

Rnd 47: (Sc in next sc, dec) 9 times—18 sc.

Rnd 48: Dec each 2 sts around—9 sc.

Rnd 49: (Dec) 4 times, sc in last sc. Add stuffing. Sl st in each st around. End off.

Legs (make 4): With gray and G hook, ch 2.

Rnd 1: 6 sc in 2nd ch from hook.

Rnd 2: 2 sc in each st around—12 sc.

Rnds 3-11: Sc in each sc. End off.

Ears (make 2): With gray and G hook, ch 6.

Row 1: Sc in 2nd ch from hook and each ch to end—5 sc. Ch 1, turn each row.

Row 2: 2 sc in first st, sc in 3 sts, 2 sc in last st.

Row 3: Sc in each sc.

Row 4: 2 sc in first st, sc in 5 sts, 2 sc in last st.

Rows 5 and 6: Sc in each sc. End off.

Tusk (make 2): With off-white sport and C hook, ch 13.

Row 1: Sl st in 2nd ch from hook and in each ch across—12 sc. Ch 1, turn.

Row 2: Sc in 10 sc. Turn.

Row 3: Sl st in first st, sc in 9 sts. Ch 1, turn. Fold work in half; sc long edges tog.

To finish: With black, embroider eyes on rnd 19 and mouth in "V" shape on rnd 16. Sew ears to head. Sew tusks to sides of mouth. For tail, attach gray to back, ch 15. Sl st in 2nd ch from hook and in next ch, sc in next 12 ch. Stuff legs and sew to body.

Old MacDonald's Farm
Combine crochet and needlepoint to make this clever farm for your youngster to play with.

SIZE

Rug, approximately 18" × 23".

MATERIALS

Knitting-worsted weight yarn, 3½-oz. skeins: 2 skeins eggshell; 1 skein each dark brown, gold, rust, gray, light green, light olive, and dark olive; 1 oz. each pink, royal blue, dark green, and grass green; few yards red. Thick bouclé or mohair-type yarn, 15 yards off-white. Rug canvas, 3½ meshes per inch, piece 21" × 27". Felt: 2½" circle, 7" square, 2" square. Stuffing. Velcro®. Waterproof marking pen. Masking tape. Crochet hook size H (5 mm). Latch hook. Large tapestry needle.

DIRECTIONS FOR CROCHETED VEGETABLES

Cabbage (make 6): With light green, ch 2.

Rnd 1: 6 sc in 2nd ch from hook. Sl st in first sc.

Rnd 2: Ch 1, sc in each sc. Sl st in first sc.

Rnd 3: (Ch 5, sk 1 sc, sl st in next sc) 3 times. End off.

Sew cabbages to section E of field (*see diagram*); or attach with Velcro® tabs.

Lettuce (make 2): With grass green, ch 4. Sl st in first ch to form ring.

Rnd 1: (Ch 4, sc in ring) 5 times.

Rnd 2: Holding ch-4 lps back, sl st in each of 5 sc around. End off.

Carrot tops (make 3): With grass green, ch 6. Sl st in first ch, (ch 6, sl st in same ch) twice. End off.

Spinach (make 3): With dark green, ch 6. Sl st in 2nd ch from hook and in next 4 chs; (ch 5, sl st in 2nd ch from hook and in next 3 chs, sl st in first ch of ch 6) twice. End off.

Sew lettuce, carrot tops, and spinach to section G; or attach with Velcro® tabs.

DIRECTIONS FOR CROCHETED ANIMALS

Horse: *Body* Beg at nose, with brown, ch 2.

Rnd 1: 8 sc in 2nd ch from hook. Sl st in first sc, ch 1.

Note: End each rnd with sl st in first sc, ch 1.

Rnds 2-4: Sc in each sc.

Rnd 5: (Sc in 2 sc, 2 sc in next sc) twice, sc in 2 sc—10 sc.

Rnd 6: Sc in each sc.

Rnd 7: Sc in 3 sc, 2 sc in next sc, sc in 2 sc, 2 sc in next sc, sc in 3 sc—12 sc.

Rnd 8: Sc in each sc.

Rnd 9: Sl st in 3 sc, sc in 6 sc, sl st in 3 sc.

Rnd 10: Sl st in 3 sts, 2 sc in next sc, sc in 4 sc, 2 sc in next sc, sl st in 3 sts—14 sts.

Rnd 11: 2 sc in each of 3 sts, sc in 8 sc, 2 sc in each of 3 sts—20 sc.

Rnd 12: Sc in 4 sc, 1 dec (to dec 1 sc, pull up a lp in next 2 sts, yo and through 3 lps on hook), sc in 2 sc, 2 decs, sc in 2 sc, 1 dec, sc in 4 sc—16 sc.

Rnd 13: (Sc in 1 sc, 2 sc in next sc) twice, sc in 8 sc, (sc in next sc, 2 sc in next sc) twice—20 sc.

Rnd 14: (Sc in 2 sc, 2 sc in next sc) twice, sc in 3 sc, 1 dec, sc in 3 sc, (sc in 2 sc, 2 sc in next sc) twice—22 sc.

Rnd 15: (2 sc in next sc, sc in 2 sc) twice, sc in 4 sc, 1 dec, sc in 4 sc, (2 sc in next sc, sc in 2 sc) twice—25 sc.

Rnd 16: (Sc in next sc, 2 sc in next sc, sc in next sc) twice, sc in 4 sc, 1 dec, sc in next sc, 1 dec, sc in 4 sc, (sc in next sc, 2 sc in next sc, sc in next sc) twice—27 sc.

Rnds 17-21: Sc in each sc.

Rnd 22: Sc in 3 sc, 1 dec, sc in 17 sc, 1 dec, sc in 3 sc—25 sc.

Rnd 23: Sc in each sc.

Rnd 24: Sc in 2 sc, 1 dec, sc in 8 sc, 1 dec, sc in 7 sc, 1 dec, sc in 2 sc—22 sc.

Rnds 25-30: Sc in each sc. Stuff horse.

Rnd 31: (1 dec) 11 times.

Rnd 32: Sc in next sc, (1 dec) 5 times.

Rnd 33: (1 dec) 3 times. End off.

Front legs (make 2): Ch 2.

Rnd 1: 6 sc in 2nd ch from hook.

Rnds 2-5: Sc in each sc.

Rnd 6: (Sc in 2 sc, 2 sc in next sc) twice.

Rnds 7 and 8: Sc in each sc—8 sc.

Rnd 9: (Sc in 3 sc, 2 sc in next sc) twice.

Rnd 10: Sc in each sc—10 sc. End off.

Back legs (make 2): Work as for front legs through rnd 10. Work 2 more rnds of 10 sc. End off.

Ears (make 2): Ch 2.

Row 1: 3 sc in 2nd ch from hook. Ch 1, turn.

Row 2: Sc in 3 sc. End off.

To finish: Stuff legs; sew in place. Sew base of ears to head, gathering ears slightly. For mane, cut strands of gold; sew several strands tog at center of strands to back of neck, having shorter strands toward front. For tail, cut 14 strands of gold 8″ long; tie tog at center; sew in place.

Cow: *Body* Beg at nose, with eggshell, ch 2.

Rnd 1: 8 sc in 2nd ch from hook. Sl st in first sc, ch 1.

Note: End each rnd with sl st in first sc, ch 1.

Rnds 2 and 3: Sc in each sc.

Rnd 4: (Sc in 2 sc, 2 sc in next sc) twice, sc in 2 sc—10 sc.

Rnd 5: Sc in each sc.

Rnd 6: Sc in 3 sc, 2 sc in next sc, sc in 2 sc, 2 sc in next sc, sc in 3 sc—12 sc.

Rnds 7 and 8: Sc in each sc.

Rnd 9: (2 sc in next sc) 4 times, sc in 4 sc, (2 sc in next sc) 4 times—20 sc.

Rnd 10: (Sc in next sc, 2 sc in next sc) twice,

sc in 12 sc, (sc in next sc, 2 sc in next sc) twice—24 sc.

Rnds 11-16: Sc in each sc.

Rnd 17: (Sc in next sc, 1 dec) twice, sc in 12 sc, (sc in next sc, 1 dec) twice—20 sc.

Rnd 18: Sc in each sc.

Rnd 19: (Sc in next sc, 1 dec) twice, sc in 8 sc, (sc in next sc, 1 dec) twice—16 sc.

Rnds 20-22: Sc in each sc. Stuff body.

Rnd 23: Dec 8 times—8 sc.

Rnd 24: Dec 4 times—4 sc. End off.

Front legs (make 2): Work as for Horse's front legs through rnd 7. End off.

Back legs (make 2): Work as for front legs through rnd 7.

Rnd 8: (Sc in 3 sc, 2 sc in next sc) twice.

Rnd 9: Sc in each sc. End off.

Ears (make 2): Work as for Horse's ears.

Horns (make 2): Ch 5.

Row 1: Sc in 2nd ch from hook and in next 2 chs, sl st in last ch. Ch 1, turn.

Row 2: Sl st in sl st, sc in 3 sc. Ch 1, turn.

Row 3: Sc in 3 sc, sl st in sl st. End off. Sew edges tog, forming point at sl st end.

Tail Ch 6. Sl st in 2nd ch from hook and in each ch. End off. Knot several short lengths in end to make tassel.

Udder With pink, ch 12. Sl st in first ch to form ring, being careful not to twist ch.

Rnd 1: Ch 1, (sc in 2 chs, ch 4, sc in 2nd ch from hook and in next 2 chs, sc in next ch on ring) 4 times, sl st in first sc.

Rnd 2: Ch 1, (pull up a lp in next 2 sc, yo and through 3 lps on hook; holding 3 sc strip in front, sc in next sc) 4 times.

Rnd 3: (Dec 1 sc in next 2 sts) 4 times. End off.

To finish: Stuff legs and udder. Sew legs, udder, ears, horns, and tail in place. With brown, embroider eyes and nostrils with French knots; embroider spots of different sizes on back with chain stitch (*see Embroidery Stitch Details, page 185.*)

Lamb: *Body* Beg at nose, with gray, ch 2.

Rnd 1: 6 sc in 2nd ch from hook. Sl st in first sc, ch 1 each rnd.

Rnd 2: Sc in each sc.

Rnd 3: (Sc in 2 sc, 2 sc in next sc) twice—8 sc.

Rnd 4: Sc in each sc.

Rnd 5: (Sc in 3 sc, 2 sc in next sc) twice—10 sc. Cut gray; join off-white bouclé yarn.

Rnd 6: Sc in each sc.

Rnd 7: (2 sc in next sc, sc in next sc) 5 times—15 sc.

Rnds 8-13: Sc in each sc. Stuff body.

Rnd 14: (Sc in next sc, 1 dec) 5 times.

Rnd 15: 5 decs. End off.

Legs (make 4): With gray, work as for Horse's front legs rnds 1-5. End off.

Ears (make 2): With off-white, ch 2; 3 sc in 2nd ch from hook. End off.

To finish: Stuff legs. Sew legs and ears in place. For tail, join off-white to back of lamb, ch 3. Embroider brown French knots for eyes.

Cat: *Body* Beg at nose, with gray, ch 2.

Rnd 1: 8 sc in 2nd ch from hook. Sl st in first sc, ch 1 each rnd.

Rnds 2-4: Sc in each sc.

Rnd 5: (Sc in next sc, 2 sc in next sc) 4 times—12 sc.

Rnds 6-9: Sc in each sc.

Rnd 10: (Sc in next sc, 1 dec) 4 times. Stuff body.

Rnd 11: 4 decs. Ch 10 for tail. Sc in 2nd ch from hook and in each ch. End off.

Paws (make 2): With eggshell, ch 6.

Row 1: Sc in 2nd ch from hook and in each ch. Ch 1, turn.

Row 2: Sc in 5 sc. End off. Fold in half lengthwise; sew edges tog.

Ears (make 2): With eggshell, ch 2; 2 sc in 2nd ch from hook. End off.

To finish: Sew paws and ears in place. Embroider brown straight stitches for eyes, pink lazy daisy stitch for nose. Pull 2" strand of eggshell through nose for whiskers; unravel yarn.

Pig: *Body* Beg at nose, with pink, ch 2.

Rnd 1: 6 sc in 2nd ch from hook. Sl st in first sc, ch 1 each rnd.

Rnd 2: Sc in each sc.

Rnd 3: 2 sc in each sc—12 sc.

Rnds 4-6: Sc in each sc.

Rnd 7: (Sc in next sc, 2 sc in next sc) 6 times—18 sc.

Rnds 8-12: Sc in each sc.

Rnd 13: (Sc in next sc, 1 dec) 6 times—12 sc. Stuff body.

Rnd 14: 6 decs. Ch 6 for tail. Sl st in 2nd ch from hook and in each ch. End off.

Legs (make 4): Work as for Horse's front legs rnds 1-4. End off.

Ears (make 2): Ch 4.

Row 1: Sc in 2nd ch from hook and in next 2 chs. Ch 1, turn.

Row 2: 1 dec, 1 sc. Ch 1, turn.

Row 3: 1 dec. End off.

To finish: Stuff legs. Sew legs and ears in place. Embroider brown French knot eyes, straight-stitch nostrils.

Dog: *Body* Beg at nose, with gold, ch 2.

Rnd 1: 6 sc in 2nd ch from hook. Sl st in first sc, ch 1 each rnd.

Rnd 2: Sc in each sc.

Rnd 3: (Sc in 2 sc, 2 sc in next sc) twice—8 sc.

Rnd 4: Sc in each sc.

Rnd 5: 2 sc in first sc, sc in 6 sc, 2 sc in last sc—10 sc.

Rnd 6: Sc in first sc, 2 sc in next sc, sc in 2 sc, 1 dec, sc in 2 sc, 2 sc in next sc, sc in last sc—11 sc.

Rnd 7: Sc in 2 sc, 2 sc in next sc, sc in 5 sc, 2 sc in next sc, sc in 2 sc—13 sc.

Rnds 8-10: Sc in each sc.

Rnd 11: 1 dec, sc in 11 sc.

Rnds 12 and 13: Sc in each sc. Stuff body.

Rnd 14: 6 decs—6 sc.

Rnd 15: 3 decs. End off.

Legs (make 4): Work as for Horse's front legs rnds 1-4.

Ears (make 2): With brown, ch 3.

Row 1: Sc in 2nd ch from hook and in next ch. Ch 1, turn.

Row 2: Sc in 2 sc. Ch 1, turn.

Row 3: 1 dec. End off.

To finish: Stuff legs. Sew legs and ears in place. For tail, join brown to back of body, ch 5. Sl st in 2nd ch from hook and next ch, sc in next 2 chs. End off. For collar, make a blue ch to fit around neck. Make brown French knots for eyes and nose.

Chicken: Beg at head, with eggshell or brown, ch 4.

Row 1: Sc in 2nd ch from hook and in next 2 chs. Ch 1, turn each row.

Row 2: 2 sc in first sc, sc in 2 sc.

Row 3: 2 sc in first sc, sc in 3 sc.

Rows 4-7: 2 sc in first sc, sc across—9 sc.

Row 8: (1 dec, 1 sc) 3 times.

Row 9: (1 dec, 1 sc) twice.

Row 10: 2 decs.

Row 11: 1 dec. End off.

To finish: Sew edges of rows tog, shaping beak with a few sts, stuffing as you go. Make 5 yarn loops for tail. With rust, embroider chain stitch along top of head; make a loop under beak.

Farmer: *Legs* (make 2): Beg at foot, with brown, ch 2.

Rnd 1: 6 sc in 2nd ch from hook. Sl st in first sc, ch 1 each rnd.

Rnd 2: Sc in each sc.

Rnd 3: 2 sc in first sc, sc in next sc, 1 dec over next 2 sc, sc in 2 sc.

Rnd 4: Sc in 3 sc, 2 sc in next sc, sc in 2 sc. Cut brown; join blue.

Rnds 5-10: Work even on 7 sc. End off for first leg; do not end off on 2nd leg.

Body

Rnd 1: Sc around 2nd leg, sc around first leg; 14 sc.

Rnds 2 and 3: Sc in each sc. Cut blue; join rust.

Rnds 4-10: Sc in each sc. End off. Stuff legs and body.

Arms (make 2): With pink, ch 2.

Rnd 1: 6 sc in 2nd ch from hook.

Rnd 2: Sc in each sc. Cut pink; join rust.

Rnds 3-10: Sc in each sc. End off.

Head With pink, ch 2.

Rnd 1: 8 sc in 2nd ch from hook.

Rnds 2-4: Sc in each sc.

Rnd 5: (1 dec, sc in 2 sc) twice—6 sc.

Rnd 6: Sc in each sc.

Hat With gold, ch 2.

Rnd 1: 8 sc in 2nd ch from hook. Sl st in first sc, ch 1 each rnd.

Rnd 2: Sc in 7 sc, 2 sc in last sc—9 sc.

Rnd 3: Sc in each sc.

Rnd 4: (Sc in next sc, 2 sc in next sc) 4 times, sc in last sc—13 sc.

Rnd 5: (Sc in 2 sc, 2 sc in next sc) 4 times, sc in last sc—17 sc.

Rnd 6: (Sc in 3 sc, 2 sc in next sc) 4 times, sc in last sc—21 sc. End off.

Bib With blue, ch 6.

Row 1: Sc in 2nd ch from hook and in next 4 ch. Ch 1, turn each row.

Rows 2-5: Sc in 5 sc. End off.

To finish: Sew shoulders. Stuff head and arms; sew in place. Sew bib to top of pants. Make blue chs for straps, cross in back. With red, embroider backstitch lines across bib between rows; make red "buttons." With red, embroider chain stitch band on hat. For beard, join gray in "chin"; (ch 3, sl st in next st along chin) 4 times. Embroider brown French knot eyes.

Farmer's wife: *Body* Beg at shoulder, with gray, ch 12. Sl st in first ch to form ring, being careful not to twist ch.

Rnd 1: Ch 1, sc in each ch around. Sl st in first sc, ch 1 each rnd.

Rnd 2: * Sc in next sc, pull up a lp in next sc, drop gray, draw gold through 2 lps on hook; with gold, pull up a lp in next sc, drop gold, draw gray through 2 lps on hook, repeat from * 3 times, carrying yarns loosely on back of work.

Rnd 3 and All Odd Rnds: With gray, sc around.

Rnd 4 and All Even Rnds: Work every 3rd sc in gold, varying placement of gold.

Rnds 5 and 6: Sc in each sc.

Rnd 7: (Sc in 2 sc, 2 sc in next sc) 4 times—16 sc.

Rnd 8: Sc in each sc.

Rnd 9: (Sc in 7 sc, 2 sc in next sc) twice—18 sc.

Rnd 10: Sc in each sc.

Rnd 11: (2 sc in next sc, sc in 5 sc) 3 times—21 sc.

Rnd 12: Sc in each sc.

Rnd 13: (2 sc in next sc, sc in 6 sc) 3 times—24 sc.

Rnds 14 and 15: Sc in each sc.

Rnd 16: Work all sc in gold. Cut gold.

Rnds 17 and 18: Work all sc in gray. End off.

Arms (make 2): Work as for Farmer's arms for 8 rnds, working 2 rnds pink, 2 rnds gray, 4 rnds gold.

Head Work as for Farmer's head.

Apron With eggshell, ch 27.

Row 1: Sc in 2nd ch from hook and in next 8 chs. Ch 1, turn each row.

Rows 2-9: Sc in 9 sc. At end of row 9, ch 18. End off. Gather apron slightly across top.

To finish: Sew 2½″ felt circle to bottom of skirt. Stuff head and arms; sew in place. For collar, make gold ch to fit around neck; tie yarn ends in bow. For hair, sew strands of eggshell to head across center top; form bun in back. Embroider blue eyes, rust mouth. Embroider apron with red lines in chain and backstitch.

House: *Front* With gray, ch 23.

Row 1: Sc in 2nd ch from hook and in each ch across—22 sc. Ch 1, turn each row.

Rows 2 and 3: Work even. Cut gray. Make small balls of eggshell, gray, and blue. Drop color not in use to wrong side of work.

Row 4: 3 sc eggshell, 7 sc blue, 12 sc eggshell.

Row 5: 12 sc eggshell, 7 sc blue, 3 sc eggshell.

Row 6: Repeat row 4.

Row 7: Repeat row 5.

Row 8: Repeat row 4.

Row 9: 3 sc eggshell, 6 sc gray, 3 sc eggshell, 7 sc blue, 3 sc eggshell.

Row 10: 3 sc eggshell, 7 sc blue, 3 sc eggshell, 6 sc gray, 3 sc white.

Rows 11-17: Repeat rows 9 and 10 alternately. Cut gray.

Row 18: Repeat row 4. Cut blue.

Row 19: 22 sc eggshell.

Row 20: 1 dec (pull up a lp in 2 sc, yo and through 3 lps on hook), sc in 18 sc, 1 dec.

Row 21: Sc across—20 sc.

Row 22: 1 dec, sc in 16 sc, 1 dec.

Row 23: 6 sc eggshell, 6 sc gray, 6 sc eggshell.

Row 24: 1 dec, 4 sc eggshell, 6 sc gray, 4 sc eggshell, 1 dec.

Row 25: 5 sc eggshell, 6 sc gray, 5 sc eggshell.

Row 26: 1 dec, 3 sc eggshell, 6 sc gray, 3 sc eggshell, 1 dec.

Row 27: 4 sc eggshell, 6 sc gray, 4 sc eggshell.

Row 28: 1 dec, 2 sc eggshell, 6 sc gray, 2 sc eggshell, 1 dec. Cut gray.

Row 29: Sc in 12 sc.

Row 30: 1 dec, 8 sc, 1 dec.

Row 31: Sc in 10 sc.

Row 32: 1 dec, 6 sc, 1 dec.

Row 33: Sc in 8 sc.

Row 34: 1 dec, 4 sc, 1 dec.

Row 35: Sc in 6 sc.

Row 36: 1 dec, 2 sc, 1 dec.

Row 37: Sc in 4 sc.

Row 38: 2 decs.

Row 39: Sc in 2 sc.

Row 40: 1 dec. End off.

Back Work as for front rows 1-3.

Rows 4-8: With eggshell, sc in 22 sc.

Rows 9-17: 3 sc eggshell, 6 sc gray, 4 sc eggshell, 6 sc gray, 3 sc eggshell. Cut gray.

Rows 18 and 19: Repeat row 4.

Rows 20-40: Work as for front.

Sides (make 2): Work as for back rows 1-19. End off.

Roof From right side, join rust to one side piece in first st.

Row 1: Ch 3, dc in next st and in each st across. Ch 1, turn.

Row 2: Sc in front lp of each st across, sc in top of ch 3. Ch 3, turn.

Row 3: Dc in back lp of next st and each st across. Ch 1, turn.

Rows 4-29: Repeat rows 2 and 3 alternately. End off.

Chimney With gray, ch 25.

Row 1: Sc in 2nd ch from hook and in each ch across. Ch 1, turn.

Rows 2 and 3: Sc in 24 sc. Ch 1, turn.

Row 4: 1 dec, sc in 14 sc, 1 dec. Ch 1, turn.

Row 5: Sc in 16 sc. Ch 1, turn each row.

Rows 6-14: Dec 1 sc each side every even row, sc in each sc across on odd rows. At end of row 14, end off. Sew sides of rows 1-3 tog. Join rust in first st of foundation ch. Ch 3, dc in each ch around. Sl st in top of ch 3. End off.

To finish: Seam house tog along edges. Sew chimney to roof. On front and back edges of roof, work scallops: Join rust in corner, * ch 3, sl st in seam, repeat from * around roof to opposite corner. With blue, outline windows in chain stitch; embroider cross in larger windows in chain stitch. Outline door with rust chain stitch. Sew on a button for doorknob. For window box, with rust, ch 12. Dc in 4th ch from hook and in each ch. End off. Sew under front window. Stuff house and chimney. Sew felt squares to bottom of house and into top of chimney.

DIRECTIONS FOR GARDEN RUG

Mark rug area on canvas with waterproof

marking pen, counting 65 meshes × 85 meshes; leave approximately 1″ margin all around. Bind edges of canvas with masking tape. Following diagram, divide rug into areas shown, counting each square on diagram as one mesh on canvas. Referring to Needlepoint Stitch Details below, work sections A through G in stitches and colors indicated, using three strands of yarn in needle. When needlepoint sections have been completed, work sections H through M with latch hook (*see How to Latch Hook, page 189*), cutting strands in lengths from 3″ to 8″ for desired height of each section and using one strand for each knot. When knotting is complete, cut and shape pile as desired.

Block rug if necessary. Turn under canvas edges to wrong side, mitering corners. Whipstitch raw edges in place with strong thread. For durability, cover hems with twill tape, or line rug with fabric.

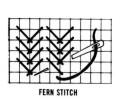

FERN STITCH

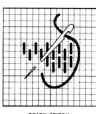

BRICK STITCH

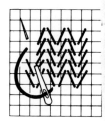

STEM STITCH

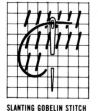

SLANTING GOBELIN STITCH

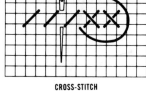

CROSS-STITCH

SATIN-STITCH SQUARES

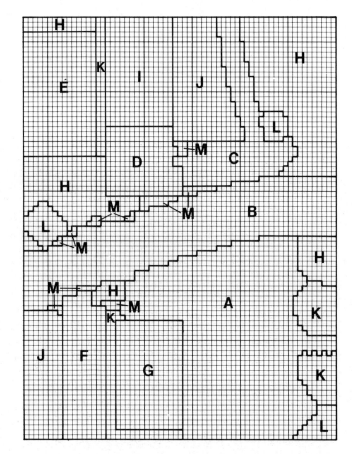

KEY FOR DIAGRAM
A. Brick Stitch—light green.
B. Half Cross-Stitch—outline random-size bricks in dark olive. Fill in bricks with satin-stitch rectangles in rust.
C. Slanting Gobelin—2 strands light green, 1 strand light olive.
D. Stem Stitch—dark brown.
E. Fern Stitch—dark brown.
F. Satin-Stitch Squares—1 strand each gray, gold, light olive; 3 squares each row, alternating direction of rows.
G. Cross-Stitch—dark brown.
H. Latch hook—light olive.
I. Latch hook—light green.
J. Latch hook—gold.
K. Latch hook—dark olive.
L. Latch hook—dark green.
M. Latch hook—grass green.

Patty *is a cheerful crocheted traveling companion.*

SIZE
17″ tall.

MATERIAL FOR DOLL AND DRESS
Worsted-weight yarn, two 3½-oz. skeins rose, 1 skein each pink and brown, small amount of white, red, navy. Crochet hook size H (5 mm). Polyester fiberfill. Yarn needle.

GAUGE
4 sc = 1″.

DIRECTIONS FOR DOLL —————
Head: Beg at top of head, with pink, ch 2.

Rnd 1: 6 sc in 2nd ch from hook. Join with sl st in first sc.

Rnd 2: Ch 1, 2 sc in each sc around. Join each rnd, ch 1.

Rnd 3: Sc in first sc, 2 sc in next sc, (sc in next sc, 2 sc in next sc) 5 times—18 sc.

Rnd 4: (Sc in 2 sc, 2 sc in next sc) 6 times—24 sc.

Rnd 5: (Sc in 3 sc, 2 sc in next sc) 6 times—30 sc.

Rnd 6: (Sc in 4 sc, 2 sc in next sc) 6 times—36 sc.

Rnds 7-9: Continue to inc 6 sc evenly around each rnd—54 sc.

Rnd 10: Sc in each sc around.

Rnd 11: (Sc in 8 sc, 2 sc in next sc) 6 times—60 sc.

Rnd 12: (Sc in 9 sc, 2 sc in next sc) 6 times—66 sc.

Rnds 13-17: Sc in each sc around.

Rnd 18: (Sc in 9 sc, work 2 sc tog) 6 times—60 sc.

Rnd 19: (Sc in 8 sc, work 2 sc tog) 6 times—54 sc.

Rnd 20: (Sc in 7 sc, work 2 sc tog) 6 times—48 sc.

Rnd 21: (Sc in 6 sc, work 2 sc tog) 6 times—42 sc.

Rnd 22: (Sc in 5 sc, work 2 sc tog) 6 times—36 sc.

Rnd 23: (Sc in 4 sc, work 2 sc tog) 6 times—30 sc. End off.

Body: Beg at neck, with rose, ch 30. Sl st in first ch to form ring. Ch 1.

Rnd 1: Sc in each ch around. Join each rnd, ch 1.

Rnd 2: (Sc in 4 sc, 2 sc in next sc) 6 times—36 sc.

Rnd 3: Sc in 10 sc, 2 sc in next sc, sc in 18 sc, 2 sc in next sc, sc in 6 sc—38 sc.

Rnds 4-16: Work even on 38 sc.

Rnd 17: Sc in 6 sc, work next 2 sc tog, sc in 18 sc, work next 2 sc tog, sc to end of rnd—36 sc. Drop lp from hook.

Turn body inside out. Sew neck edge firmly to neck edge of head, having ends of rnds at back. Turn right side out. Stuff head firmly. Stuff body. Pick up lp and continue with body, stuffing lower body before closing bottom.

Rnd 18: (Sc in 4 sc, work 2 sc tog) 6 times—30 sc.

Rnd 19: (Sc in 3 sc, work 2 sc tog) 6 times—24 sc.

Rnd 20: (Sc in 2 sc, work 2 sc tog) 6 times—18 sc.

Rnd 21: (Sc in 1 sc, work 2 sc tog) 6 times—12 sc. Work 2 sc tog around. Sew opening closed, sewing 3 sts for front to 3 sts for back.

Legs: Beg at shoes, with rose, ch 12.

Rnd 1: Sc in 2nd ch from hook and in next 9 ch, 3 sc in last ch (toe); work on opposite side of ch, sc in each ch. Do not join rnds.

Rnd 2: Sc in each sc around, inc 3 sc evenly around toe—26 sc.

Rnds 3-6: Work even.

Rnd 7: Sc to 4 sts before toe, (work next 2 sc tog, sc in next sc) 3 times, sc to end of rnd—23 sc.

Rnd 8: Sc to 2 sts before toe, (work next 2 sc tog) twice, sc to end of rnd—21 sc.

Rnds 9-12: Work even. Cut rose.

Rnd 13: With white, sc in each sc around. Cut white.

Rnd 14: Working in back lps only, with pink, sc in each sc around.

Rnds 15-31: Work even. Stuff leg.

Rnds 32-34: * Sc in next sc, work next 2 sc tog, repeat from * around until hole is closed. Sew legs to bottom of body. Join white in front lp of rnd 13. Working from left to right, sc in each st around.

Left arm: Beg at top, with pink, ch 2.

Rnd 1: 6 sc in 2nd ch from hook. Do not join rnds.

Rnd 2: 2 sc in each sc around—12 sc. Mark end of rnds.

Rnd 3: Sc in 3 sc, (2 sc in next sc) twice, sc around—14 sc. Incs are at outer edge of arm.

Rnds 4-9: Work even.

Rnd 10: Sc in 5 sc, 2 sc in next sc, sc around—15 sc.

Rnds 11-13: Work even.

Rnd 14: Sc in 5 sc, work 2 sc tog, sc around—14 sc.

Rnd 15: (Sc in 1 sc, work 2 sc tog) 4 times, sc in 2 sc—10 sc.

Rnd 16: (2 sc in next sc, sc in next sc) 5 times—15 sc.

Rnd 17: 2 sc in next sc, sc in next sc, 2 sc in next sc (5 sts for thumb), (2 sc in next sc, sc in next sc) 3 times, sc to end of rnd.

Rnd 18: Sk thumb sts, sc around—15 sc.

Rnd 19: Sc around, work 2 sc tog on edge opposite thumb—14 sc.

Rnd 20: Sc around, work 2 sc tog on palm—13 sc. Stuff arm firmly.

Rnds 21 and 22: Work 2 sc tog until hole is closed.

Thumb: Join pink in first thumb st, sc in 3 sts; end off. Sew thumb sts tog.

Right arm: Work as for left arm through rnd 2.

Rnd 3: Sc in 7 sc, (2 sc in next sc) twice, sc to end.

Rnds 4-9: Work even.

Rnd 10: Sc in 8 sc, 2 sc in next sc, sc to end—15 sc.

Rnds 11-13: Work even.

Rnd 14: Sc in 8 sc, work 2 sc tog, sc around—14 sc.

Rnd 15: Sc in 2 sc, (work 2 sc tog, sc in 1 sc) 4 times—10 sc.

Rnd 16: (2 sc in next sc, sc in next sc) 5 times—15 sc. Finish as for left arm.

Sleeve (make 2): Beg at top, with rose, ch 3, sl st in first ch to form ring. Ch 1.

Rnd 1: 6 sc in ring. Do not join rnds.

Rnd 2: 2 sc in each sc around—12 sc.

Rnd 3: (Sc in next sc, 2 sc in next sc) 6 times—18 sc.

Rnd 4: Sc around, inc 2 sc in rnd—20 sc.

Rnds 5-7: Work even.

Rnd 8: * Ch 3, sk 1 sc, sc in next sc, repeat from * around. End off.

Place arm in sleeve. Sew top of arm to inside top of sleeve. Sew sleeve to body at rnds 3 and 6 of body with thumbs pointing toward front.

Skirt: With rose, ch 40. Sl st in first ch to form ring. Ch 1.

Rnd 1: Sc in each ch around. Join each rnd.

Rnd 2: Ch 1, sc in each sc around.

Rnd 3: Ch 3, 2 dc in each sc around.

Rnds 4-12: Ch 3, dc in each dc around.

Rnd 13: * Ch 3, sk 1 dc, sc in next dc, repeat from * around. End off.

Sew skirt to doll at waist.

To finish: *Hair* Starting at one side of forehead, loop brown yarn across forehead (about 24 2″ loops), sewing or gluing back edges of loops to head. Cut remainder of skein of brown yarn into 15″ lengths. Place on head. Stitch through center of strands for part, stitching to head from top of bangs to back of head. Glue or sew inner layers of hair to head. Trim hair ends evenly around. Tie red yarn bow to hair each side. *Features* Embroider navy eyes in satin stitch, red nose (a short straight stitch), red mouth in outline or couching stitch.

Crochet a white ch long enough to go around neck. Tie around neck.

MATERIALS FOR CAPE, BERET, AND HATBOX

Four-ply handknitting yarn, two 3½-oz. pull-skeins light blue; small amount white. Crochet hook size H (5 mm). Round elastic. One button.

DIRECTIONS FOR CAPE, BERET, AND HATBOX

Cape: Beg at lower edge, with light blue, ch 90.

Row 1: Dc in 3rd ch from hook and in each ch across—88 dc. Ch 2, turn.

Rows 2-8: Dc in each dc across.

Divide for arm opening Work 3 rows on first 12 sts. End off. Join yarn in next st on last long row. Work dc in each of 64 dc. Ch 2, turn. Work 2 more rows, dec 6 sts evenly spaced across each row—52 dc. End off. Work 3 rows dc on last 12 sts. Working across all sts, work dc until 16 rows from start, dec 6 sts each row. End off.

Edging With white, working from left to right, work 1 row sc (crab st) around each arm opening and around outer edge of cape. With white, make ch; draw through last row around neck edge. Tie ends into bow.

Beret: Ch 3, 11 dc in 3rd ch from hook; join with a sl st in top of ch 3.

Rnd 2: Ch 3, dc in joining, 2 dc in each dc around—24 dc, counting ch 3 as 1 dc. Join with a sl st in top of ch 3 each rnd.

Rnd 3: (Dc in next dc, 2 dc in next dc) 12 times—36 dc.

Rnd 4: (Dc in each of next 2 dc, 2 dc in next dc) 12 times—48 dc.

Rnd 5: (Dc in each of next 3 dc, 2 dc in next dc) 12 times—60 dc.

Rnd 6: (Dc in each of next 4 dc, 2 dc in next dc) 12 times—72 dc.

Rnd 7: Dc in each dc around.

Rnds 8 and 9: Dec 12 dc evenly spaced around.

Rnd 10: Dec 10 dc evenly spaced around. End off; join white. With white, work 1 rnd reverse sc over elastic. Adjust elastic to fit doll head.

Hatbox: Ch 3; sl st in first ch to form ring.

Rnd 1: Ch 1, 6 sc in ring. Sl st in first sc.

Rnd 2: Ch 3 (counts as 1 dc), 2 dc in first sc, 3 dc in each sc around—18 dc. Join each rnd.

Rnd 3: Ch 3, dc in first dc, 2 dc in each dc around—36 dc.

Rnd 4: Ch 3, 2 dc in next dc, * dc in next dc, 2 dc in next dc, repeat from * around—54 dc.

Rnd 5: Working in back lps only, sc in each dc around.

Rnds 6 and 7: Sc in each sc around. End off.

Work another piece the same through rnd 5. At end of rnd 5, ch 12 for buttonloop. Sk 2 sts, sl st in next st. End off.

Sew pieces tog ⅔ of the way around with buttonloop at center of opening. Sew button at center of sc section opposite buttonloop. For strap, work a piece on 2 sc about 7" long. Sew ends to top of box. Insert circles of cardboard to keep shape of box.

Curly  Dolls

The large own, dressed jumper and Mary Janes. *doll has a doll of her in matching*

SIZES
Large doll, 15½″; small doll, 6″.

EQUIPMENT
Pencil. Ruler. Masking tape. Tapestry and sewing needles. Scissors. Straight pins. **For blocking:** Softwood surface such as pine or plywood. Brown paper. T- or carpenter's square. Rustproof thumbtacks.

MATERIALS
Mono needlepoint canvas, 12 mesh-to-the-inch, one piece at least 22″ × 30″. Persian-type yarn in 12-yard skeins: 7 skeins off-white; 6 skeins light turquoise; 5 skeins rust; 4 skeins light pink; 2 skeins dark orange; 1 skein each, black, magenta, medium pink. Polyester fiberfill. Matching sewing threads. **For large doll only:** 4-ply handknitting yarn, one 3½-oz. skein bronze. White cotton pre-pleated trim, ¾″ wide, 1⅛ yards. Aqua grosgrain ribbon ⅜″ wide, ¾ yard. Five ¼″-diameter white buttons.

DIRECTIONS FOR DOLLS
Needlepoint: With pencil, mark the following rectangles on canvas as general guidelines for doll pieces, placing them 1″ in from canvas edges and 1″ apart. For large doll, mark two of each: 5″ × 5¾″ (front and back of head), 7″ × 8″ (body front and back), 5″ × 6½″ (legs); also mark four of each: 2½″ × 4¼″ (arms) and 1¾″ squares (hands). For small doll,

mark two of each: 2″ × 2½″ (head front and back), 2½″ × 3″ (body front and back), 3″ × 3″ (legs), and 1½″ × 2½″ (arms). Do not cut out individual pieces until directed.

To work needlepoint, cut yarn into 18″ lengths. Separate the three strands and work with two strands in needle throughout. When starting first strand, leave 1″ of yarn on back of canvas and cover it as work proceeds; the first few stitches will anchor it in place. To end strand or to begin a new one, run yarn under a few stitches on back of work; do not make knots. Keep yarn tension firm and even. Stitching tends to twist the working strand; now and then let needle and yarn hang freely to untwist.

Following stitch details, color key, and charts, work needlepoint on all pieces in either continental or diagonal stitch. For each doll head, body, arm, hand, or leg, begin in upper right corner of marked rectangle and count to left for first stitch; each square on chart represents one mesh of canvas or one needlepoint stitch. Fill in numbered areas with a single color, following key; also follow key to work symboled stitches of faces and small doll's arm. After filling large doll's face and head front with needlepoint, add several long straight stitches in nose area indicated by box on chart, using light pink yarn and working over needlepoint; see photograph.

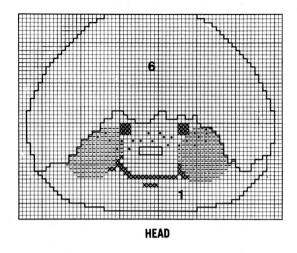

HEAD

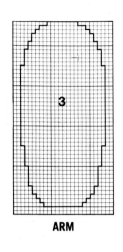

ARM

LARGE DOLL

HAND

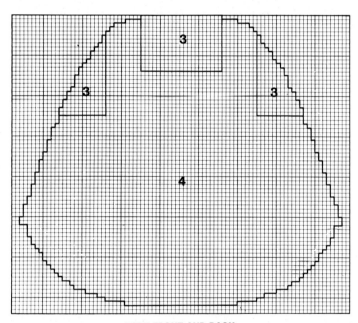

BODY FRONT AND BACK

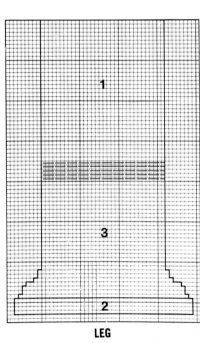

LEG

For small doll, add pink nose as for large doll; also add fly stitch mouth with black yarn and make a reversed stitch over each eye stitch, forming an "X." For head backs, fill in with hair color as for front, leaving bottom three rows to be worked in light pink. For large doll's leg, work sock cuffs with bars of long horizontal stitches over three threads as shown, using white yarn and beginning and ending each bar in same meshes as adjacent bars.

Color Key

1 Light Pink
   Med. Pink
2 Black
3 Off-White
4 Light Turquoise
5 Magenta
6 Rust
7 Dark Orange

When needlepoint is completed, block entire canvas as follows: Cover wood surface with brown paper. Mark canvas outline on paper for guide, making sure corners are square. Mark horizontal and vertical center lines on paper and on wrong side of canvas. Place canvas, right side down, over guide. Match center markings on canvas and paper. Fasten canvas to wood with rustproof tacks; tack corners first, then the center of each side; continue placing tacks until there is a solid border of tacks around entire edge, dividing and subdividing spaces between tacks already placed. Test yarns for colorfastness. Wet thoroughly with cold water, adding salt to water if yarns are not colorfast. Let dry. If piece is badly warped, block again.

To assemble: Disregarding pencil guidelines, cut out doll pieces three canvas meshes beyond last row of stitches all around. Fold unworked canvas to wrong side of pieces. For large doll, sew three buttons to front of dress, ¼" below top and ¼" apart. For both dolls, place bodies together, wrong sides facing and matching folded edges; whipstitch together, using matching yarns, working through last row of needlepoint on each edge, and leaving top edge open. Stuff body firmly with fiberfill; stitch opening closed. Assemble head pieces as for body. For large doll, assemble arms and hands as for body; slipstitch hands to arms. Fold leg pieces in half vertically; stitch and stuff in same manner as for body. For small doll, assemble arms and legs as for large doll's legs. For both, slipstitch legs to body at skirt edge with toes pointing outward. Having seams at front and back

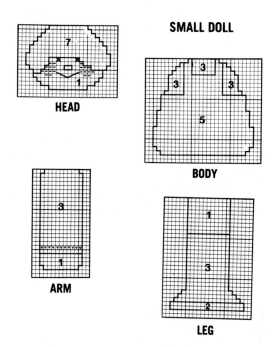

SMALL DOLL

HEAD

BODY

ARM

LEG

(back only for small doll), stitch arms to body at shoulders. Attach head to neck edge; wrap pink yarn around joining several times and secure. Cover scalp with turkey work "curls," using handknitting yarn instead of Persian on large doll (*see Embroidery Stitch Details, page 185*). Using black yarn, make two straight stitches across instep for shoe strap (*see photograph*).

For large doll only Sew a ¼" button to end of each shoe strap at back of feet. Tie ribbon into bow around head. Slipstitch pleated trim to wrists and lower edge of dress, turning in raw edges. Gather remaining trim and place around neck. Stitch ends of trim together at center back.

egina & Randi

Regina the graceful Southern belle wears a romantic lace-trimmed gown. Randi is a pixie with her flower-petal cap, leaf-soled shoes, and sunny smile.

Regina

SIZE
About 20″ tall.

EQUIPMENT
Pencil. Ruler. Paper for patterns. Tape measure. Dressmaker's tracing (carbon) paper. Dry ball-point pen. Small embroidery hoop. Embroidery and regular scissors. Embroidery and sewing needles. Knitting needle. Straight pins. Small safety pin. Sewing machine with zigzag attachment. Iron.

MATERIALS
For doll: Closely woven cotton fabric such as muslin or kettle cloth 45″ wide, ½ yard desired flesh color. Flesh-color sewing thread and heavy-duty sewing thread. Yellow sport-weight yarn, 3 ozs. Six-strand embroidery floss: one skein yellow; small amounts brown, white, pink, and red. Scraps of navy and white felt. Coral crayon. Polyester fiberfill for stuffing. Glue.

For clothes: Sheer cotton fabric 44″ wide, 1½ yards white. Small amounts white closely woven cotton fabric and satin. White flat lace: ½″ wide, 12 yards; 1¾″ wide, ¾ yard. Pink satin ribbon ½″ wide, 2½ yards. Flat elastic ⅛″ wide, 1 yard. Three small snap fasteners. Tiny pink artificial flowers, seven small bunches. White sewing thread. Pink seed beads, 13.

DIRECTIONS FOR DOLL
Enlarge patterns by copying on paper ruled in 1″ squares. Complete half- and quarter-patterns indicated by long dash lines; fine lines are for placement or embroidery.

Use dressmaker's carbon and dry ball-point pen to transfer patterns to wrong side of flesh-color fabric, placing them ½″ from fabric edges and ½″ apart; reverse leg and body patterns to make a front and a back for each. Cut out one head center, two bodies, two arms, two soles, and four legs, leaving ¼″ seam allowance around all pieces.

Mark one head on fabric, for face; center and transfer actual-size pattern for face to right side of fabric, including fine lines for embroidery. Do *not* cut out.

Face: From felt, cut two complete white eyes and two navy irises, omitting seam allowances. Glue eyes to face; let dry. Insert face area in embroidery hoop. Embroider as follows, referring to Embroidery Stitch Details, page 185: Using two strands floss in needle and outline stitch, make brown eye outlines, lashes, and brows, pink nose, and red mouth.

With white floss and satin stitch, make small highlight in each eye. When embroidery is completed, remove fabric from hoop. Steam-press gently, wrong side up. Cut out face; use as pattern to cut head back.

To assemble: Pin head center to face and head back with bottom straight edges even. Stitch around sides and top, leaving neck edge open. Fold neck ¼" to wrong side; baste. Turn head to right side. Stuff firmly with fiberfill. "Rouge" cheeks with coral crayon.

Fold arms in half lengthwise, right side in. Stitch raw arm and hand edges, leaving top straight edges open. Turn; stuff firmly. Baste each arm closed ⅛" from raw edges, enclosing stuffing. Stitch legs together in pairs at front

and back, leaving top and bottom edges open. Stitch soles to bottom openings, matching dots; turn and stuff. Baste each leg top as for arm, but with seams centered. On right side of one body (front), pin arms ½" down from shoulders, so that arms cross, thumbs point down, and side edges are even; stitch. Pin and stitch legs to body bottom in similar manner, so that toes point toward shoulders. Place body front on work surface with limbs on top, extending outward. Fold left arm across body, so that hand extends above right shoulder and seam allowance faces out. Pin left side of body back, wrong side up, to body front; stitch. Pin and stitch right side of body in same manner (body will look like a tube with hands extending above and legs below). Push legs up through tube, so that only

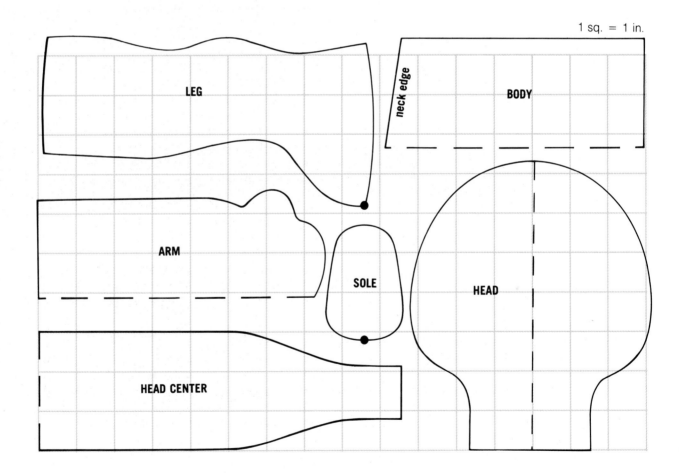

1 sq. = 1 in.

LEG

ARM

HEAD CENTER

SOLE

neck edge

BODY

HEAD

seam allowance extends at bottom; pin and stitch body bottom. Turn and stuff. Turn raw edges ¼" to inside; slipstitch opening closed. Using heavy-duty thread, slipstitch head, centered, over shoulders.

Hair: Cut 200 26" lengths of yarn. Working with all six strands of matching embroidery floss, stitch center of each length to front head-center seam, working from left side of head to right side of head. Pull ends into ponytail, leaving some strands free at front for bangs. Trim bangs to about 3½" long at forehead, longer along sides of face. Wrap all loose ends tightly around pencils; dampen, then let dry, for curls.

DIRECTIONS FOR CLOTHES

Bloomers: On closely woven cotton fabric, mark two bloomers, adding ¼" to each waist edge; cut out, adding seam allowance all around. Press leg bottoms ¼" to wrong side. Cut ½" lace trim to fit leg bottoms. Pin lace in place on wrong side, so that ruffles extend below folds; topstitch on right side close to folds, using wide zigzag stitch. Cut four 5" lengths of elastic. Starting at a side edge of each leg with one end, pin elastic to wrong side 1½" above fold; zigzag-stitch in place. Press waist edges ½" to wrong side. Pin and stitch elastic to wrong side of waist ¼" below fold as for leg. Reset machine for straight stitch. Stitch bloomers together at center front and back from waist to crotch. Stitch each inseam from lace to crotch; turn to right side.

Dress: *Bodice* From satin fabric, cut one bodice front, using complete pattern, and two bodice backs, using half-pattern and adding ¼" to each center back. For decorative inset: Mark a 3¾" × 11" rectangle on sheer fabric. Cut 3¾" length of 1¾"-wide lace; baste to center of rectangle, matching edges at top and bottom. Stitch four ¼" tucks on each side of lace; press tucks toward lace. Trim inset to fit bodice front within marked "V" on pattern; baste in place on bodice. Stitch bodice front to backs at shoulders. Press raw edges at center backs ¼" to wrong side twice; topstitch in place. From sheer fabric, cut a 44" × 1½" strip for bodice ruffle. Press one long edge ¼" to wrong side. Topstitch 44" length of ½" lace to pressed edge, so that lace extends beyond edge. Press opposite long edge ¼" to wrong side; baste close to fold and gather to 20". Pin center of strip to bottom of "V" inset, with lace facing downward. Pin remainder of strip along "V," repeating "V" shape on bodice back; stitch. Cut a 20" length of ½" lace. Topstitch lace over gathered edge of front bodice ruffle. Sew seed beads along center of strip, placing beads ½" apart. *Collar* From sheer fabric, cut one 1½" × 30" strip; press one long edge ¼" to wrong side. Stitch 30" length of ½" lace to pressed edge. Gather long raw edge to 10¼". From satin, cut one 1½" × 10¼" strip for binding. Stitch binding to neck edge of bodice; press seam down. Stitch gathered edge of ruffle to opposite long edge; press seam down, so ruffle extends above binding. Turn all short edges under; slipstitch. Sew snap fasteners, evenly spaced, to center back edges. *Each sleeve* Cut sleeve from sheer fabric. Press wrist edge under ¼". Stitch ½" lace to wrist edge. Cut 12" length of 1¾" lace; baste to sleeve between light lines on pattern. On each side of lace, stitch two ¼" tucks; press tucks toward lace. Zigzag-stitch a 4½" length of elastic to sleeve bottom, 1" from wrist edge. Reset machine for straight stitch. Baste upper curved edge of sleeve between X's. Pin lower curved edge of sleeve to front and back armhole of bodice below X's. Gather upper edge to fit armhole; pin and stitch. Stitch each underarm and side in a continuous seam. *Skirt* From sheer fabric, cut 8" × 44" skirt and six 4½" × 44" ruffles. Stitch ruffles together in pairs at short edges, for three 87½"-long ruffles. Gather one long (waist) edge of skirt to fit bodice waist. Trim one long (bottom) edge of each ruffle with ½" lace. Gather top edge of each ruffle to 44". Stitch one ruffle to waist edge, second ruffle

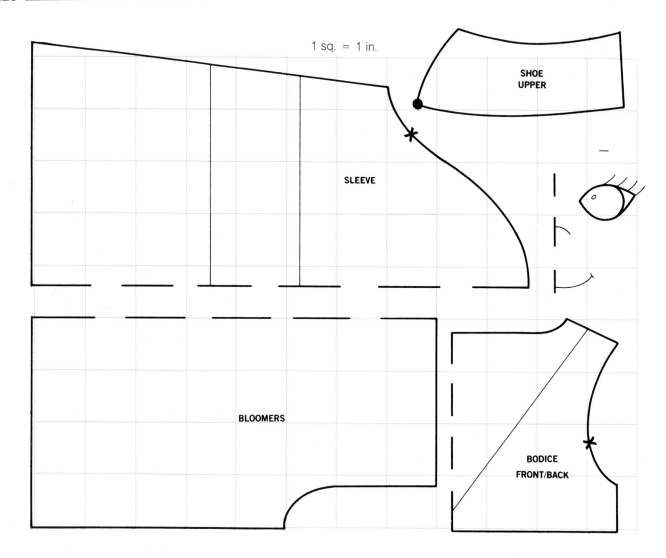

1 sq. = 1 in.

SHOE UPPER

SLEEVE

BLOOMERS

BODICE FRONT/BACK

3″ below, and third ruffle to skirt bottom, for three tiers. Beginning at bottom, stitch center back edge together to 2½″ below waist. Above seam, press edges ¼″ to wrong side; slipstitch. Cut 36″ length of satin ribbon, for waist tie, and 18″ length for hair tie. Make six small bows from remaining ribbon. Tack a cluster of flowers to each bow, then tack bows to dress, having one at center front of neck binding, and one at center of ribbon waistband. Tack remaining cluster of flowers to center of hair tie; tie around top of ponytail as shown in color photograph.

Shoes: From satin, cut four uppers and two soles. Press top edge of each upper ¼″ to wrong side; topstitch close to fold. Stitch uppers together in pairs at center front and back. Stitch soles to uppers, matching dots; turn.

Randi

SIZE
About 20″ tall.

EQUIPMENT
Pencil. Ruler. Paper for patterns. Tape measure. Dressmaker's tracing (carbon) paper. Dry ball-point pen. Small embroidery hoop. Embroidery and regular scissors. Embroidery and sewing needles. Knitting needle. Straight pins. Sewing machine with zigzag attachment and attachment for making scalloped hems. Iron.

MATERIALS
For doll: Closely woven cotton fabric such as muslin or kettle cloth 45″ wide, ½ yard flesh color. Flesh-color sewing thread and heavy-duty sewing thread. Sport-weight yarn, 3 ozs. pale yellow. Six-strand embroidery floss: one skein to match hair; small amounts blue, black, white, and pink. Coral crayon. Polyester fiberfill for stuffing. **For clothes:** Lightweight cotton fabric 45″ wide, ¾ yard pale pink. Sheer cotton fabric 45″ wide, ½ yard medium pink. Small amount light green moire fabric. Fusible interfacing. Flat elastic ¼″ wide, 1 yard. Two small snap fasteners. Double-faced satin ribbon ¼″ wide, 3 yards pale pink. Tiny silk flowers for braids. Scraps of pink and green felt. Ten yellow seed beads. Sewing thread to match fabrics.

DIRECTIONS FOR DOLL
Enlarge patterns by copying on paper ruled in 1″ squares. Complete half- and quarter-patterns indicated by long dash lines; fine lines are for placement or embroidery.

Use dressmaker's carbon and dry ball-point pen to transfer patterns to wrong side of flesh-color fabric, placing them ½″ from fabric edges and ½″ apart; reverse leg and body patterns to make a front and a back for each. Cut out one head center, two bodies, two arms, two soles, and four legs, leaving ¼″ seam allowance around all pieces.

Mark one head on fabric, for face; center and transfer actual-size pattern for face to right side of fabric, including fine lines for embroidery. Do *not* cut out.

Face: Insert face area in embroidery hoop. Embroider as follows, referring to Embroidery Stitch Details, page 185: Using three strands of floss in needle, work blue eyes in vertical satin stitch; work a white double cross-stitch near center of each eye. Using two strands of floss and outline stitch, work black eye outline and pink mouth. Work black straight-stitch lashes. When embroidery is completed, remove fabric from hoop. Press gently, wrong side up. Cut out face; use as pattern to cut head back.

To assemble: Pin head center to face and head back with bottom straight edges even. Stitch around sides and top, leaving neck edge open. Fold neck ¼″ to wrong side; baste. Turn head to right side. Stuff firmly with fiberfill. "Rouge" cheeks with coral crayon.

Fold arms in half lengthwise, right side in. Stitch raw arm and hand edges, leaving top straight edges open. Turn; stuff firmly. Baste each arm closed ⅛″ from raw edges, enclosing stuffing. Stitch legs together in pairs at front and back, leaving top and bottom edges open. Stitch soles to bottom openings, matching dots; turn and stuff. Baste each leg top as for arm, but with seams centered. On right side of one body (front), pin arms ½″ down from shoulders, so that arms cross, thumbs point down, and side edges are even; stitch. Pin and stitch legs to body bottom in similar manner, so that toes point toward shoulders. Place body front on work surface with limbs on top, extending outward. Fold left arm across body, so that hand extends above right

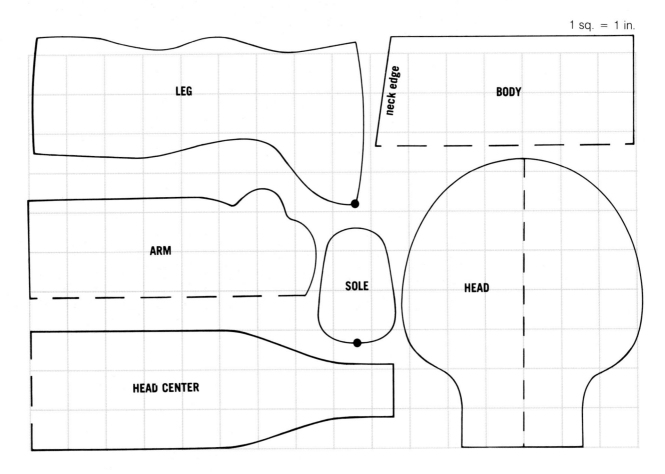

1 sq. = 1 in.

LEG

BODY

neck edge

ARM

SOLE

HEAD

HEAD CENTER

shoulder and seam allowance faces out. Pin left side of body back, wrong side up, to body front; stitch. Pin and stitch right side of body in same manner (body will look like a tube with hands extending above and legs below). Push legs up through tube, so that only seam allowance extends at bottom; pin and stitch body bottom. Turn and stuff. Turn raw edges ¼" to inside; slipstitch opening closed. Using heavy-duty thread, slipstitch head, centered, over shoulders.

Hair: Mark center part from front head seam to nape of neck. For braids, cut 120 30" lengths of yarn. Working with groups of 10 strands at a time and all six strands of matching embroidery floss, stitch center of each group to part, working from front seam to back. Cut pink ribbon into six 18" lengths. Divide yarn

on each side of head into three equal sections and braid, including a length of ribbon in braid; tie each braid with short length of yarn. Tack top of braids to head near cheeks to secure. Tie a ribbon bow around top and bottom of each braid. Insert silk flowers into bottom bows. For bangs, cut 50 6" lengths of yarn; bundle together with ends even. Stitch center of bundle to front of part. Finger-comb bangs down over forehead; trim ends; do not tack down.

DIRECTIONS FOR CLOTHES
Bloomers: On pale pink fabric, mark two bloomers, adding ¼" to each waist edge; cut out, adding seam allowance all around. Use matching thread and machine scallop to finish each leg bottom; trim fabric close to machine scallops. Cut four 5" lengths of

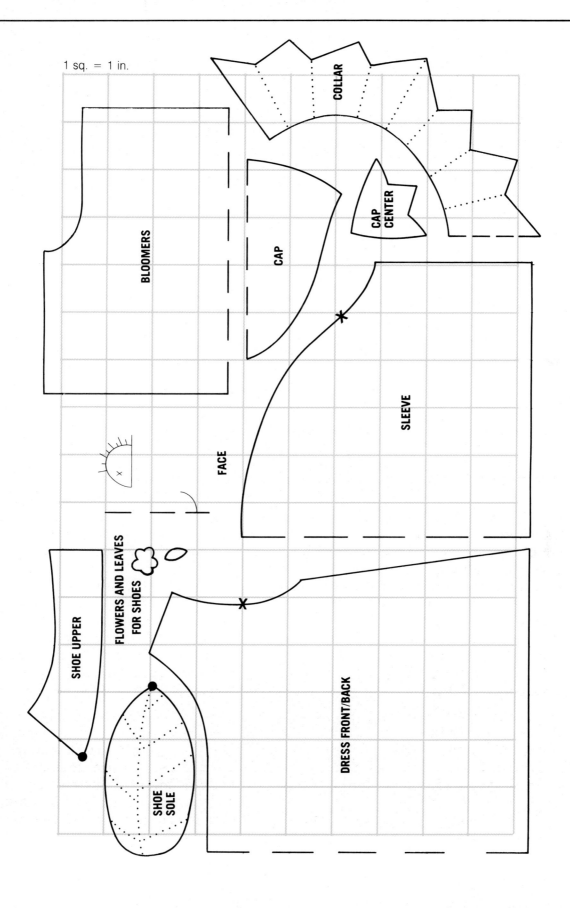

1 sq. = 1 in.

BLOOMERS

COLLAR

CAP

CAP CENTER

SLEEVE

FACE

FLOWERS AND LEAVES FOR SHOES

SHOE UPPER

DRESS FRONT/BACK

SHOE SOLE

elastic. Starting at a side edge of each leg with one end, pin elastic to wrong side ¾" above scallops; zigzag-stitch in place. Press waist edges ½" to wrong side. Pin and stitch elastic to wrong side of waist ¼" below fold as for leg. Reset machine for straight stitch. Stitch bloomers together at center front and back from waist to crotch. Stitch each inseam from scallops to crotch; turn to right side.

Dress: From sheer fabric, cut dress front, using complete pattern, and two dress backs, using half-pattern and adding 1¼" to each center back. From pale pink fabric, cut a second dress for lining, adding ¼" to each bottom edge. Also cut two sleeves from sheer fabric. On moire, mark two collars; add ¼" to long curved edges, then cut out, adding seam allowance all around. Finish bottom edges of dress, sleeves, and lining with scallops as for bloomers. Stitch dress front to backs at shoulders. *Each sleeve* Baste upper curved edge of sleeve between X's. Pin lower curved edges to front and back armhole below X's. Gather basted edge to fit armhole; pin and stitch. Stitch underarm and side in a continuous seam. Stitch lining front and backs together at shoulders; baste lining to dress along neck edge. Press all center back edges under ¼" twice; slipstitch in place. Stitch collars along bottom (pointed) and short-side edges; turn to right side. Using matching thread, topstitch lines on collar following dotted lines on pattern. Press long curved edges ¼" to one (wrong) side. Place collar over neck edge of dress as shown in color photograph; slipstitch in place on wrong side. Sew snap fasteners to dress back, one at neck, one 3" below neck edge.

Cap: From sheer fabric, cut five cap sections. From pale pink fabric, cut five cap sections, adding 1¼" to curved (bottom) edges. Stitch sheer sections together along straight edges. Finish edges with machine-scallops as for bloomers. Assemble pale pink sections and finish edges in same manner. Tack caps together at center tops, with wrong side of sheer cap centered over right side of pale pink cap. From moire, cut four cap centers and 1½" × 1¼" rectangle for "stem." Press one 1½" edge ¼" to wrong side, then fold piece in half widthwise twice; whipstitch long edges together. Stitch cap centers together along straight edges, catching end of stem in center of seam. Press raw edges of cap center under ⅛" twice; topstitch. Tack cap center to center of sheer cap, with stem extending upward.

Shoes: From moire, cut four uppers and two soles. Fuse interfacing to wrong side of pieces, following manufacturer's directions. Using matching thread, topstitch lines on soles, following dotted lines on pattern. Stitch uppers together in pairs at fronts and backs. Stitch soles to uppers, matching dots. Turn top edges under ⅛", then ¼"; slipstitch in place. From felt, cut four green leaves and two pink flowers, omitting seam allowance. Thread five seed beads on a length of green sewing thread. Tie thread ends together, forming a small ring; leave long thread ends. Thread remaining five seed beads on another length of thread in same manner. Tack two leaves, one flower, and one seed-bead flower center to center front of each shoe.

usannah & Sweet Pea

Susannah is made of warm calico and polka-dot fabric. Sweet Pea, her faithful feline friend, has bright blue eyes.

SIZES

Susannah, about 12½″ tall. Sweet Pea, about 10″ tall.

EQUIPMENT

Paper for patterns. Pencil. Colored pencil. Ruler. Scissors. Embroidery needles. Large-eyed needle. Compass. Sewing machine with zigzag attachment. Iron.

MATERIALS

For Susannah: Brown calico 45″ wide, ¼ yard. Brown polka-dot fabric 45″ wide, ½ yard. Pink-beige cotton knit, 7″ square. Scrap ⅜″-wide lace or tatted edging. Three ¼″-diameter pearl buttons. Small amount of gray yarn for hair. **For Sweet Pea:** Brown polka-dot fabric 45″ wide, ½ yard. Scrap brown calico. Scrap beige felt or chamois. **For both:** Matching sewing thread. Scrap six-strand embroidery floss in bright blue, black, and rose. Dacron polyester for stuffing.

DIRECTIONS FOR SUSANNAH

Complete half-patterns indicated by dash lines and enlarge patterns for body, face, bonnet back and front, arm, and hand by copying on paper ruled in 1″ squares. Cut pieces as follows, adding ½″ seam allowance all around unless otherwise indicated. From brown polka-dot fabric, cut two bodies and two arms, using patterns (reverse arm pattern for right and left side and add seam allowance to straight edges only); also cut 9″-diameter circle. From brown calico, cut one bonnet back and one bonnet front, using patterns; also cut 7″ × 18″ piece for apron, two 2″ × 9″ strips for apron ties, and one 2½″ × 18″ strip for bonnet ruffle. From pink-beige cotton knit, use pattern to cut face and single hand, adding seam allowance to wrist of hand only.

Make ¼″ hems along 7″ side edges of apron. Along one 18″ edge, machine-stitch two rows of long basting stitches. For apron ties, fold each 2″ × 9″ strip in half lengthwise, wrong side inward and with raw edges tucked in; topstitch along open long edge. Tuck in raw edges at one end on each tie; topstitch. With right sides facing, pin bonnet back to bonnet front, easing at top as necessary; stitch. For bonnet ruffle, fold 2½″ × 18″ strip in half lengthwise, wrong side inward; stitch along 18″ edge. Turn in raw edges at each end; topstitch. Pleat ruffle strip to

measure about 11"; press and stitch to hold pleats along raw edge. Pin ruffle to right side of front edge of bonnet; stitch. Trim bonnet along ruffle with lace edging as in photograph; slipstitch in place. Pin right side of face to wrong side of bonnet front edge; stitch. Referring to pattern, mark placement and embroider facial features and hair (*see Embroidery Stitch Details, page 185*). Work eyes in six strands of blue and black floss as indicated. Work mouth and nose in two strands of rose floss as indicated. Satin-stitch yarn hair from center part to outer edges of face as in photograph. Seam body pieces together, right sides facing. Machine-stitch two rows of long basting stitches along bottom edge of body (skirt). Gather skirt edge to fit circle. With right sides facing, pin and stitch circle to body; turn.

To assemble: Gather long edge of calico apron to fit between dots marked X on body; baste in place. Pin arms in place, lining up dots on arm and neck edge of body marked Y and overlapping left arm, wrist edge on top of right arm. Make certain lower edge of arms overlaps apron top edge. Tuck in raw end of apron tie at lower back edge of arm. Appliqué arms to body, using white thread and close zigzag stitch. Do not stitch overlapped wrist edges. With right sides facing, pin hand to left wrist; stitch. Add lace edging and slipstitch in place. Attach open edges of hand to right arm, using buttonhole stitch and matching sewing thread. Lightly pad arms. With right sides facing, pin head to neck edge; stitch, leaving opening to stuff. Stuff fully; tuck in raw edges at opening; slipstitch closed. Pin and hem lower edge of apron. Add 3 small

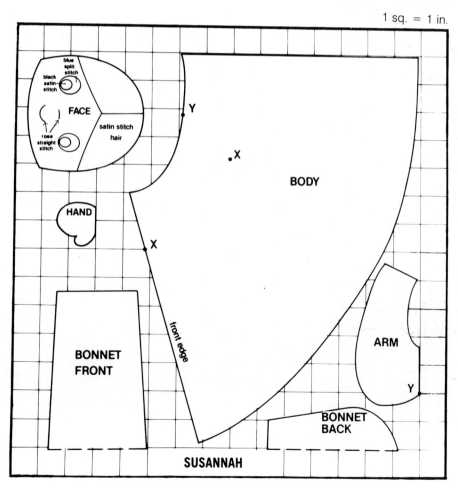

1 sq. = 1 in.

SUSANNAH

buttons down back seam of body, beginning at neck edge. Tie apron ties in bow.

DIRECTIONS FOR SWEET PEA

Enlarge patterns for cat as described for Susannah. Adding ½" seam allowance all around, unless otherwise indicated, use patterns to cut two body pieces, one tail, two ears, and back and front head pieces from brown polka-dot fabric. Also cut an 8"-diameter circle from polka-dot fabric. Referring to pattern, mark placement for leg details on body front along lower edge. Use close zigzag stitch to embroider details in brown thread. With right sides facing, stitch body pieces together at side seams. Machine-stitch two rows of long basting stitches along bottom edge of body. Fold tail in half lengthwise,

right side inward; stitch and turn tail. Also make basting stitches around head back piece. Use patterns to cut two beige felt or chamois ears and one nose. Fold and press raw side edges of polka-dot ears to wrong side. With wrong sides facing, use buttonhole stitch and matching thread to join beige ear to polka-dot ear. Use buttonhole stitch to attach nose to head front piece. Referring to pattern, mark placement for eyes and mouth on front. Work eyes in six strands of blue and black floss as indicated. Work mouth in two strands of rose as indicated. For whiskers, use doubled strands of black floss, and thread needle so that doubled ends go through needle eye. Following dots around mouth, insert needle; remove needle and thread loose ends of floss through loop at opposite end; pull up and knot. Trim to 2½".

To assemble: Pull up basting stitches at lower edge of body to fit circle. With right sides facing, pin circle to body, adding tail at dots marked X, center back; stitch. Turn. Pull up basting stitches around back of head and with right sides facing, pin back to front. Add ears at dots marked Y. Stitch, leaving neck edge open. With right sides facing, pin head to body; stitch, leaving opening. Turn; stuff cat; turn in raw edges and slipstitch opening closed. Make collar from scrap calico. Cut collar strip to 2" × 7". Fold and press long edges to center on wrong side, then fold strip in half again lengthwise. Fit collar around neck; sew in place.

1 sq. = 1 in.

SWEET PEA

attach tail
centered on
back

X

X

BODY
FRONT AND BACK

TAIL

piece on fold

HEAD BACK

EAR
(cut 4)

HEAD FRONT

blue
split
stitch

black
satin
stitch

nose

black
straight
stitch

ess & Ted

An adorable brother and sister pair knitted in Phildar yarn.

SIZE
12" tall.

MATERIALS
Phildar Pronostic, 1 ball each of flesh, pink, brown, and light green for Tess, 1 ball each of flesh, pink, brown, and dark green for Ted. Knitting needles No. 3 (3 mm). Crochet hook size C (2½ mm). Stuffing. Two buttons.

GAUGE
7 sts = 1".

DIRECTIONS FOR TESS
Head: With flesh, cast on 58 sts. Work 38 rows in stockinette st (k 1 row, p 1 row). Thread yarn through last row of sts, draw up for top of head.

Arms: With flesh, cast on 25 sts. Work 20 rows in stockinette st. * Work 1 row green, 1 row pink, 1 row flesh, repeat from * 14 times more. Work 1 row green, 20 rows flesh. Thread yarn through last row of sts, draw up. Thread yarn through cast-on sts, draw up. Sew seam at each end of work for 28 rows leaving center open.

Legs and body: With brown, cast on 27 sts. Work 8 rows in stockinette st. * Work 1 row pink, 1 row flesh, 1 row green, repeat from * twice more. Work 1 row pink, 30 rows flesh. Put stitches on a spare needle.

Work 2nd leg to match. Place both legs on needle, bind off 1 st on each leg at center of work for seam—52 sts. Work 22 rows flesh. Bind off.

Skirt: With green, cast on 75 sts. Work 3 rows in stockinette st, k 1 row on wrong side for hem. Work 4 rows green, then 2 rows pink, 2 rows green, 2 rows flesh, 34 rows light green.

Next Row: Bind off, knitting tog every 2nd and 3rd st before binding them off.

Apron: With flesh, cast on 20 sts. Work 30 rows in stockinette st.

Next Row: (K 2 tog) 10 times. Work 7 rows in stockinette st. Bind off.

Straps (make 2): With crochet hook, ch 23. Sc in 2nd ch from hook and in each ch across. End off.

To finish: From wrong side, sew leg seams, sew center back seam. Gather cast-on edge of foot and draw up. Turn right side out and stuff. Stuff arms and sew to body. Sew back head seam. Gather neck edge of head, turn right side out, stuff and sew to body.

Embroider cheeks in pink, 1 st in brown for mouth, and 2 sts in green for each eye in duplicate st.

Sew brown yarn to top of head for bangs. Cut yarn in 12" lengths and sew to head for hair. Tie yarn around hair at each side of head and sew to head.

Sew back seam of skirt. Turn up lower edge and hem in place. Place skirt on doll and catch-stitch in place.

With crochet hook, work 1 row sc around outer edge of apron, then work 1 row crab st

(sc worked from left to right). Place apron on doll and sew straps in place.

DIRECTIONS FOR TED

Work head, arms, legs, and body as for Tess.

Trousers (make 2 pieces): With green, cast on 34 sts. Work 3 rows in stockinette st, then k 1 row on wrong side for hem. Work 4 rows in stockinette st.

Next Row (right side): P 1 row. Continue in stockinette st beg with a p row for 12 rows. Bind off 2 sts at beg of next 2 rows. Bind off 1 st at beg of next 2 rows—28 sts. Work even for 12 rows, then work 2 rows in k 1, p 1 ribbing. Bind off in ribbing.

Straps (make 2): With green, cast on 5 sts. Work in ribbing of k 1, p 1 for 38 rows. Bind off in ribbing.

To finish: Make up head, arms, legs, and body as for Tess. Embroider face.

Cut brown yarn in 5" lengths and sew to head for hair.

Sew back, front, and leg seams of trousers. Turn up lower leg edge and hem in place. Place trousers on doll and sew straps to trousers. Sew small buttons to front of straps.

Under the Big Top Puppets

The ringmaster, his assistant, the lion, and the clown can all be stored in the corduroy circus tent tote.

Ringmaster, Circus Lady, and Clown

SIZE
10″ tall.

EQUIPMENT
Pencil. Ruler. Scissors. Paper for patterns. Dressmaker's tracing (carbon) paper. Dry ball-point pen. Sewing and embroidery needles. Straight pins.

MATERIALS
For all: Felt: three 9″ × 12″ sheets white (for Clown) or flesh-colored (for others). Scrap of red felt. Light blue six-strand embroidery floss. Sewing thread to match fabrics below. Lightweight cardboard. White glue. Yellow grosgrain ribbon 1″ wide, 12″ piece. **For Circus Lady:** Scraps of pink felt, red satin, and red nylon netting. Silver-colored strung sequins, one yard. Red satin ribbon ⅜″ wide, 12″ piece. Yellow knitting worsted. **For Ringmaster:** Scraps of pink felt; blue, black, brown, and red satin; gold fringed braid; and black cord. Red satin ribbon ⅜″ wide, 10″ piece. Four gold ½″ shank buttons. Brown knitting worsted. Dowel, ⅛″ in diameter, 4″ piece,
painted black. **For Clown:** Scraps of black felt, red satin, black six-strand embroidery floss, and navy/white polka-dot fabric. Two red ⅝″ buttons. Red pompon 1¼″ wide. Yellow pompon 1″ wide. Orange knitting worsted.

GENERAL DIRECTIONS
Enlarge patterns by copying on paper ruled in 1″ squares; complete half-patterns indicated by heavy dash lines; make separate patterns for parts A, B, and C, and for B/C combined. Use patterns to cut pieces from felt and fabric as directed below, adding ½″ seam allowances all around, except where otherwise indicated; do not add seam allowance to cardboard pieces. When assembling felt and fabric pieces, stitch together with right sides facing and edges even, making ½″ seams and using matching thread.

DIRECTIONS FOR RINGMASTER, CIRCUS LADY, AND CLOWN
Using pattern, cut two bodies from flesh-colored or white felt, adding no seam allowance along bottom. Omitting all seam allowances, cut two felt hands and, for Clown and Ringmaster only, two ears. Using dressmaker's carbon and dry ball-point pen, transfer

desired face, centered, to head of one body piece. Read How to Appliqué, page 179. Using patterns and omitting seam allowances, cut face pieces from felt as follows: For Circus Lady and Ringmaster, cut mouth from red and cheeks from pink; for Clown, cut outside mouth from black, cheeks and inside mouth from red. Machine-appliqué pieces to head over markings; for Clown, appliqué outside mouth first, then inside mouth as shown. Using all six strands of light blue floss in an embroidery needle, embroider eyes, using French knots for Ringmaster and Circus Lady and crossed straight stitches for Clown (see *Embroidery Stitch Details, page 185*). Using black floss and outline stitch, embroider arches over Clown's eyes. Tack red pompon "nose" to Clown face at open circle. For Ringmaster's mustache, cut eight 2" strands of brown knitting worsted, bundle together, and tack at centers above mouth as shown. Pin hands flat against arms, thumbs up, and matching wrist edges; baste 3⁄8" in from edge. For Ringmaster and Clown, pin ears against head between dots; baste. Using color specified above, cut 54 8" pieces of knitting worsted for hair. Fold each in half and pin along crown so that ends are against face and centers align with edge of piece; distribute hair evenly between dots Y for Ringmaster and Clown and dots Z for Circus Lady; baste. Stitch front and back body pieces together, catching in hands, ears, and hair and leaving bottom open; turn puppet right side out. Trim hair on Clown or Ringmaster to 1" long. For Circus Lady, leave most of hair long but cut several 1"-long bangs in front; then fold ends of remaining hair under and form "roll" across back of head; tack in place. Dress puppet following directions below.

DIRECTIONS FOR CLOTHES

Ringmaster's uniform: Use pattern to cut the following from satin: two A pieces from brown, one B piece from black, two C pieces and one B/C piece from blue. Cut red satin ribbon to fit and stitch to piece B along fine lines (see *pattern*). Using original pattern as a guide, join pieces as follows: Stitch A to B/C to make uniform back. Stitch C pieces to sides of B, then stitch B/C made to A to make uniform front. At dots, clip into seam allowances 1⁄2"; finish "neck" edge between dots by turning fabric 1⁄4" to wrong side twice and stitching; finish bottom and cuffs in same manner. Sew gold buttons to uniform front at X's. To make epaulets, cut two from cardboard and two from red satin. Place satin pieces, wrong side up, on flat surface. Cover one side of each cardboard piece with white glue and place, glue side down, in center of satin piece. Glue seam allowances to back of cardboard. Cut fringed braid to fit curved edge and glue to right side of each epaulet as shown; let dry. Glue or slipstitch epaulets to shoulders as shown.

Clown suit: Using pattern, cut two clown suit pieces from navy dotted fabric for front and back. Turn edges along neck, bottom, and cuffs 1⁄4" to wrong side twice and stitch. Stitch front and back together along sides and underarm in one continuous seam, then stitch seam along top of sleeve. Turn suit right side out. Sew red buttons to suit front at X's. Tie grosgrain ribbon into bow and tack to neck front as shown; place suit on puppet. To make hat, cut one from cardboard and one from red satin, using pattern. Lay satin piece, wrong side up, on flat surface. Cover one side of cardboard with white glue and place, glue side down, in center of satin piece; glue seam allowance to back of cardboard; let dry. Curl piece to form cone, overlapping flat edges, and glue to make hat; glue yellow pompon to point; let dry. Glue or slipstitch hat brim to head as shown.

Lady's dress: Using pattern, cut two dress pieces from red satin for front and back. Fold edges along neck, armholes, and bottom 1⁄4" to wrong side twice and stitch. Cut pieces of strung sequins to fit and stitch to neck and armhole edges as shown. Stitch front and back together along side and shoulder seams; turn dress right side out. To make tutu, cut 8" × 20" piece red nylon netting and fold

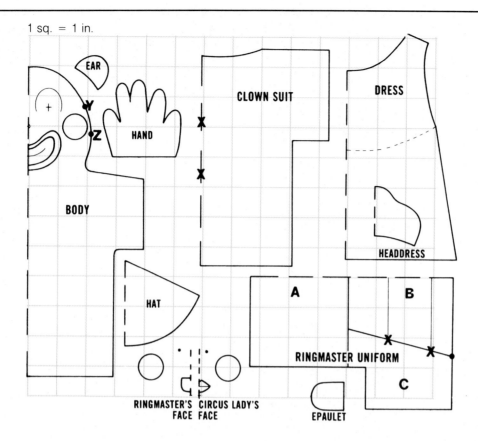

1 sq. = 1 in.

EAR

HAND

CLOWN SUIT

DRESS

BODY

HEADDRESS

HAT

A

B

RINGMASTER UNIFORM

C

RINGMASTER'S
FACE

CIRCUS LADY'S
FACE

EPAULET

in half lengthwise. Baste along fold ¼" in from edge; pull basting thread and gather piece to 12" length. Cut 12" piece red ribbon and stitch to tutu over basting to make waistband. Cut strung sequins to fit and stitch along waistband as shown. Using dash line on pattern as a guide for placement, slipstitch waistband of tutu to dress, overlapping ends in back. Place dress on puppet. To make headdress, cut one cardboard and two satin pieces, adding seam allowance to only one fabric piece (front). Lay front, wrong side up, on flat surface. Cover one side of cardboard with white glue and place, glue side down, in center of satin; glue seam allowances to back of cardboard, then glue remaining satin piece, wrong side down, to back, aligning edges with edges of cardboard. Cut strung sequins to fit and glue to edges of front as shown. Glue or stitch headdress to puppet's head.

Lion

SIZE
11" long.

EQUIPMENT
Pencil. Ruler. Scissors. Paper for patterns. Dressmaker's tracing (carbon) paper. Dry ball-point pen. Cardboard, 2" × 20" piece. Sewing machine with zigzag attachment. Straight pins.

MATERIALS
Corduroy: wide wale, 15" × 20" piece gold; pinwale, 10" square pink. Felt scraps, gold, black, red. Yellow rug yarn, 15 yards. Two black shank-type buttons, ½" diameter. Red six-strand embroidery floss. Black heavy-duty thread. Sewing threads to match fabrics and felt.

1 sq. = 1 in.

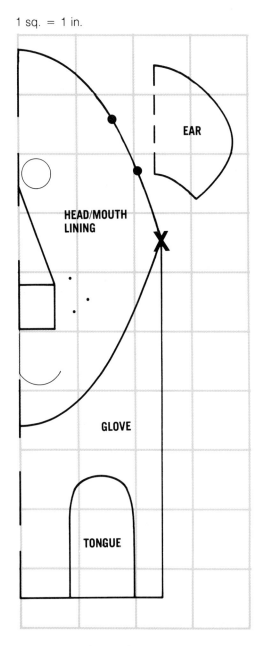

EAR

HEAD/MOUTH
LINING

GLOVE

TONGUE

DIRECTIONS FOR LION

Enlarge patterns by copying on paper ruled in 1″ squares; complete half-patterns indicated by dash lines. Using dressmaker's carbon and dry ball-point pen, transfer pattern outlines and X's to wrong side of fabric or felt, as directed below. When marking more than one piece on same fabric, leave at least ½″ between pieces. Cut out pieces as directed.

Using matching sewing thread, stitch pieces together as directed, with right sides facing, raw edges even, and making ¼″ seams; turn to right side.

On gold corduroy, mark one head, two ears, and two complete gloves, omitting inner lines. On pink corduroy, mark head again for mouth lining and two ears. Mark upper nose on gold felt, lower nose on black, tongue on red. Cut out all pieces, adding ¼″ seam allowance to corduroy pieces only. Using dressmaker's carbon and dry ball-point pen, transfer face to right side of head. Set machine for wide zigzag stitch (⅛″ or wider) and appliqué upper and lower nose pieces to head, using matching thread. Sew button eyes at open circles. With full six strands of red floss in embroidery needle, outline-stitch muzzle. For whiskers, pass doubled heavy-duty black thread back and forth through each side of nose, leaving 1½″ loops on either side; cut loops. For each ear, stitch a gold and pink ear together, leaving short end open; clip curve and turn; fold sides in ½″, as shown in photograph; baste. Pin ears, pink side down, to right side of head between dots (*see pattern*) so that raw edges of ears and head are even; baste. Stitch glove pieces together at sides from X to bottom, leaving bottom and top edges open. To make hair, closely wrap yarn around 2″ width of cardboard. Stitch across loops on one side; cut loops on opposite side; remove cardboard; trim ends. On right side, pin hair strip around curved opening of both glove sections so that stitched edge of strip and raw edge of fabric are even; baste. Pin mouth lining to head and stitch along "chin" between X's. Matching X's, pin raw edges of head/mouth lining piece to each curved edge of glove. Stitch together all around, beginning and ending at a glove side seam and catching in ears and hair. Turn bottom of glove ¼″ to wrong side; stitch all around; turn to right side. With matching thread, slipstitch tongue to center of mouth lining along flat edge.

Circus Tent Tote

SIZE
About 10″ high.

EQUIPMENT
Pencil. Ruler. Scissors. Plain paper and tracing paper for patterns. Glue. Lightweight card-board. Compass. Sewing and embroidery needles. Straight pins. Sewing machine with zipper foot and zigzag attachment.

MATERIALS
Pinwale corduroy 45″ wide: ½ yard red, ¼ yard ecru. Red/white striped cotton fabric 36″ wide, ¾ yard for lining. Sewing thread to match fabrics. Red 6″ zipper. Red satin ribbon ⅛″ wide, 1½ yards. Green fringe 1½″ wide, one yard. Scraps of six-strand embroidery floss: red, gold, blue, green, orange, and pink. Wooden dowel ⅛″ in diameter, 3½″ piece. Polyester quilt batting. Two snap fasteners. Scrap of blue cardboard.

DIRECTIONS FOR TOTE
Trace actual-size patterns and markings for roof segment and scallop; complete half-patterns, indicated by dash lines. Using com-pass, mark 11¼″-diameter circle on plain paper. Glue papers to lightweight cardboard; cut out on marked lines for three templates. Use templates to mark pieces on wrong sides of fabrics as follows: Using pencil or pin, indicate direction of nap on wrong side of corduroy; when marking pieces, place them so nap runs in direction of arrows on pattern. Place templates ½″ from fabric edges and 1″ apart. Using pencil, draw around templates on ecru fabric for six scallops and three roof segments; mark three roof segments and one circle on red corduroy; also mark two circles on lining fabric. Cut out pieces ½″ beyond marked lines. Cut out additional pieces as directed; seam allowance is included in measurements. With right sides facing, edges even, and making ½″ seams, join pieces for

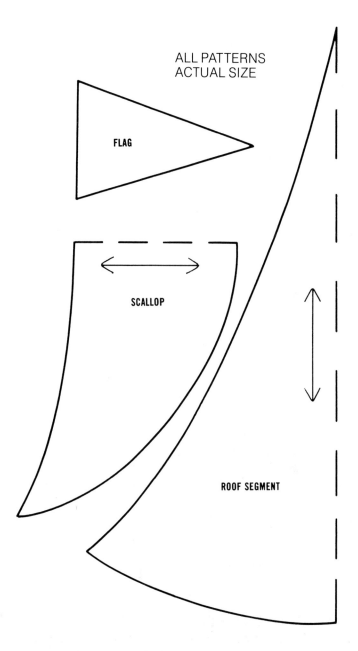

ALL PATTERNS
ACTUAL SIZE

FLAG

SCALLOP

ROOF SEGMENT

tote as directed below; use matching thread.

Alternating colors, stitch long sides of roof segments together to make roof (see photo-graph). To make handles, cut two 4″ × 21″ straps from red corduroy, with nap running lengthwise. Double-fold straps lengthwise and stitch ¼″ in from each long edge for 1″-

wide straps. Pin straps to roof as shown; baste. Turn longest (bottom) edge of each scallop ⅛" to wrong side twice and stitch close to fold. Cut six 8" pieces of red satin ribbon; topstitch one to each scallop, ¼" in from bottom edge. Pin top of each scallop to bottom of a roof segment; stitch roof edge all around, catching in strap ends. From red corduroy cut 7" × 37" piece for tent wall, with nap running lengthwise. Place piece on flat surface with long edges at top and bottom; mark bottom with tailor's tack or chalk; measure 4" up and 1½" in from lower left corner and mark point with pin for placement of appliqué. To make appliqué, place a scrap of ecru corduroy about 5" square right side up on flat surface; carefully print the word "CIRCUS" in center, using pencil and making letters about ⅜" high. Embroider letters in outline stitch (*see Embroidery Stitch Details, page 185*), using all six strands of floss in embroidery needle and a different color floss for each letter. When embroidery is completed, trim appliqué to measure 1" × 2½". Placing lower left corner at pin, baste sign to tent wall, so that long edges are parallel with bottom. Set sewing machine for wide zigzag stitch (⅛" or wider) and appliqué to wall around edges; removing basting. At short ends of wall, press ½" to wrong side; with right side out, baste pressed edges together to form tube. With zipper pull at bottom and zipper front facing wrong side of fabric, pin zipper to inside of tube, so that teeth align with basting and ends are ½" in from raw edges. Using zipper foot, topstitch ¼" from

each side of basting, catching in zipper; remove basting; do not open zipper.

Use template to cut two circles from batting; do not add seam allowance. Baste each to center of a lining circle on wrong side. Cut 7" × 37" piece from lining fabric for wall lining. Cut 6½" × 36½" piece batting and baste to center of wall lining on wrong side. Press short edges of wall lining ¼" to wrong side. Placing ends even with zipper, pin one long edge of lining to bottom edge of tube. Stitch along bottom edge for 3" on either side of zipper to make bottom of tent flap; open zipper. Pin remainder of bottom edge of wall lining to outside of one lining circle; ease to fit all but 6" of circumference; stitch. In same manner, stitch wall bottom to corduroy circle, then stitch raw edges of circles together; turn, so that right side of lining is out; slipstitch side edges of lining to wall. Baste remaining (top) edges of wall and lining together, ⅜" in from the edge. Pin combined edges to roof; stitch all around; trim seam; do not turn. Press seam allowance of remaining circle to wrong side. Pin piece to inside of roof, with wrong sides facing, so that edge covers seam; slipstitch all around. Remove any visible basting threads from lining; turn tote right side out. Cut a piece of green fringe to fit and slipstitch around bottom of wall as shown. Sew snaps to inside of tent flap on either side of zipper. Using pattern, cut flag from blue cardboard and glue to one end of dowel. Use other end to push any visible raw edges of roof point to inside; push end of flag into point; glue or tack in place.

 Valarie & Vanessa

They're the best of friends all year round. They can trade clothes, too.

SIZE
Each doll, about 23″ tall.

EQUIPMENT
Pencil. Ruler. Paper for patterns. Beam compass. Sewing and embroidery scissors. Dressmaker's tracing (carbon) paper. Dry ballpoint pen. Tailor's chalk. Straight pins. Sewing and embroidery needles. Knitting needle. Safety pin. Sewing machine with zigzag attachment. Iron.

MATERIALS
For each doll: Heavyweight cotton knit fabric, such as double-knit, 45″ wide, ½ yard flesh color. White heavy-duty sewing thread. Two black half-ball buttons (shank type) ¾″. Sportweight yarn, 3 ozs. desired color for hair. Embroidery floss, one skein to match yarn; small amount red. Polyester fiberfill for stuffing. Coral crayon. **For clothes** (Note: All clothes will fit each doll shown): **For dress and matching bloomers:** Voile fabric 54″ wide: ¾ yard desired print; ⅛ yard white. Nylon net 72″ wide, ½ yard white. White nylon pre-gathered lace trim ½″ wide, 1 yard. White flat elastic ¼″ wide, ⅝ yard. Grosgrain ribbon ⅝″ wide, 1 yard to match dress fabric. Two small snaps. **For shoes:** Black "patent leather" vinyl, piece 12″ square. Two white ½″ buttons. **For socks:** Purchased stretch socks with ruffled trim, size 1 year. **For cape:** Wool fabric 54″ wide, ¾ yard red. Fabric for lining 45″ wide, ¾ yard red. Baby rickrack, 2½ yards yellow. Flat elastic ¼″ wide, ½ yard.

Two tiny snaps. **For coat, muff, and earmuffs:** Teal blue wool fabric, 22″ × 25″ piece. Same-size piece lining fabric. White long-pile fake fur, piece 18″ square. Scrap of white cotton fabric. Three white ⅜″ buttons (shank type). Child's plastic hairband. White 4-ply yarn. **For each:** Sewing thread to match fabrics and trims.

GENERAL DIRECTIONS
Enlarge patterns by copying on paper ruled in 1″ squares. Complete half-patterns, indicated by heavy dash lines. Following individual directions below, use dressmaker's carbon and dry ball-point pen to transfer patterns to wrong side of fabrics and fake fur, unless otherwise directed, placing them ½″ from fabric edges and ½″ apart. When marking pieces on knit fabric, corduroy or fake fur, follow arrows on patterns for placement on ribs of fabric or nap on fur. Cut out pieces ¼″ beyond marked lines for seam allowance, unless otherwise indicated. When cutting additional pieces without patterns, do not add seam allowance. After cutting out knit and fake fur pieces, zigzag-stitch raw edges to prevent raveling. To assemble doll and clothes, pin pieces together with right sides facing and raw edges even; stitch on marked lines with matching thread, making ¼″ seams, unless otherwise directed. Clip into seam allowance at curves and across corners; turn piece to right side and poke out corners with

knitting needle. Referring to photograph, assemble and finish pieces as directed below.

DIRECTIONS FOR DOLLS

(for each): Read General Directions. Prepare patterns following General Directions. From knit fabric, cut three heads (front, back, and lining), two bodies, two arms, two soles, and four legs, reversing pattern for second and fourth legs; also cut 2½" × 25½" strip for head center. Mark eyes and mouth on right side of one head piece (front). With wrong sides facing, stitch head front and lining together, leaving neck edge open. Do not turn; stuff evenly with fiberfill (or use layer of batting), so that face resembles a plump pancake; stitch neck opening closed. Attach buttons for eyes with needle and thread, stitching through all layers and pulling thread tight; buttons will sink into padding slightly. With red embroidery floss, straight-stitch mouth in same manner (*see Embroidery Stitch Details, page 185*). "Rouge" cheeks with coral crayon. With right sides facing, pin long side edges of head center to face and head back with bottom straight edges even. Stitch, leaving neck edge open. Fold neck ¼" to wrong side; baste. Turn head to right side. Stuff firmly.

Fold arms in half lengthwise, right side in. Stitch raw arm and hand edges, leaving top straight edges open. Turn and stuff. Baste each arm closed ⅛" from raw edges, enclosing stuffing. Stitch legs together in pairs at front and back, leaving top and bottom edges open. Stitch soles to bottom openings, matching dots; turn and stuff. Baste each leg top as for arm, but with seams centered. On right side of one body (front), pin arms ½" down from shoulders, so that arms cross, thumbs point down, and side edges are even; stitch. Pin and stitch legs to body bottom in similar manner, so that toes point toward shoulders. Place body front on work surface with limbs on top. Fold left arm across body, so that hand extends above right shoulder and seam allowance faces out. Pin left side of body

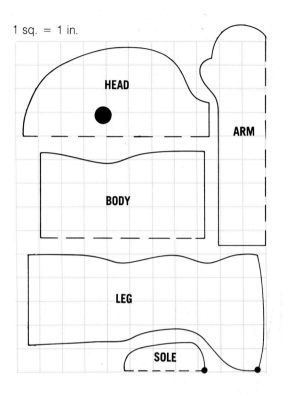

1 sq. = 1 in.

HEAD
ARM
BODY
LEG
SOLE

back, wrong side up, to body front; stitch. Pin and stitch right side of body in same manner (body will resemble a tube with hands extending above and legs below). Push legs up through body, so that only seam allowance extends at bottom; pin and stitch body bottom. Turn and stuff. Turn raw edges ¼" to inside; slipstitch opening closed. Using heavy-duty thread, slipstitch head, centered, over shoulders.

Hair: *For Vanessa* Cut 200 27" strands of yarn. To make set of curls, wind a strand of yarn around four extended fingers of one hand; tie together at center with matching floss. Make 200 sets of curls in this manner. Tack two sets of curls to center of front head seam. Working down toward cheeks, tack nine sets of curls along seam on each side. Tack ten sets across nape of neck between side curls. Tack remaining curls to crown, covering head. *For Valarie* Starting at center of front head seam, mark center part to nape of neck with pencil. Cut 156 14″ strands of yarn. Working with groups of 12 strands at a time and all six strands of matching floss in needle, stitch center of each group to part, working from front head seam to back; tack to head near cheeks to secure; trim ends. For two side puffs and bangs, cut 24 27″ strands of yarn. Following directions above, make 24 sets of curls. Referring to photograph for placement, tack 11 sets of curls to each side of head near cheeks for puffs; tack two curls to front of part for bangs.

DIRECTIONS FOR CLOTHES

Read General Directions. Prepare patterns for clothes. Make separate patterns for the following: dress bodice front and back; coat front, back, and lining.

Additional directions: *To assemble* When assembling pieces, press seams open after stitching, unless otherwise directed; do not press fake fur or vinyl. *To gather* Hand- or machine-baste piece ⅛″ from raw edge. Pull basting to gather edge to fit as specified. Pin piece in place; adjust gathers evenly and stitch. *To finish edges with lace trim* Press fabric edge ¼″ to wrong side. Cut lace trim to fit. Pin lace to fabric on wrong side, so that ruffle extends beyond fold. Topstitch close to fold. *To bind neck edges* Following individual directions, cut a fabric strip same length as neck, plus ½″. Press short edges and one long edge ¼″ to wrong side, unless otherwise specified. Place strip on neck, right sides facing and with raw edges even; pin and stitch. Fold strip to inside of garment, then slipstitch in place.

Bloomers (not shown): From voile print fabric, cut two bloomers. Press waist edges ¼″ to wrong side. Cut two 5½″ lengths of elastic. Pin elastic across wrong side of each waist ⅛″ from fold; stitch, using machine set for wide zigzag stitch. Reset machine for straight stitch. Finish leg bottoms with lace

trim, following directions above. Cut two 5″ lengths of elastic. Starting at inseam, pin elastic to leg bottom on wrong side 1¼″ above fabric edge; zigzag-stitch in place. Reset machine for straight stitch. Stitch bloomers together at center front and back from waist to crotch. Stitch each inseam from lace to crotch; turn to right side.

Dress: From voile print fabric, cut two sleeves, one bodice front, and two bodice backs, reversing for second back; also cut 48¼″ × 8″ skirt. From white voile, cut four collars, reversing for second and fourth pieces. Mark open dots on bodice front and collars; make tailor's tacks through dots to mark right side. From nylon net, cut two 48¼″ × 6¾″ pieces for underskirt. Stitch bodice front and backs together at shoulders. *Each sleeve* Press sleeve bottom ¼″ to wrong side. Cut 4½″ length of elastic. Stitch to sleeve bottom as for bloomers waist. Reset machine for straight stitch. Baste upper curved edge of sleeve between X's. Pin lower curved edges of sleeve to front and back armhole of bodice below X's. Gather upper curved edge to fit armhole; pin and stitch. Stitch underarm and side in a continuous seam. Turn assembled bodice to right side. *Collar* Cut two lengths of lace trim to fit outer curved edges of collar. Place collars together in pairs, right sides facing; sandwich one length of lace between each pair with ruffles facing in and outer edges even; pin and stitch. Turn collars to right side; press. Stitch collars to right side of neck, matching raw edges and tailor's tacks; clip into seam allowance through all thicknesses. From white voile, cut 1½″-wide strip and bind neck, following directions above. *Skirt* Stack net underskirt pieces on work surface with long edges at top and bottom. Place skirt right side up on underskirt with top (waist) edges even; pin. Machine-baste close to waist through all thicknesses. Pull threads to gather waist of skirt and underskirt to fit bodice waist; stitch. *To finish dress* Press center back edges ⅛″ to wrong side; topstitch. Starting at hem, stitch center backs together to 2″ below waist; press seam open. Above seam, press edges under ⅛″; stitch. Turn dress to right side. Press hem ¼″ then 1″ to wrong side; slipstitch. Sew snaps to neck opening and center back. For belt, trim ribbon ends on an angle. Pin belt, centered, across bodice front between side seams, so that bottom edge of belt is even with waist; slipstitch in place along bottom edge.

Shoes: On wrong side of vinyl, mark two soles; also mark four uppers, marking strap on two pieces only and reversing for each second piece. Cut out, omitting seam allowance on each upper at top and strap edges. Stitch uppers together in pairs at front and back. Stitch soles to uppers, matching dots; turn. Test-fit shoes on doll; mark placement for strap ends and remove shoes. Tack strap ends in place; sew a button over each tack.

Cape: From wool fabric, cut hood. Also mark and cut out cape as follows: Using compass, mark two concentric circles with diameters of 3½″ and 22½″; mark center. Using ruler and tailor's chalk, draw a line (radius) from center point to outer circle. Cut on marked lines, cutting away inner circle for neck opening. Use cape and hood to cut matching lining pieces. *Hood* Stitch darts on hood and lining; press darts to one side. Stitch hood and lining together at curved edges, leaving straight edge (neck) open; turn to right side; press; baste close to neck edge. Topstitch ⅛″ then ⅝″ from curved edge to form casing. Use safety pin to work elastic through casing; topstitch each end to secure. *To assemble cape* Stitch cape and lining together at outer curved edges (hem) and straight edges (center front), leaving neck edge open; turn and press. Center neck edge of hood and hood lining along cape neck, right sides facing; pin and stitch, being careful not to catch cape lining beneath. Turn seam allowance to inside, between cape and lining; baste. Press neck edge of cape lining ¼″ to inside; slip into fold

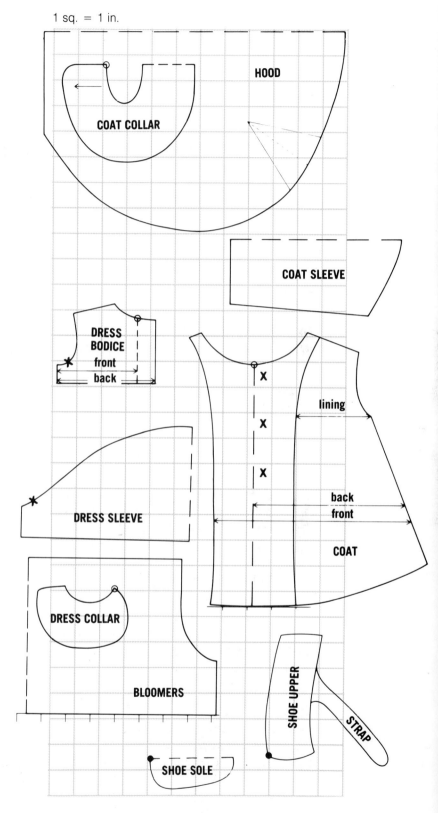

1 sq. = 1 in.

HOOD

COAT COLLAR

COAT SLEEVE

DRESS BODICE
front
back

lining

X

X

X

back
front

COAT

DRESS SLEEVE

DRESS COLLAR

BLOOMERS

SHOE UPPER

STRAP

SHOE SOLE

allowance at curves. Pin neck lining in place, covering seam allowance of hood; slipstitch. Following photograph, pin and stitch rickrack in place around cape. Sew on snaps at neck edge and center front.

Coat: From wool fabric, cut two coat fronts, one coat back, and two sleeves. From lining fabric cut two lining fronts and one back. Stitch coat fronts and back together at shoulder seams. *Each sleeve* Baste upper edge of sleeve and ease to fit sleeve opening; pin and stitch sleeve and underarm, making continuous seam. Press coat fronts to wrong side along dash line for facing. *Lining* Stitch shoulder seams and attach sleeves as for coat. Place coat and lining together and stitch curved edge of lining front to facing edge of coat front; stitch neck edges of coat and lining together. Turn, so that right side of lining is outside, and push coat sleeves into lining sleeves. Turn cuff edge of coat sleeves ¾" to wrong side; press. Turn cuff edge of each lining sleeve ¾" to wrong side and slipstitch to coat sleeve ½" above crease. Turn hem of coat 1½" to wrong side and press. Turn lining hem 1½" to wrong side and slipstitch ½" above coat hem. From white fake fur, cut one collar and slipstitch inside edge to neck edge of coat, matching open circles (*see pattern*). Sew buttons to right coat front at X's; sew snaps to inside right front and left front to correspond with buttons. **Muff:** From fake fur, cut piece 8" square. Fold in half; stitch edges opposite fold together. Turn remaining edges ½" to wrong side and slipstitch; turn muff to right side. **Earmuffs:** Using compass, draw two 3"-diameter circles on wrong side of fake fur and cut out. Draw two 2½"-diameter circles on heavy cardboard and cut out. To wrong side of each fake fur circle, glue a cardboard circle; fold edge to back and glue. Closely wrap or cast on loops of white yarn to cover hairband. Glue muffs to ends on each side.

illiam & Wendy *are ready for summertime fun in their machine-appliquéd bathing costumes.*

SIZES
Tote, 13″ × 18¼″. Dolls, about 23″ high.

EQUIPMENT
Pencil. Ruler. Paper for patterns. Scissors. Masking tape. Dressmaker's tracing (carbon) paper. Dry ball-point pen. Straight pins. Sewing and embroidery needles. Knitting needle. Sewing machine with zigzag attachment. **For inner tube:** Compass. Zipper-foot attachment.

MATERIALS
For each doll and matching tote: Sturdy pre-washed cotton fabric such as lightweight canvas or kettle cloth 45″ wide, 1 yard off-white. Jumbo rickrack, 1½ yards navy (tote). Vogart® Ball Point Paint Tubes, one tube each color shown on tote (*see photograph*). Polyester fiberfill for stuffing. **For William:** Closely woven cotton fabric 36″ wide, ⅓ yard each: white, red. Navy/white striped cotton belting ¾″ wide, ⅔ yard. White lightweight non-woven interfacing 18″ wide, ¼ yard. Fusible bonding 18″ wide, ¼ yard. Sewing thread to match fabrics and trim. Yellow sport-weight yarn. Yellow six-strand cotton embroidery floss. Polyester braided cord ⅛″ diameter, ⅓ yard red. Two silver-colored metal D rings 1″ diameter. Whistle. **For Wendy:** Calico fabric 45″ wide, ½ yard yellow; scrap of blue. Blue satin ribbon ⅜″ wide, 16″. Sewing thread to match fabrics and trim. Dark brown sport-weight yarn. Dark brown six-strand cotton embroidery floss. **For inner tube:** Calico fabric 45″ wide, ¼ yard red; scraps of yellow, blue, green. Lightweight cotton welting ⅛″ diameter, 1½ yards red. Red sewing thread.

DIRECTIONS FOR TOTES
(for each): Enlarge patterns by copying on paper ruled in 1″ squares. From off-white fabric, cut two 14″ × 20″ rectangles for tote front and back and two 3¼″ × 12¾″ straps. On wrong side of front and back, mark a line 1¼″ below top edge; on front, mark another line ½″ up from bottom edge. Baste lines to mark right side. **To paint:** Place tote front, right side up, on work surface; tape edges to secure. Place pattern face up on fabric, centering it between basted lines. Slip light-color dressmaker's carbon between; transfer pattern, using dry ball-point pen. Color design with ball-point paint tubes as follows; before beginning, read manufacturer's directions and test paints on scrap. Go over design lines first, then fill in areas solidly: Paint facial features, referring to photograph for colors. Go over remaining design lines with black,

1 sq. = 1 in.

except for Wendy's pail, go over stripes on sails with yellow, waves with medium blue. Fill in areas as shown. **To assemble:** Pin together tote front and back with right sides facing and raw edges even; stitch sides and bottom with matching thread, making ½" seams; trim bottom corners. Still wrong side out, turn bag so a side seam is facing you. Spread corner to flatten into triangle and stitch across triangle, 1½" above end of seam. Repeat on opposite corner, thus "boxing" bottom of tote. Press top edge of tote ¼" then

½" to wrong side; turn tote to right side. Cut 27" length of rickrack. Starting at one side seam, pin rickrack around top of tote, with bottom edge even with basting; topstitch with matching thread. On each strap, fold and press one long edge 1" to wrong side; press other long edge ⅜", then ¾" to wrong side, overlapping first fold; pin. Cut two pieces of rickrack same length as straps. Stitch rickrack, centered, to front of each strap. With right side of strap ends facing wrong side of tote, pin a strap to tote front and back

2¼″ from side seams, so that ends are even with hem; topstitch on right side over previous stitching.

GENERAL DIRECTIONS FOR DOLLS

Enlarge patterns by copying on paper ruled in 1″ squares. Complete half-patterns indicated by long dash lines. Use dressmaker's carbon and dry ball-point pen to transfer patterns to wrong side of fabric, unless otherwise directed; place pieces ½″ from fabric edges and ½″ apart. Cut out ¼″ beyond marked lines for seam allowance. When cutting additional pieces without patterns, do not add seam allowance.

To cut out body: Following directions above, transfer outline of body front only to off-white fabric for William and Wendy; cut out. Use body front as pattern to cut body back.

To paint face and shoes: Place body front, right side up, on work surface; tape edges to secure. Center pattern face up on fabric; slip light-color dressmaker's carbon between; transfer fine solid lines only. Remove pattern and carbon. Transfer shoe backs to body back in same manner, reversing Wendy's shoe for opposite foot. Color design with ball-point paint tubes as follows; before beginning, read manufacturer's directions and test paints on scrap. Go over design lines first, then fill in areas solidly: Paint facial features, referring to photograph, for colors. Go over remaining design lines with black. Fill in shoe fronts as shown, extending sides and bottom of each to ⅛″ from fabric edges. Fill in shoe backs in same manner, using red for Wendy.

To appliqué clothes: Transfer appliqué pieces, indicated by heavy lines, to right side of fabrics, following individual directions. Referring to How to Appliqué, page 179, cut out pieces for machine appliqué; you need not make cardboard patterns for these dolls. Following directions for machine appliqué and individual directions, pin, baste, and stitch pieces in place on backgrounds (*see original patterns for placement*).

To assemble body: Pin pieces together with right sides facing and raw edges even; stitch on marked lines with matching thread, making ¼″ seams and leaving 3″ opening at top. Clip into seams at curves and across corners; turn to right side and poke out corners with knitting needle. Stuff firmly with fiberfill. Turn raw edges ¼″ to inside; slip-stitch opening closed. Finish each doll as directed below.

DIRECTIONS FOR WILLIAM

Read General Directions. Cut out body front and back, following General Directions. Paint facial features on body front. Transfer appliqué pieces for two white shirts and two red bathing trunks; transfer lettering, centered, to right side of one shirt (front) for placement guide; cut out. From red fabric, cut 5″ × 8″ rectangle. Cut one matching piece each from fusible bonding and interfacing. Fuse interfacing to wrong side of matching fabric piece with fusible bonding, following manufacturer's directions. Transfer lettering to right side of fused fabric; cut on marked lines, using tips of scissors for internal cutouts on A, R, and D. Pin and baste individual letters to shirt front, matching outlines. Set machine as for machine appliqué with red thread. Stitch around letters and cutouts, covering raw edges. Appliqué clothing pieces on body front and back, using same thread. Reset machine for straight stitch. From red fabric, cut two 1⅛″ × 1¾″ rectangles for belt loops. On each piece, fold under 1¾″ edges, overlapping at center back; press. Using white thread, topstitch ⅛″ from folds. Fold under ends of each loop ¼″; baste. With short folded edges at top and bottom, pin loops to front of bathing trunks 2¼″ from side seams, so that top of each is even with shirt/trunks joining; tack in place at corners. Assemble body, following General Directions.

1 sq. = 1 in.

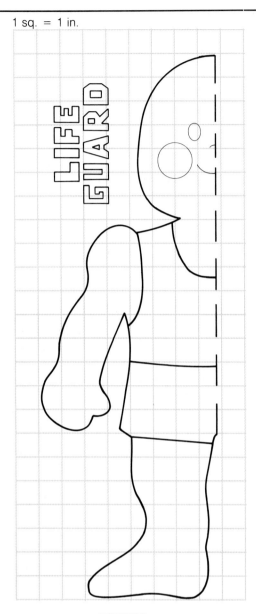

WILLIAM

Hair: Cut four 3-yard lengths of yarn; bundle together with ends even. Tack one end of bundle to head 2″ above right eye, using all six strands of floss in needle. Bring yarn down to right cheek, tack in place, back to top, tack, down again, continuing around back of head to left cheek but leaving center top uncovered; do not end off. Bring yarn up to starting point; tack. Working from this point, lap yarn back and forth, tacking as

before, to cover top and make forelock over left eye. At end of last full lap, fold under yarn ends and tack in place with invisible stitches.

Belt: Fold ends of belting ¼″ to wrong side; topstitch. Thread one end of belt through D rings; slipstitch in place on wrong side. Fold under free end of belt 4″; slipstitch. Thread belt through loops and fasten. *To finish* Thread whistle onto braided cord; place around neck and tie ends together.

DIRECTIONS FOR WENDY

Read General Directions. Cut out and paint body front and back, following General Directions. When all painting is complete, transfer appliqué pieces for two bathing suits to yellow calico; cut out. Appliqué pieces to body front and back, using blue thread. Reset machine for straight stitch. Assemble body, following General Directions.

Hair: Starting 2″ above eyes, use pencil to mark center part to nape of neck. Cut 156 12″ lengths of yarn. Working with groups of 12 strands at a time and all six strands of matching floss in needle, stitch center of each group to part, working from forehead back; tack to head near cheeks to secure; trim ends. For two curly buns, cut 22 27″ lengths of yarn. To make a set of curls, wind a strand of yarn around four extended fingers of one hand; tie together at center with floss. Make 11 sets of curls for each bun. Referring to color photograph for placement, tack curls to head near cheeks. *To finish* Cut ribbon ends on an angle. Tie into bow and tack to bathing suit front as shown.

Skirt: From yellow calico, cut piece full fabric width to depth of 5″. From blue calico scrap, cut 1½″ × 26″ strip for waistband/ties, piecing together as necessary. Press selvages and one long edge of skirt ¼″ to wrong side; topstitch. Baste ⅛″ in from other long edge. Pull basting to gather to 12¾″; press. Press

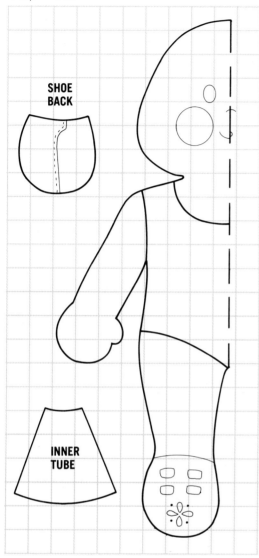

SHOE BACK

INNER TUBE

WENDY

joining welting ends

one long edge of waistband/ties ¼" to wrong side. Center other long edge over gathered edge of skirt, right sides facing; pin and stitch, making ½" seam. Turn waistband to wrong side of skirt, so that folded tie edges are even; topstitch. Knot tie ends to prevent raveling. Turn up 1" hem at skirt bottom; stitch.

DIRECTIONS FOR INNER TUBE

Read General Directions. Using pattern, cut two inner tube pieces from each color calico, for eight pieces. Referring to photograph, stitch pieces together along straight edges to form inner tube front as shown; press seams open. Use assembled front as pattern to cut matching back from red calico. Measure inner and outer edges of tube; cut welting to each measured length, plus 1". Pin welting to right side of tube front, matching raw edges; overlap ends 1". Using zipper-foot attachment and starting 2" from beginning of welting, stitch all around tube to 1" from end of welting. Snip out 1" of cord from overlapping end. Turn under ½" of excess fabric and, butting ends of cord, fit it over the start of welting (*see diagram*). Finish stitching welting in place. Stitch together tube front and back at outer edges; turn to right side. On tube back, press under raw inner edge ¼", clipping into seam allowance as necessary. Pin inner opening closed about halfway around; slipstitch. Stuff tube firmly, slipstitching opening closed as you work around.

-Traordinary Animals *This knitted menagerie is full of wonderful characters —all made from soft yarn.*

Lamb

SIZE
16″ long.

MATERIALS
Phildar Nebuleuse, 2 balls Agneau (A). Phildar Pronostic, 1 ball Champagne (B). Knitting needles No. 3 (3¼ mm) and No. 11 (8 mm). Steel crochet hook No. 2. Stuffing. Two buttons for eyes. **Note:** Each square on chart equals 1 st. Work in stockinette st (k 1 row, p 1 row) throughout.

DIRECTIONS FOR LAMB
Underbody: Follow Chart 1. Beg at front leg, with B and No. 3 needles, cast on 8 sts. Work to top of chart. Bind off.

Sides: Follow Chart 2. With A and No. 11 needles, cast on 28 sts. Work to top of chart. Bind off. Make another piece, beg with a p row instead of a k row so that the two sides will face the same way. Use p side for right side.

Head: Follow Chart 3. With A and No. 11 needles, cast on 4 sts. Work to top of chart. Bind off. Use p side for right side.

Face: Follow Chart 4. With B and No. 3 needles, cast on 24 sts. Work to top of chart. Bind off.

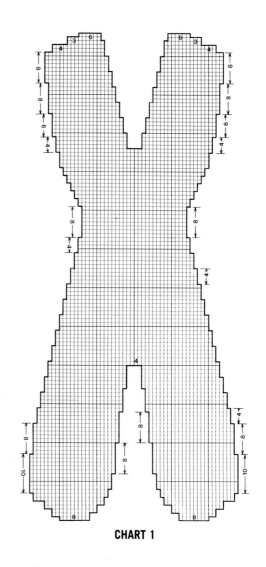

CHART 1

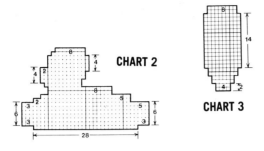

CHART 2

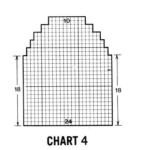

CHART 3

CHART 4

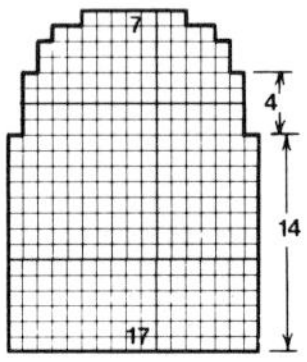

CHART 5

Ears (make 2): Follow Chart 5. With B and No. 3 needles, cast on 17 sts. Work to top of chart. Bind off. Work 2 rows of sc around sides and top of ear.

To finish: Sew pieces tog *(see photograph),* stuffing firmly before closing last seam. Sew on buttons for eyes. Embroider pink nose.

Baby Rabbit

SIZE
9½" long.

MATERIALS
Phildar Anouchka, 1 ball each Apricot (A), and White (W). Knitting needles No. 3 (3¼ mm). Stuffing. Felt or buttons for eyes. Small amount of pink or brown yarn for nose. **Note:** Use double strand of yarn throughout. Work in stockinette st (k 1 row, p 1 row) throughout.

DIRECTIONS FOR BABY RABBIT
Body: With A, cast on 9 sts. Following Chart 1, work to top of chart; bind off. Make another piece reversing shaping.

Front inside leg: Beg at lower edge of front leg, with W, cast on 9 sts. Following Chart 2, work to top of chart; bind off. Make another piece, reversing shaping.

Head gusset: Beg at top of back, with A, cast on 7 sts. Following Chart 3, work 40 rows, change to W and complete light portion of chart. Bind off (front neck).

Body gusset: Beg at top of back, with A, cast on 7 sts. Following Chart 4, work to top of chart changing to W as shown on light portion of chart.

Back leg: Beg at base of foot, with A, cast on 6 sts. Following Chart 5, work to top of chart. Work 2nd piece using W and reversing shaping. Work 2nd leg to match, reversing shaping.

Ears (make 4 pieces): With W, cast on 5 sts. Following Chart 6, work to top of chart.

Tail: With W, cast on 4 sts. Following Chart 7, work to top of chart.

To finish: Purl side of stockinette is right side of body. Sew inside front leg to body. Join in center. Insert head and body gussets. Turn right side out, stuff and close seam. Join back legs, turn right side out, stuff, and close seams. Sew leg to body. Join ear pieces and sew to top of head. Gather outside edge of tail, draw up, stuff, and sew to body. Cut oval eyes from felt and sew in place or sew on buttons. Embroider nose. Brush to make yarn fluffy.

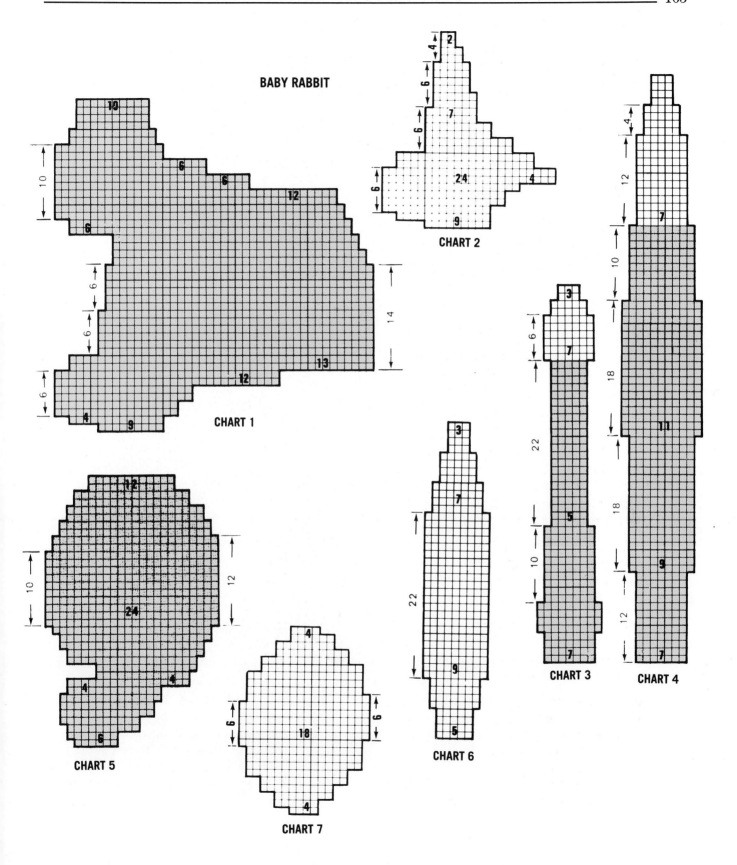

BABY RABBIT

CHART 1

CHART 2

CHART 3

CHART 4

CHART 5

CHART 6

CHART 7

Mama Rabbit

SIZE
16″ long.

MATERIALS
Phildar Dedicace, 3 balls pink (P). Phildar Anouchka, 2 balls white (W). Knitting needles No. 3 (3¼ mm). Stuffing. Felt or buttons for eyes. Small amount of gray yarn for nose.
Note: Use double strand of yarn throughout. Work in stockinette st (k 1 row, p 1 row) throughout.

DIRECTIONS FOR MAMA RABBIT
Body: With P, cast on 18 sts. Following Chart 1, work to top of chart; bind off. Make another piece reversing shaping.

Front inside leg: Beg at lower edge of front leg, with W, cast on 8 sts. Following Chart 2, work to top of chart; bind off. Make another piece reversing shaping.

Head gusset: Beg at top of back, with P, cast on 9 sts. Following Chart 3, work to top of chart. Bind off (front neck).

Body gusset: Beg at top of back, with P, cast on 9 sts. Following Chart 4, work to top of chart.

Back leg: Beg at base of foot, with P, cast on 6 sts. Following Chart 5, work to top of chart. Work 2nd piece using W and reversing shaping. Work 2nd leg to match, reversing shaping.

Ears (make 4 pieces): With W, cast on 6 sts. Following Chart 6, work to top of chart.

Tail: With W, cast on 6 sts. Following Chart 7, work to top of chart.

To finish: Finish as for Baby Rabbit.

MAMA RABBIT

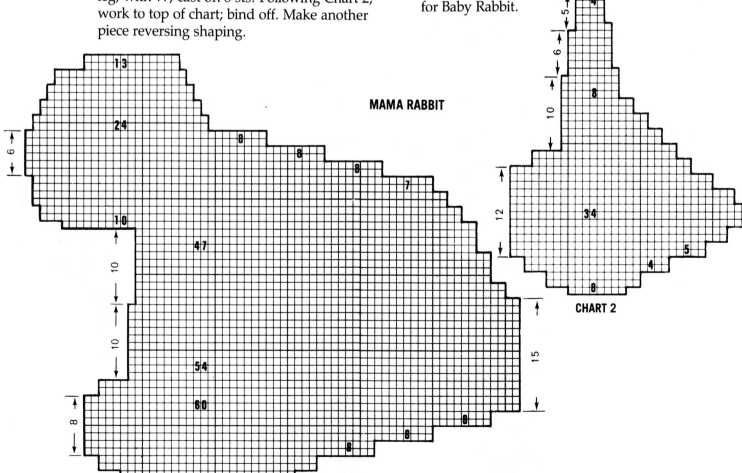

CHART 1

CHART 2

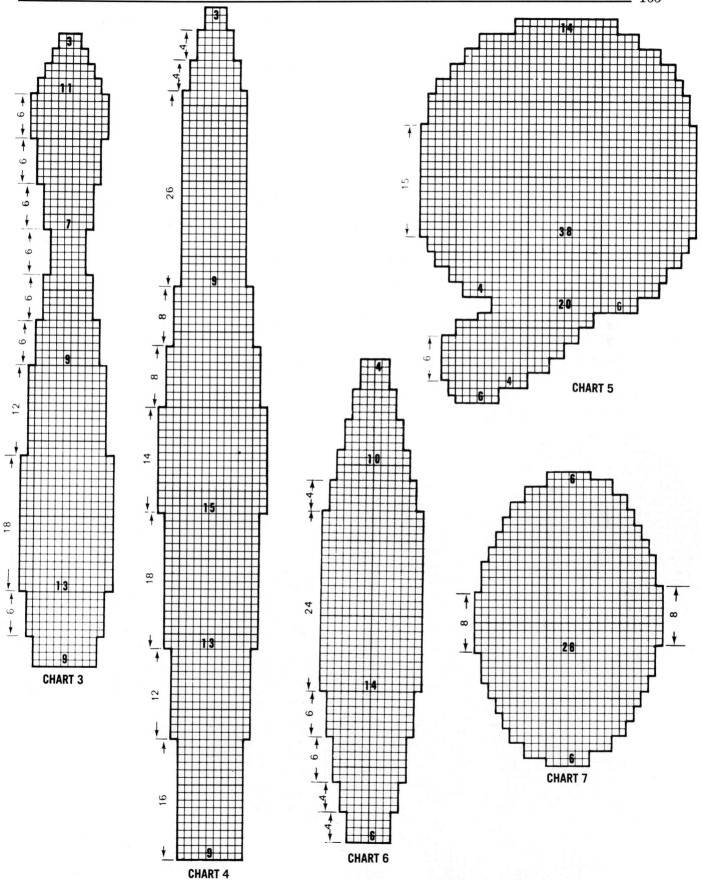

CHART 3

CHART 4

CHART 5

CHART 6

CHART 7

Piglet

SIZE
12″ long.

MATERIALS
Phildar Sagittaire, 2 balls pink (A), 1 ball each royal (B), mauve (C), and blue (D). Knitting needles No. 4 (3½ mm). Crochet hook size G/6 (4¼ mm). Stuffing. Two buttons. Felt or buttons for eyes.

DIRECTIONS FOR PIGLET AND CLOTHES

Back: Beg at lower body, cast on 50 sts A. Following Chart 1, work in stockinette st.

Left front: Beg at lower edge, cast on 24 sts A. Following Chart 2, work in stockinette st. Work right front to match, reversing all shapings.

Base: Beg at front edge, cast on 20 sts A. Following Chart 3, work in stockinette st.

Arms (make 2): Beg at top of arm, cast on 33 sts A. Following Chart 4, work in stockinette st.

Legs (make 2): Beg at foot, cast on 48 sts A. Following Chart 5, work in stockinette st.

Soles (make 2): Beg at heel edge, cast on 7 sts A. Following Chart 6, work in stockinette st.

Nose: Cast on 5 sts A. Following Chart 7, work in stockinette st. With crochet hook and A, ch 5. Sl st in first ch to form ring.

Rnd 1: 10 sc in ring; sl st in first sc.

Rnd 2: Ch 1, * 2 sc in next sc, sc in next sc, repeat from * around. Repeat rnd 2 until piece is 1″ in diameter.

Ears: Beg at lower edge, cast on 14 sts A. Following Chart 8, work in garter st (k every row). Work 2nd ear to match, reversing shaping.

Pullover: With C, cast on 94 sts. Work in k 1, p 1 ribbing for 3 rows.

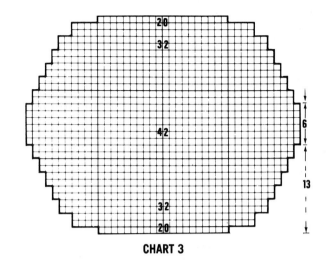

CHART 3

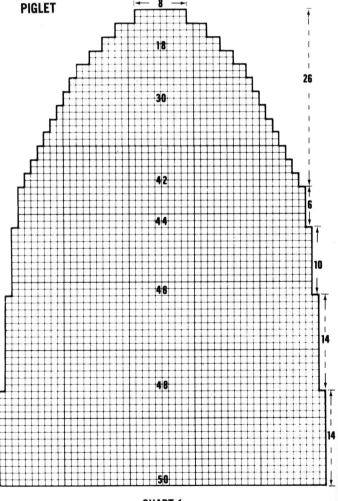

PIGLET

CHART 1

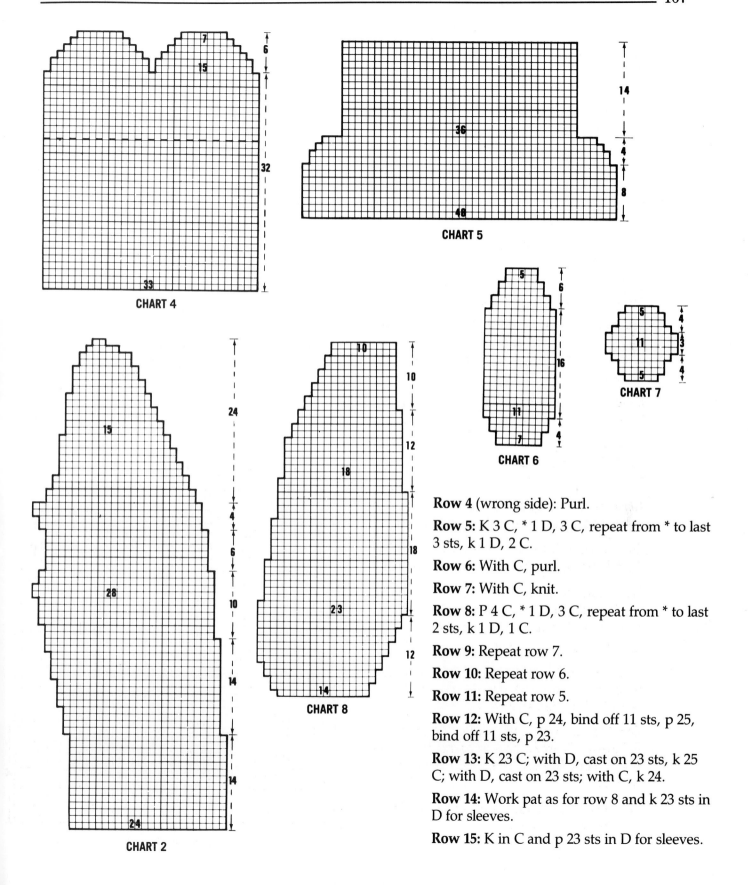

CHART 4

CHART 5

CHART 6

CHART 7

CHART 2

CHART 8

Row 4 (wrong side): Purl.

Row 5: K 3 C, * 1 D, 3 C, repeat from * to last 3 sts, k 1 D, 2 C.

Row 6: With C, purl.

Row 7: With C, knit.

Row 8: P 4 C, * 1 D, 3 C, repeat from * to last 2 sts, k 1 D, 1 C.

Row 9: Repeat row 7.

Row 10: Repeat row 6.

Row 11: Repeat row 5.

Row 12: With C, p 24, bind off 11 sts, p 25, bind off 11 sts, p 23.

Row 13: K 23 C; with D, cast on 23 sts, k 25 C; with D, cast on 23 sts; with C, k 24.

Row 14: Work pat as for row 8 and k 23 sts in D for sleeves.

Row 15: K in C and p 23 sts in D for sleeves.

Row 16: P all sts in C.

Row 17: Repeat row 5.

Row 18: Repeat row 8. Repeat last 2 rows 4 times more.

Row 27: With D, * K 9, k 2 tog, repeat from * to last 8 sts, k 8—108 sts. Continue with D, beg with a k row, work 6 rows in reverse stockinette st. Bind off.

Pants: Beg at lower leg, with B, cast on 66 sts.

Row 1: * K 1, p 1, repeat from * across.

Row 2: * P 1, k 1, repeat from * across. Repeat last 2 rows 3 times more. Keeping to seed st, bind off 3 sts at beg of next 2 rows, 2 sts at beg of next 4 rows, 1 st at beg of next 4 rows. Work even in seed st for 18 rows. Work in ribbing of k 1, p 1 for 2 rows. Bind off in ribbing.

Basset

SIZE
20″ long.

MATERIALS
Phildar Anouchka, 2 balls color Cuivre (A). Phildar Gin Fizz, 2 balls color Chaudron (B). Knitting needles Nos. 8 (5 mm) and 2 (2¾ mm). Stuffing. Two buttons for eyes. Dog collar. **Note:** Each square on chart equals 1 st. Work in stockinette st throughout. Purl side is right side of work.

DIRECTIONS FOR BASSET
Back: *First side* With No. 8 needles and B, cast on 21 sts. Follow Chart 1 to top of chart. Bind off. Make another piece reversing shaping.

Head back: Beg at center back, with No. 8 needles and B, cast on 10 sts. Follow Chart 2 to top of chart.

Head top: Beg at front of head, with No. 8 needles and B, cast on 19 sts. Follow Chart 3 to top of chart.

Make another piece to match.

To finish: Join front body seam above and below nose opening. Sew knitted nose piece into opening. Join side seams of front and back. Sew base in place leaving opening. Turn right side out, stuff, and close opening.

Join front leg seam. Sew sole in place. Turn right side out, stuff, and sew leg to base.

Join arm seam, turn right side out, stuff, close opening, and sew to body. Gather arm at wrist, pull up, and fasten off.

Join front, back, and leg seams of pants. Join pullover at center back.

Sew ears to top of head. Sew crocheted circle on nose. Cut out eyes from felt and sew in place or use buttons for eyes. Sew buttons to lower edge of pullover.

Front leg: Beg at top of leg, with No. 8 needles and B, cast on 8 sts. Follow Chart 4 to top of chart. Make another piece reversing shaping.

Back leg: Beg at top of leg, with No. 8 needles and B, cast on 10 sts. Follow Chart 5 to top of chart. Make another piece reversing shaping.

Lower body: Beg at back edge, with No. 2 needles and A, cast on 8 sts. Follow Chart A to top of chart (neck edge).

Lower head: Beg at muzzle, with No. 2 needles and A, cast on 20 sts. Follow Chart B to top of chart (neck edge).

Muzzle: Beg at nose, with No. 2 needles and A, cast on 16 sts. Follow Chart C to top of chart (sides of eyes).

Front leg: Beg at top of leg, with No. 2 needles and A, cast on 15 sts. Follow Chart D to top of chart. Work 2nd piece to match reversing shaping.

Back leg: Beg at top of leg, with No. 2 needles and A, cast on 20 sts. Follow Chart E to top of chart. Work 2nd piece to match reversing shaping.

Ears: Beg at top of ear, with No. 2 needles

CHART G 12 8 18 10 10 6 4 4 12

CHART E 11 30 20

CHART C 10 14 40 16

CHART B 25 24 40 20

CHART F 6 22 10 8 8 22 8 8 11 14

CHART D 12 6 4 4 6 6 6 6 6 8 6 6 4 4 6 15

BASSET

CHART A 6 16 30 8 8 8 8 21 20

CHART 1 9 6 13 35 17 8 7 21

CHART 2 6 34 10

CHART 3 15 12 19

CHART 4 6 6 6 6 6 8

CHART 5 10 8 16 8 10

and A, cast on 14 sts. Follow Chart F to top of chart. Work 2nd piece to match reversing shaping. Work another ear the same.

Tail: Beg at base of tail, with No. 2 needles and A, cast on 12 sts. Follow Chart G to top of chart. Work 2nd piece to match reversing shaping.

To finish: Make up all B pieces with purl side out. Join back and side darts on top head piece. Sew muzzle and back head to top head. Join body and sew to back head. Join lower head and lower body and sew in place leaving an opening. Turn to right side, stuff, and close opening.

Join front and back leg pieces with one A and one B to each leg. Turn out legs, stuff, and sew to body. Join tail; stuff and sew in place. Join ear piece and sew to head. Sew on button eyes.

Yuletide Characters *A chubby Santa Claus, his little elves, and a soft plush reindeer are cuddly friends.*

Santa and Elves

SIZE
Santa, about 18" high; elf, about 9" high.

EQUIPMENT
Soft pencil. Ruler. Paper for patterns. Small compass. Beam compass. Dressmaker's tracing (carbon) paper. Dry ball-point pen. Embroidery and regular scissors. Straight pins. Sewing and embroidery needles. Sewing machine.

MATERIALS FOR SANTA AND SIX ELVES
Stretch terry fabric 45" wide, ⅝ yard each red and green. Cotton knit fabric 45" wide, ⅓ yard flesh color. White plush or short-pile fake fur 60" wide, ⅛ yard. Sewing thread to match fabrics and fur. Six-strand cotton embroidery floss: red, blue. Rose crayon. Polyester fiberfill. Seven ½" jingle bells.

DIRECTIONS FOR SANTA OR ELF
Enlarge patterns by copying on paper ruled in 1" squares; complete half-patterns indicated by dash lines. Following directions below, transfer patterns to wrong side of fabrics or fur, using dressmaker's carbon and dry ball-point pen. Mark additional pieces without patterns, using compass or ruler and pencil. Cut out pieces on marked lines, unless otherwise directed. Directions given are for

Santa and, where different, are in parentheses for elf. Mark and cut out the following pieces: From red (green) terry, cut hat, adding ¼" seam allowance at each back edge; also cut circles with the following diameters: body 17" (8"), two arms 9" (4"). From knit fabric, cut the following circles: head 9" (4"), two hands 3½" (1¼"); for Santa, also cut 1¼" circle for nose. From plush or fake fur, mark and cut 13" × 3½" (8" × 1½") rectangle for hat brim, marking short edges parallel to nap; for Santa, also cut beard, referring to arrow on pattern for placement on nap and adding ¼" fold allowance at top edge.

On right side of fabric, baste all around body ¼" from edge, using doubled thread in needle and long running stitches; pull thread to gather slightly, forming "pouch." Stuff lightly with fiberfill, then pull thread tightly to gather opening closed; secure thread. Construct head, hands, and Santa's nose in same manner. **Each arm:** Fold arm in half right side in, matching edges; pinch center of fold gently between thumb and index finger of one hand. Flatten assembled hand and slip it into arm, so that gathered edge is centered on fold and caught between thumb and index finger; pin through all thicknesses. Topstitch hand ⅜" from fold; remove pins. Construct arm as for body. Place body on work surface

with gathered edge (neck) at top. Pin arms against body sides as shown in photograph, so that gathered edges of arms are even with neck and spaced 3″ (1½″) apart; slipstitch. **Head:** Flatten head so that gathered edge is at center back. Following large or small diagram, use pencil to mark eyes and mouth on head front. To embroider, work with six (three) strands of blue floss in needle for eyes, three strands of red for mouth. Begin a length by knotting one end and running needle through head from back to front; tug floss gently so that knot passes through fabric and is embedded in stuffing. To end off, run needle through head from front to back; tug floss gently and clip excess. When making stitches, pull floss tightly to form facial contours. (*See Embroidery Stitch Details, page 185.*) For Santa, work eyes in straight stitch; outline mouth in backstitch. For elf, work mouth in horizontal straight stitch; for each eye, work a cross-stitch over a vertical straight stitch. When embroidery is complete, slipstitch Santa's nose in place as indicated by dotted line on diagram. "Rouge" cheeks with crayon; color tip of Santa's nose and inner mouth. **Hat:** Fold hat in half lengthwise right side in. Machine-stitch ¼″ from back edges; turn to right side. Stuff bottom half of hat lightly. Place hat on head so that seam is at center back and raw edge frames face; backstitch in place close to edge. Fold long edges of hat brim ⅞″ (⅜″) to wrong side; slipstitch. With right sides facing, whipstitch ends together to form a ring; turn to right side. Slip brim over hat, matching seams in back and covering raw edge; pin. Slipstitch brim edges in place. **To finish:** Pin head to body between arms as shown; slipstitch in place. Sew jingle bell to hat top. For Santa, fold top edge of beard ¼″ to wrong side; slipstitch. Pin beard to face as shown; slipstitch top edge in place.

Fuzzy Reindeer

SIZE
18″ high.

EQUIPMENT
Pencil. Ruler. Paper for patterns. Dressmaker's tracing (carbon) paper. Dry ball-point pen. Scissors. Pinking shears. Straight pins. Sewing needle. Knitting needle. Sewing machine.

MATERIALS
Reddish-brown plush or short-pile fake fur 60″ wide, ½ yard. White plush or short-pile fake fur, piece 13″ square. Red cotton fabric with tiny holly print, strip 3″ × 34″. Felt: white, piece 9″ × 12″; scraps of red, green, and black. Sewing thread to match fabrics and felt. Heavy-duty sewing thread. Brown ¾″ pompon. Two amber plastic animal eyes ¾″ diameter, with shank and washer for backing. White craft glue. Polyester fiberfill for stuffing.

DIRECTIONS FOR REINDEER
Enlarge patterns by copying on paper ruled in 1″ squares. Complete half-patterns indicated by long dash lines. Referring to arrows on patterns for placement on nap, transfer patterns to wrong side of designated fabrics as follows, using dressmaker's carbon and dry ball-point pen; place pieces ½″ from fabric edges and ½″ apart. On reddish-brown plush or fake fur, mark two head sides, two body sides, two front legs, and two back legs, reversing each second piece; also mark two ears and one tail (backs) and one head center. On white plush or fake fur, mark two under-bodies and two muzzles, reversing each second piece; also mark two ears and one tail (fronts). On felt, mark eight black hooves and four white antlers. Cut out pieces ¼″ beyond marked lines for seam allowance, but omit seam allowance at bottom edge of antlers. Zigzag-stitch raw edges of plush and fake fur pieces to prevent raveling; reset machine for straight stitches.

To assemble: Pin pieces together with right sides facing and raw edges even; stitch on marked lines, making ¼″ seams unless otherwise directed; ease in fullness where necessary. Clip into seam allowance at curves and across corners.

Stitch head sides to head center, matching A's and B's. Stitch muzzles together at center front. Stitch muzzle to head, matching C's and D's. Stitch head sides together at center front, matching D's and E's; leave neck edge open. Machine-baste around neck edge; turn to right side. Attach an eye to each side of head (*see pattern for placement*). Stuff head with fiberfill until firm. Pull basting thread gently to gather neck edge. Stitch ear fronts and backs together in pairs, leaving bases open; turn. Turn raw edges ¼″ to inside and slipstitch openings closed. Pin one ear to each side of head as shown, pinching base tightly from back for shaping; slipstitch in place, using heavy-duty thread. Stitch pompon "nose" to muzzle as shown.

Make a left and right half of body as follows: For each, stitch hooves to bottom of front and back legs and body side, matching F's and G's. Stitch front and back legs to body side, leaving top edges open. Pin underbody to body side/legs, matching letters, open dots, and darts (fine dash lines on patterns); stitch together between H and I. Stitch darts at underbody/leg joinings for shaping.

To finish: Stitch assembled body sides together, leaving neck edge open; turn. Stuff body until firm, using knitting needle for hooves. Slipstitch head over neck, turning it slightly as shown. Construct tail as for ear. Pinch base of tail tightly and slipstitch to rear seam. Stitch antlers together in pairs, leaving bottom edges open; turn and stuff; slipstitch openings closed. Slipstitch antlers to head top as shown. Pink long edges of cotton fabric strip; notch ends with scissors. Tie strip into bow around neck. On felt, mark two green holly leaves and four red berries; cut on marked lines. Glue two berries to each leaf; let dry. Tack holly to top of head between antlers as shown.

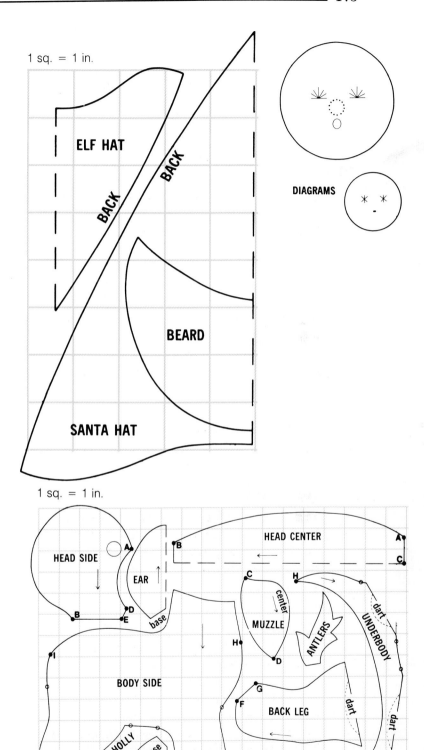

1 sq. = 1 in.

ELF HAT

BACK

BACK

BACK

BEARD

SANTA HAT

DIAGRAMS

1 sq. = 1 in.

HEAD CENTER

HEAD SIDE

EAR

base

MUZZLE

center

ANTLERS

UNDERBODY

dart

BODY SIDE

HOLLY

base

TAIL

BACK LEG

dart

FRONT LEG

dart

HOOF

Zara

In her satin tutu and matching slippers she's sure to be a star.

Zara Ballerina

SIZE
About 20" tall.

EQUIPMENT
Pencil. Ruler. Paper for patterns. Tape measure. Dressmaker's tracing (carbon) paper. Dry ball-point pen. Small embroidery hoop. Embroidery and regular scissors. Embroidery and sewing needles. Knitting needle. Straight pins. Sewing machine with zigzag attachment. Iron.

MATERIALS
For doll: Closely woven cotton fabric such as muslin or kettle cloth 45" wide, ½ yard flesh color. Flesh-color sewing thread and heavy-duty sewing thread. Sport-weight yarn, 4 ozs. pale yellow for hair. Six-strand embroidery floss: one skein to match hair; small amounts blue, brown, white, light pink, and dark pink. Coral crayon. Brown felt-tipped marking pen. Polyester fiberfill for stuffing. **For clothes:** Nylon tulle 45" wide, ¾ yard pink. Satin fabric 45" wide, ½ yard pink. Grosgrain ribbon ⅜" wide, 2½ yards pink. Flat lace trim ½" wide, ½ yard pink. Flat elastic ⅜" wide, 1 yard. Two small snap fasteners. Sewing thread to match fabrics.

DIRECTIONS FOR DOLL

Enlarge patterns by copying on paper ruled in 1" squares. Complete half- and quarter-patterns indicated by long dash lines; fine lines are for placement or embroidery.

Use dressmaker's carbon and dry ball-point pen to transfer patterns to wrong side of flesh-color fabric, placing them ½" from fabric edges and ½" apart; reverse leg and body patterns to make a front and a back for each. Cut out one head center, two bodies, two arms, two soles, and four legs leaving ¼" seam allowance around all pieces.

Mark one head on fabric, for face; center and transfer actual-size pattern for face to right side of fabric, including fine lines for embroidery. Do *not* cut out.

Insert face area into embroidery hoop. Using three strands of blue floss in needle, work eyes in vertical satin stitch. Using two strands in needle, outline-stitch light pink nose, dark pink mouth and chin, and brown eye outline; work matching lashes in straight stitch. Work a white double cross-stitch in each eye as shown in color photograph. When embroidery is completed, remove fabric from hoop. Press gently, wrong side up. Cut out face; use as pattern to cut head back.

To assemble: Pin head center to face and head back with bottom straight edges even. Stitch around curved sides and top, leaving neck edge open. Fold neck ¼" to wrong side; baste. Turn head to right side. Stuff firmly with fiberfill. "Rouge" cheeks with crayon. Mark freckles with felt-tipped pen.

Fold arms in half lengthwise, right side in. Stitch raw arm and hand edges, leaving top

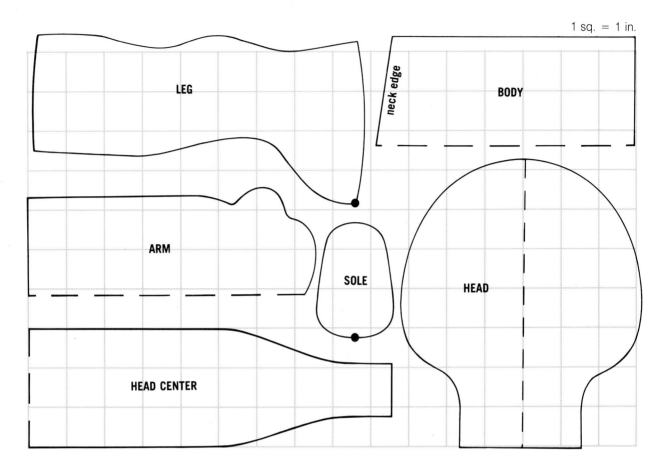

1 sq. = 1 in.

LEG

neck edge

BODY

ARM

SOLE

HEAD

HEAD CENTER

straight edges open. Turn; stuff firmly. Baste each arm closed ⅛″ from raw edges, enclosing stuffing. Stitch legs together in pairs at front and back, leaving top and bottom edges open. Stitch soles to bottom openings, matching dots; turn and stuff. Baste each leg top as for arm, but with seams centered. On right side of one body (front), pin arms ½″ down from shoulders, so that arms cross, thumbs point down, and side edges are even; stitch. Pin and stitch legs to body bottom in similar manner, so that toes point toward shoulders. Place body front on work surface with limbs on top, extending outward. Fold left arm across body, so that hand extends above right shoulder and seam allowance faces out. Pin left side of body back, wrong side up, to body front; stitch. Pin and stitch right side of body in same manner (body will look like a tube

with hands extending above and legs below). Push legs up through tube, so that only seam allowance extends at bottom; pin and stitch body bottom. Turn and stuff. Turn raw edges ¼″ to inside; slipstitch opening closed. Using heavy-duty thread, slipstitch head, centered, over shoulders. Take several small stitches through both sides of each knee and elbow, for "dimples."

Hair: Mark center part from front head seam to nape of neck. For braids, cut 120 36″ lengths of yarn. Working with groups of 10 strands at a time and all six strands of matching embroidery floss, stitch center of each group to part, working from front seam to back. Divide yarn on each side into three equal sections and braid; tie each braid with short length of yarn. Tack top of braids to head

1 sq. = 1 in.

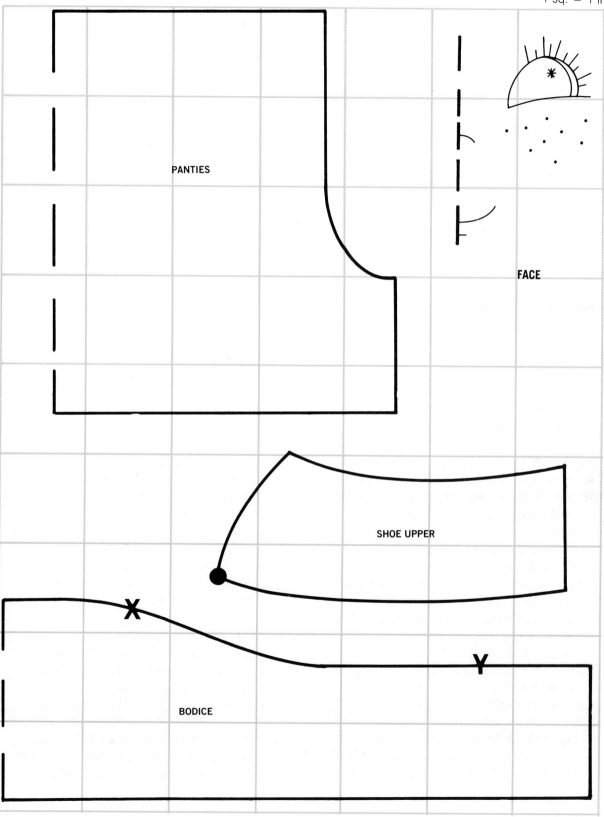

PANTIES

FACE

SHOE UPPER

BODICE

near cheeks to secure, then bring braids to top of head; tuck ends in and tack securely in place.

DIRECTIONS FOR CLOTHES

Panties: From satin fabric, cut two panties. Press waist edges and leg bottoms ¼" to wrong side. Cut two 7½" lengths of elastic. Starting at side edge of each leg with one end, pin elastic to wrong side close to fold; zigzag-stitch in place. Pin and stitch elastic to wrong side of waist as for leg. Reset machine for straight stitch. Stitch panties together at center front and back from waist to crotch. Stitch each inseam; turn to right side.

Dress: From satin fabric, cut one bodice; also cut four straps 1½" × 6½". From lace, cut two 6½" lengths. From width of tulle, cut five 5"-wide layers for tutu and six 1¾" × 8" pieces for strap trim. Stack tutu layers together with edges even. Baste along one long edge, through all layers. Press all edges of bodice under ¼". Gather tutu to fit waist edge of bodice; pin in place on wrong side. *Each strap* Stack three layers of tulle together. Baste along one long edge through all layers. Gather to 6½" length. Press long edges of two satin straps under ¼". Place strap front and back together, wrong sides facing, with gathered edges of tulle and unfinished edge of lace in between. Topstitch close to pressed edges, securing tulle and lace. Pin strap to wrong side of bodice front where indicated by X on pattern, making sure tulle and lace extend outward. Pin opposite end to bodice back (Y on pattern). Topstitch around entire bodice close to pressed edges, securing tutu and straps. Stitch snap fasteners to bodice back.

Shoes: From satin, cut four uppers and two soles. Press top edge of each upper ¼" to wrong side; topstitch close to fold. Stitch uppers together in pairs at front and back. Stitch soles to uppers, matching dots; turn. Place shoes on doll. Cut two 34" lengths of grosgrain ribbon. Center a ribbon across top of foot; pin ribbon to shoe edge at each side; remove shoe. Topstitch ribbon to shoe at edges, then fold ribbon back over itself, angling back slightly; topstitch again over previous stitches. Replace shoe on doll; wrap ribbons around ankle "toe-shoe" style as shown in photograph. Tie ends in bow.

To finish: Cut 18" length of grosgrain ribbon; tie in bow around neck. Baste unfinished edge of remaining lace trim. Gather lace tightly behind grosgrain bow; secure gathers.

How-To

APPLIQUÉ

Choose a fabric that is closely woven and firm enough so a clean edge results when the pieces are cut. Cut a pattern piece for each shape out of thin, stiff cardboard, and mark the right side of each pattern. Press fabric smooth.

Place cardboard pattern on right side of fabric. Using sharp, hard pencils (light-colored pencil on dark fabric and dark pencil on light fabric), mark the outline on the fabric. When marking several pieces on the same fabric, leave at least ½" between pieces. Mark a second outline ¼" outside the design outline. Proceed as directed below, appliquéing by hand or by machine.

BY HAND

Using matching thread and small stitches, machine-stitch all around design outline, as shown in **Fig. 1.** This makes edge easier to turn and neater in appearance. Cut out the appliqué on the outside line, as in **Fig. 2.** For a smooth edge, clip into seam allowance at curved edges and corners. Then turn seam allowance to back, just inside stitching as shown in **Fig. 3,** and press. Pin and baste the appliqué on the background, and slipstitch in place with tiny stitches, as shown in **Fig. 4.**

BY MACHINE

Pin and baste appliqués in place; do not turn under excess fabric. Straight-stitch around appliqués on marked lines. Trim away excess fabric to ⅛" from straight stitching. Set sewing machine for close zigzag stitch as directed (¼" wide or less). Zigzag around appliqués, covering straight stitching and excess fabric.

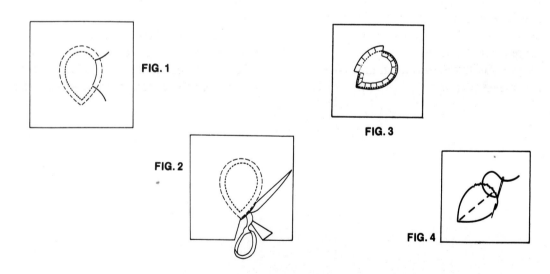

FIG. 1

FIG. 2

FIG. 3

FIG. 4

CROCHET

All crochet work begins with a chain, a series of loops made by pulling yarn through a loop on your crochet hook to make a new loop. Many beautiful and intricate patterns can be made in crochet, most of them a variation of a few basic stitches which are illustrated here—chain stitch, single crochet, double crochet, and slipstitch.

CHAIN STITCH

To make first loop on hook, grasp yarn about 2″ from end between left thumb and index finger. With right hand, lap long strand over short end, forming a loop. Hold loop in place with left thumb and index finger. Grasp hook in right hand, insert hook through loop, catch strand with hook and draw it through loop. Pull end and long strand in opposite directions to close loop around hook.

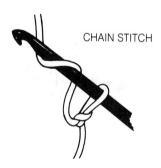

CHAIN STITCH

FIGURE 1 To make your first chain stitch, pass hook under yarn on index finger and catch strand with hook.
   Draw yarn through loop on hook. This makes one chain stitch. Repeat last step until you have as many chains as you need. One loop always remains on hook. Practice making all chains uniform.

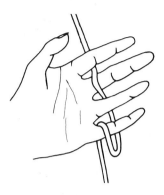

FIGURE 2 Weave yarn through left hand.

SINGLE CROCHET

FIGURE 1 Insert hook in second chain from hook. Yarn over hook.

FIGURE 2 Draw yarn through chain. Two loops on hook.

FIGURE 3 Yarn over hook. Draw yarn through 2 loops on hook. One single crochet has been made.

FIGURE 4 Work a single crochet in each chain stitch. At end of row, chain 1 and turn work around.

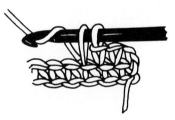

FIGURE 5 Insert hook under both top loops of first stitch, yarn over hook, and draw through stitch. Yarn over and through 2 loops on hook. Work a single crochet in same way in each stitch across row.

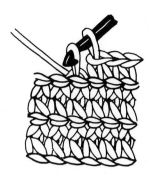

FIGURE 6 To make a ridge stitch or slipper stitch, work rows of single crochet by inserting hook in back loop only of each single crochet.

HOW TO INCREASE

To Increase 1 Single Crochet

To increase 1 single crochet, work 2 stitches in 1 stitch.

HOW TO DECREASE

To Decrease 1 Single Crochet

To decrease 1 single crochet, pull up a loop in 1 stitch, pull up a loop in next stitch (3 loops on hook), yarn over hook, draw through all 3 loops at once.

SLIPSTITCH

Insert hook in work. Yarn over hook and draw through both the stitch and the loop on hook. Slipstitch makes a firm finishing edge. A single slipstitch is used for joining a chain to form a ring.

HALF DOUBLE CROCHET

FIGURE 1 Yarn over hook. Insert hook in 3rd chain from hook.

FIGURE 2 Yarn over hook, draw through chain. Yarn over hook again.

FIGURE 3 Draw through all 3 loops on hook. One half double crochet has been made.

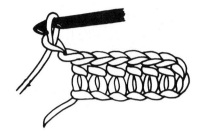

FIGURE 4 Work a half double crochet in each chain across. At end of row, ch 2 and turn work.

DOUBLE CROCHET

FIGURE 1 Yarn over hook. Insert hook in 4th chain from hook.

FIGURE 2 Yarn over hook. Draw through chain. There are 3 loops on hook.

FIGURE 3 Yarn over hook. Draw through 2 loops on hook. There are 2 loops on hook. Yarn over hook.

FIGURE 4 Draw yarn through remaining 2 loops on hook. One double crochet has been made. When you have worked a double crochet in each chain across, chain 3 and turn work. In most directions, the turning chain 3 counts as first double crochet of next row. In working the 2nd row, skip the first stitch and work a double crochet in the 2 top loops of each double crochet across. The last double crochet of each row is worked in the top chain of the chain 3 turning chain.

TREBLE OR TRIPLE CROCHET With 1 loop on hook put yarn over hook twice, insert in 5th chain from hook, pull loop through. Yarn over and draw through 2 loops at a time 3 times. At end of a row, chain 4 and turn. Chain 4 counts as first treble of next row.

DOUBLE TREBLE Put yarn over hook 3 times and work off 2 loops at a time as for treble.

TREBLE TREBLE Put yarn over hook 4 times and work off 2 loops at a time as for treble.

HOW TO TURN YOUR WORK

In crochet a certain number of chain stitches are needed at the end of each row to bring work into position for the next row. Then work is turned so reverse side is facing the crocheter. Follow the stitch table below for the number of chain stitches to make a turn.

Single crochet	Chain 1 to turn
Half double crochet	Chain 2 to turn
Double crochet	Chain 3 to turn
Treble crochet	Chain 4 to turn
Double treble crochet	Chain 5 to turn
Treble treble crochet	Chain 6 to turn

CROCHET ABBREVIATIONS

ch—chain stitch		**sc**—single crochet	
st—stitch		**sl st**—slipstitch	
sts—stitches		**dc**—double crochet	
lp—loop		**hdc**—half double crochet	
inc—increase		**tr**—treble or triple crochet	
dec—decrease		**dtr**—double treble crochet	
rnd—round		**tr tr**—treble treble crochet	
beg—beginning		**bl**—block	
sk—skip		**sp**—space	
p—picot		**pat**—pattern	
tog—together		**yo**—yarn over hook	

HOW TO FOLLOW DIRECTIONS

An asterisk (*) is often used in crochet directions to indicate repetition. For example, when directions read "*2 dc in next st, 1 dc in next st, repeat from * 4 times," this means to work directions after first * until second * is reached, then go back to first * 4 times more. Work 5 times in all.

When parentheses ( ) are used to show repetition, work directions within parentheses as many times as specified. For example, "(dc, ch 1) 3 times" means to do what is within ( ) 3 times altogether.

"Work even" in directions means to work in same stitch without increasing or decreasing.

MEASURING YOUR GAUGE

Most knitting and crochet directions include a stitch gauge. The stitch gauge gives the number of stitches to the inch with the yarn and hook or needles recommended in the pattern stitch. The directions are based on the given gauge. The gauge (or tension) at which you work controls the size of each finished piece. It is therefore essential to work to the gauge given for each item if you want it to be the correct size. To test your gauge, cast on 20–30 stitches, using the hook or needles specified. Work in the pattern stitches for 3". Smooth out your swatch and pin it down. Measure across 2" and place pins 2" apart. Count number of stitches between pins. If you have more stitches to the inch than directions specify, you are working too tightly; use a larger hook or needles. If you have fewer stitches to the inch, you are working too loosely; use a smaller hook or needles.

Most patterns give a row gauge too. Although the proper length does not usually depend on the row gauge (directions usually give lengths in inches rather than rows), in some patterns it is important to have the proper row gauge too.

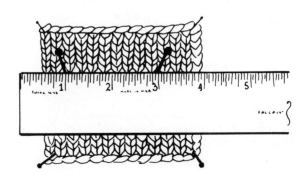

EMBROIDER

TO PREPARE FABRIC

To prevent fabric from raveling, bind all raw edges with masking tape, whipstitch edges by hand, or machine-stitch ⅛" in from all edges.

FRAMES/HOOPS

Work embroidery in a frame or hoop. With the material held tautly and evenly, your stitches are more likely to be neat and accurate than if the fabric were held in hand while working.

TO BEGIN AND END A STRAND

Cut floss or yarn into 18" strands. To begin a strand, leave an end on back and work over it to secure; to end, run needle under four or five stitches on back or take a few tiny backstitches. Do not make knots. Fasten off the thread when ending each motif, rather than carrying it to another motif.

TO REMOVE EMBROIDERY

When a mistake has been made, run a needle, eye first, under the stitches. Pull the embroidery away from the fabric; cut carefully with small scissors pressed hard against the needle. Pick out the cut portion of the embroidery and catch loose ends of the remaining stitches on back by pulling the ends under the stitches with a crochet hook.

FOR COUNTED CROSS-STITCH

For counted cross-stitch on even-weave fabrics, work stitches over a counted number of threads both hori-zontally and vertically, following a chart. Each symbol on the chart represents one stitch. Different symbols represent different colors.

For fabrics such as Aida cloth or Zweigart's "Herta," follow the mesh of the coarse flat weave (much like needlepoint canvas), where holes are obvious. Each "thread" is actually made up of four or more fine threads in a group and stitches are worked from hole to hole.

For counted cross-stitch on gingham fabric, work stitches over checks, so that one complete cross-stitch covers one check.

When working cross-stitches, work underneath stitches in one direction and top stitches in the opposite direction, making sure all strands lie smooth and flat; allow needle to hang freely from work occasionally, to untwist floss. Make crosses touch by inserting needle in same hole used for adjacent stitch (see stitch details).

TO FINISH

When your embroidered piece is completed, finish off the back neatly by running ends into the back of the work and clipping off any excess threads. Place piece face down on a well-padded surface and press, using a steam iron, or regular iron and damp pressing cloth. Press lightly from the center outward. For embroidery that is raised from the surface of the background, use extra thick, soft padding, such as a thick blanket.

EMBROIDERY STITCH DETAILS

Backstitch

Bullion Stitch

Cable Stitch

Chevron Stitch

Chain Stitch

Couching

Cross-Stitch

Double Cross-Stitch

Fly Stitch

French Knot

Honeycomb

Laid Filling Stitch

Lazy Daisy Stitch

Outline Stitch

Satin Stitch

Seed Stitch

Raised Rose Stitch

Stem Stitch

Straight Stitch

Turkey Work

Woven Stitch

KNIT

Knitting is based on two stitches, **KNIT STITCH** and **PURL STITCH.** Many knitted sweaters and accessories can be made with these two stitches alone. Before starting any knitted piece, it is necessary to **CAST ON** a certain number of stitches; that is, to place a series of loops on one needle so that you can work your first row of knitting. After you have finished your piece of knitting, it is necessary to **BIND OFF** your stitches so that they will not ravel out.

CASTING ON There are many ways of casting on stitches. The method shown here is only one of them. It gives you a strong and elastic edge.

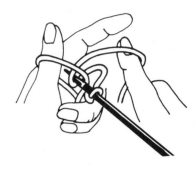

FIGURE 3 Bring needle forward to make a loop over left thumb. Insert needle from left to right in loop; bring yarn in right hand under, then over point of needle and draw yarn through loop with tip of needle.

FIGURE 1 Allow enough yarn for the number of stitches to be cast on (about ½″ per stitch for lighter weight yarns such as baby yarns, 1″ per stitch for heavier yarns such as knitting worsted, more for bulky yarns on large needles). Make a slip loop on needle and tighten knot gently.

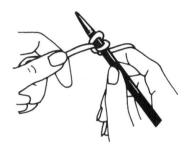

FIGURE 4 Keeping right hand in same position, tighten stitch on needle gently with left hand. You now have 2 stitches on needle. Repeat Figures 3 and 4 for required number of stitches.

KNIT STITCH

FIGURE 2 Hold needle in right hand with short end of yarn over left thumb. Weave strand that comes from ball through right hand, over index finger, under second, over third and under fourth finger.

FIGURE 5 Hold needle with cast-on stitches in left hand and yarn in same position as for casting on in right hand. Insert point of needle from left to right in first stitch.

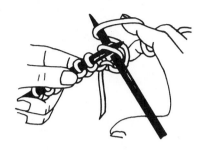

FIGURE 6 Bring yarn under and over point of right needle.

FIGURE 7 Draw yarn through stitch with point of needle.

FIGURE 8 Allow loop on left needle to slip off needle. Loop on right needle is your first knit stitch. Repeat from Figure 5 in each loop across row. When you have finished knitting one row, place needle with stitches in left hand ready to start next row.

GARTER STITCH

GARTER STITCH If you work row after row of knit stitch, you are working garter stitch.

PURL STITCH

PURL

FIGURE 9 To purl, insert needle from right to left in stitch on left needle. Bring yarn over and under point of right needle. Draw yarn back through stitch and allow loop on left needle to slip off needle.

STOCKINETTE STITCH

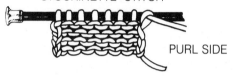

PURL SIDE

STOCKINETTE STITCH If you work one row of knit stitch and one row of purl stitch alternately, you are working stockinette stitch.

KNIT SIDE

BINDING OFF

FIGURE 10 Knit the first two stitches. Insert left needle from left to right through front of first stitch. Lift first stitch over second stitch and over tip of right needle. One stitch has been bound off, one stitch remains on right needle. Knit another stitch. Again lift first stitch over second stitch and off right needle. Continue across until all stitches have been bound off. One loop remains on needle. Cut yarn, pull end through loop, and tighten knot.

TO INCREASE ONE STITCH There are several ways to increase a stitch. **Method 1** is illustrated. Knit 1 stitch in the usual way but do not slip it off left needle. Bring right needle behind left needle, insert it from right to left in same stitch (called "the back of the stitch"), and make another knit stitch. Slip stitch off left needle. To increase 1 stitch on the purl stitch, purl 1 stitch but do not slip it off left needle. Bring yarn between needles to back, knit 1 stitch in back of same stitch.

To Increase 1 Stitch

Method 2 Pick up horizontal strand between stitch just knitted and next stitch, place it on left needle. Knit 1 stitch in back of this strand, thus twisting it.

Method 3 Place right needle behind left needle. Insert right needle in stitch below next stitch, knit this stitch, then knit stitch above it in the usual way.

To Decrease 1 Stitch

TO DECREASE ONE STITCH On the right side of work, knit 2 stitches together as in illustration, through the front of the stitches (the decrease slants to the right), or through the back of the stitches (the decrease slants to the left). On the purl side, purl 2 stitches together. Another decrease stitch is called "psso" (pass slipstitch over). When directions say "sl 1, k 1, psso," slip first stitch (take it from left to right needle without knitting it), knit next stitch, then bring slipstitch over knit stitch as in binding off.

MEASURING YOUR GAUGE (see page 183) _____

TO CAST ON AT BEGINNING OF ROW

FIGURE 1 Draw a loop of yarn through first stitch as if to knit.

FIGURE 2 Pull out the loop on right needle.

FIGURE 3 Turn loop and place it on left needle as shown. One stitch has been cast on. Without removing right needle, repeat from Figure 1 for required number of cast-on stitches.

KNITTING ABBREVIATIONS

k—knit	**psso**—pass slipstitch over
p—purl	**inc**—increase
st—stitch	**dec**—decrease
sts—stitches	**beg**—beginning
yo—yarn over	**pat**—pattern
sl—slip	**lp**—loop
sk—skip	**MC**—main color
tog—together	**CC**—contrasting color
rnd—round	**dp**—double-pointed

LATCH HOOK

Fold yarn over shank of hook, **Fig. 1;** hold ends with left hand. With hook in right hand and latch down, push hook down through mesh under double horizontal thread and up, **Fig. 2;** draw hook toward you, placing yarn ends inside hook, **Fig. 3.** Be sure the yarn is completely inside hook when the latch closes. Pull hook back through canvas, drawing yarn through loop. Tighten knot, **Fig. 4,** by pulling yarn ends.

Fig. 1   Fig. 2

Fig. 3   Fig. 4

NEEDLEPOINT

TO PREPARE CANVAS

Bind all raw edges of canvas with masking tape to prevent raveling. Find center of canvas by basting a line from center of one edge to center of opposite edge, being careful to follow one row of mesh across. Then baste another line from center of third edge to center of fourth edge. Basting threads will cross at center; they will aid in blocking canvas after work is completed.

TO WORK NEEDLEPOINT

Cut strands into 18″ lengths. When starting first strand, leave 1″ of yarn on back of canvas unless otherwise directed and cover it as work proceeds; your first few stitches will anchor it in place. To end a strand or begin a new one, run strand under four or five stitches on back of work; do not make knots. Keep tension of stitches firm and even. Stitching tends to twist the working strand; now and then let needle and strand hang freely to untwist. Follow charts and individual directions to work each design.

BLOCKING MATERIALS Softwood surface, such as pine or plywood. Brown paper. T- or carpenter's square. Rustproof thumbtacks.

Directions: Cover wood surface with brown paper. Mark canvas outline on paper for guide, making sure corners

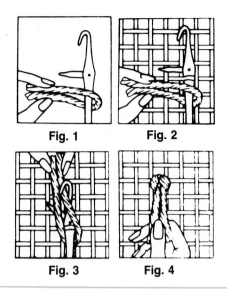

CONTINENTAL STITCH

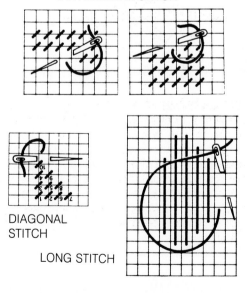

DIAGONAL STITCH

LONG STITCH

are square. Mark horizontal and vertical center lines on paper outline and on canvas. Place canvas, right side down, over guide. Match center markings on canvas with those on paper. Fasten canvas to wood with rustproof tacks; tack corners first, then the center of each side; continue placing tacks until there is a solid border of tacks around entire edge, dividing and subdividing spaces between thumbtacks already placed. Wet thoroughly with cold water; let dry. If piece is badly warped, block again.

Note: If yarn is not colorfast, dissolve salt in cold water and block with salt water.

QUILT

BY HAND

There are three ways of quilting by hand: You can stretch your quilt on a frame or in a hoop or hold the quilt a section at a time in your lap.

On a frame: Sew the top and bottom edges of the lining to the fabric strips attached to the long parallel bars of the frame. Sew several rows of stitches with strong thread.

In a hoop: Pull quilt taut in hoop, moving any extra fullness toward the edges. Work center first. As you move toward the edges, substitute smaller embroidery hoops for the large quilting hoop, to keep the fabric always taut.

Use a short, strong needle, between #7 and #10. Buy the special silicone-coated quilting thread if you can find it. If you can't, choose a strong mercerized cotton (#50 to #30) or a cotton-covered polyester. If the thread knots, frays, or breaks as you quilt, run strands across a cake of beeswax.

Whatever method you choose, start in the center of the quilt and stitch toward you. Shift position often so that you work around the center and out toward the edges in even stages.

Quilting Stitch Cut 18″ strand of thread. Knot one end. Bring needle up from lining through quilt top; give a little tug to thread so that knot passes through lining only and lies buried in batting. Sew on marked line with running stitch, in two separate motions: Push needle straight down through the three layers with one hand, take needle with other hand, pull thread through, and push up close to the first stitch (see Quilting Stitch Detail below). An experienced quilter may be able to take two or three stitches before pulling needle through, holding quilt down at quilting line with thumb of other hand; do not try this method unless using a frame. Depending on thickness of fabric and batting, make stitches as small and close as you can (5 to 10 per inch); the longer the stitch, the less durable the quilting. Space stitches evenly, so they are the same length on both sides of quilt. From time to time, look underneath to check your stitches. To end off, backstitch and take a long stitch through the top and batting only; take another backstitch and clip thread at surface; the thread end will sink into batting. If you are a beginner, practice first on a small piece in an embroidery hoop, to find the easiest and best-working method for you.

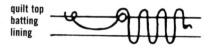

quilt top
batting
lining

By machine Machine quilting can be done with or without a quilting foot. When working on a sewing machine, the best quilting patterns to use are sewn on the diagonal or on the bias. Fabric gives a little when on the bias, making it easier to keep the area you are working on flat. Cotton batting should be quilted closely with quilting lines running no more than 2″ apart; Dacron lining may be quilted with the lines no more than 3″ apart.

As a rule, machine quilting is done with a straight stitch. Stitch length control should be set from 6 to 12 per inch. Pressure should be adjusted so that it is slightly heavier than for medium-weight fabrics.

If you are using a scroll or floral design, it is best to use the short open toe of the quilting foot, which allows you to follow the curved lines with accuracy and ease.

SMOCK

OUTLINE STITCH

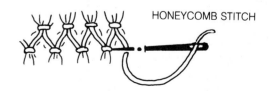

HONEYCOMB STITCH

INDEX